The author, Donal Rocca, also known as Don Rocca was born on 5th August 1941 in Dublin, Ireland to an Irish mother and Italian father. After a formal education by nuns, lay teachers and Christian brothers, he started his third level education in Atlantic College Dublin followed by Kevin St College, Dublin. Further third level education spanning more than forty years took place in Plymouth Technical College and Company courses run by Marconi, AEI, and Racal—to name but a few.

Don became a seagoing radio officer with Marconi Marine in 1960 and in 1966 he joined their staff as a marine technical assistant. In 1974, he joined the Decca Radar Co. later Racal Decca rising to Dublin area manager in 1984. In 1993, Don in association with Kieran Campbell started their own marine electronics company. Camroc Electronic Ltd. CAMROC…CAMPBELL ROCCA. Don is still owner and joint managing director of Camroc Electronic Ltd.

This book is dedicated to my late wife, Rita, with encouragement from my daughter Bernice.

D. D. Rocca

MEMORIES OF THE WAY WE WERE

AUSTIN MACAULEY PUBLISHERS™
LONDON * CAMBRIDGE * NEW YORK * SHARJAH

A CIP catalogue record for this title is available from the British Library.

ISBN 9781035802364 (Paperback)
ISBN 9781035802371 (ePub e-book)

www.austinmacauley.com

First Published 2023
Austin Macauley Publishers Ltd®
1 Canada Square
Canary Wharf
London
E14 5AA

Table of Contents

The Secrets of Cross Guns

I'll start my tale sometime in the early decades of the last century.

My father, Egidio Rocca, from Parma, Italy, was the first Alien to become a citizen of the Irish Free State in the 1930s. During the early 1920s, he was part of the Italian team repairing and restoring the bomb-damaged GPO and Four Courts. When the work was completed, most Italians went home though some went to America.

One of those who decided on the American route was a man called Verso. He had been my father's mentor and before leaving, he gifted him his tools, and with these tools my father started to seek out little jobs of his own. The reason he stayed was because he fell in love with a girl called Agnes Cunningham, and they were married in Berkeley Road Church in 1927.

My brother, Paddy, was born the following year. Things went well for a while and then the Wall Street crash of 1929 hit the world and every pound in people's pockets became a prisoner. My father told me he walked the streets of Dublin seeing if any pub or shop would like him to install a Terrazzo floor or even a porch, but no one was interested. As he walked home one evening with one last shilling in his pocket, he was approached in Gardner Street by a beggar who looked tired, hungry and dirty.

He took the shilling from his pocket and gave it to the poor wretch, and to his dying day, my father said it was the best and luckiest good deed he ever did in his life. The very next day as he again walked the streets, he decided to try his luck with the builder's providers McNaughton & Sons Ltd. They offered him a small job in Limerick City, but he'd have to make his own way there.

He didn't have money for train or bus fare but what he did have was a motor bike which he had restored himself. On the morning of his departure, he woke up with a bad cold but in those days, they made them tough in Northern Italy, and with Verso's tools strapped to the back of his born-again motorbike, he left the city on a cold winter's day Limerick bound. The Norton bike spluttered its way down past Naas, Newbridge.

Portlaoise, Roscrea and all roads south to Limerick city. There would have been one or two comfort breaks on the way to consume the small beef sandwiches provided by Agnes, washed down with tea kept warm in a flask. A large swig of cough mixture and the traveller was on his way, eventually reaching his destination some five hours after leaving Dublin.

The job must have gone well because more and more McNaughton contracts followed. Nano managed to upgrade from a motorbike to a Ford prefect car, supplemented later with a red coloured Ford van. With encouragement and finance provided by the West British owners of McNaughton's, my father started to employ his own workers to whom he divulged the secrets of the Terrazzo formula.

The numbers eventually grew to a workforce of over fifteen. Names like Scully and Billy Orr are some of those I remember. Much of their work can still be seen today in old schools, hospitals, shops and garda stations throughout the twenty-six counties, and probably some in the other six as well. Things went well for the Rocca family, with Nano regularly changing up to a new Waldens purchased motor every two years.

The best of these was a Ford V8 and filled with six family members out for a Sunday drive, people would stop and stare. Things went so well it was also possible for Nano and Agnes to take us all on holidays to Italy starting in 1947, but this is the subject of one other story I wrote.

Things didn't always go right though. Let me start by saying that sometime in the late 1930s when Nano, my father, was driving home from Drogheda, he stopped to help a fellow motorist who had broken down at the side of the road. As already indicated, Nano was a competent amateur when it came to anything mechanical and he soon had the distressed driver up and running.

Before they parted company, the relieved driver handed my father his card and told him to make contact if he ever needed help. The card read, 'Captain Gordon, Dublin Castle'.

It was the following year when a letter arrived from the Aliens Department, signed by a man called Meehan, addressed to my father stating he had two weeks to leave Ireland. War in Europe was imminent and it mattered not that Nano was married to an Irish woman with five children—Patrick, Eda, Seamus, George and Albert. He and all other Aliens, had to get out of de Valera's Ireland.

Agnes pondered the problem. She considered contacting her mother's old friend, Willie, WB Yeats, who had helped the family in the past but he was old now and probably his influence had waned. She then remembered the card— 'Captain Gordon, Dublin Castle'.

Donning her best dress from Clerys' ladies department and accompanied by Paddy, she entered Dublin Castle and requested to see Captain Gordon. Initially, this request was refused but Agnes in her youth was not a person to take no for an answer, and eventually she was granted entry to the captain's office. True to his word and with assistance from *Freenys Solicitors,* Nano was the first Alien to become a citizen of the Irish Free State.

My brother, Paddy, and Seamus enjoyed a day or two in the Sun as the event was published in the newspapers. Both brothers were pupils at St Patrick's National school, Drumcondra, where a number of the teachers, probably 1916/1922 veterans, were very interested in them and the story.

The Second World War commenced and almost immediately all Italians were rounded up and incarcerated in the Curragh camp (The British did the same by erecting an internment camp in Douglas Isle of Man). This gave the government a problem. What to do with their fellow Catholics? It didn't go down well in the Vatican, particularly as one of their favourites, John Charles McQuaid, was Archbishop of Dublin.

The problem was partly solved when people like my father agreed to employ many of the internees. My father, Nano, took four and then wondered what to do with them? They gave him the solution—charcoal! These men were expert at making charcoal and explained in detail what they would require—'wood, and a field'.

Hardly items readily available but then Nano had a light bulb moment. The family regularly visited Enniskerry and the Powerscourt estate during Sunday drives, so on the next visit, Nano contacted the estate manager. It was agreed he would hire a small field and he could have all the fallen trees and branches free of charge.

The timber was perfect for the manufacture of charcoal, so the project began. The first thing was accommodation for the new employees. Wooden huts were erected fitted with camp beds and cooking facilities. With fresh food collected daily by Paddy from nearby Enniskerry, and the wonderful Glendalough close by, this was a perfect way to sit out the war.

Paddy often wondered where the fresh venison meat, he hadn't purchased, came from, but suspected illegally from the estate deer herd! The next step was to dig out a large pit into which the four experts placed layers of wood and straw, which they then covered in sods of earth, after which they set the sunken pyre on fire and let it smoulder away for days. After that, they removed the charcoal and began the whole process again.

The charcoal was high quality and subsequently sold to Rourke's Bakery, Dublin with some going to the Irish Army. The charcoal gas was used to run cars and trucks. As Nano had to collect and deliver the charcoal, he received permission to do likewise. The car had to have a tank fitted into the boot, from which a one inch pipe, ran over the roof and into the engine space.

The initial outlay was high but as he was the fuel manufacturer, it cost him virtually nil to run his new Ford. Nano also had a small hidden petrol tank in case the charcoal gas ran out. You might say a get me home reserve. It should be noted that running a vehicle in this manner was highly dangerous, but in wartime some niceties are abandoned.

It often happened that while driving back to Dublin via the Scalp, the trailer load would start to re-burn. Nano carried a spare bucket which he would fill with water from a local farmhouse or whatever to douse the flames.

Nano and Agnes were regular visitors to the Savoy cinema on Sunday night. On several occasions, on reaching the foyer, they would see curious Dubliners viewing, what was one of the very few vehicles in O'Connell Street. Feeling ashamed, they would walk around until the streets were empty before driving back home to 41, Home farm Park, Drumcondra.

It happened one evening that a knock came on the door at 41. It was the local police with information that an Italian Alien was living at this address. Agnes invited them in and once she showed them the new Free State passport, they left and never came back. It must be understood that everyone was struggling during the emergency, but perhaps the Roccas less than most.

Agnes wasn't a particularly warm mother, but she saw to it that we were well fed, had a warm bed to sleep in and more particularly were dressed in the best clothes available. She never ran out of tea as she bought most of it on the black market. It was also not unknown for Nano to buy meat from under the counter, particularly a pig or two from a country farmer, which at the time was illegal.

Observing this affluence, I suppose it was understandable that some locals, possibly with sons fighting in the sands of North Africa, might have got a bit peeved. The vast majority of our neighbours were very kind and very friendly, but sometimes remarks like, 'taking the jobs of decent Irish people', could be heard. During the war years, the Terrazzo business waned very badly as there was no marble from Italy and no white Portland cement from the UK.

Once the war ended, the McNaughton Company, who also had offices in Belfast and London, were able to supply the white cement which then left the problem of acquiring marble. As you'll gather by now, my father who probably left school before his teen years, was a great problem solver. He drove to Kilkenny where he met the manager of the local marble works.

They had a large quantity of unusable offcuts of no use to them but to Nano it was like gold-dust. He bought it up at a bargain price. He then bought an old open backed lorry and with this, the marble offcuts were driven back to Dublin, where it was crushed using a crusher, actually built by my father.

It took several years till all the Kilkenny marble was depleted but by that stage, marble offcuts could be acquired from Connemara, Italy and Earlys, the Dublin Co. who supplied church altars to the whole of Ireland.

Nano also built his own terrazzo tile machine. You might be wondering where all this work was taking place and I'm going to tell you. 'Erne Street', which is located off Pearse Street, Dublin.

He bought an old tenement property in Erne Street, which had been the home of an old Irish gentry family. The rooms were converted for multiple family occupations, for which Nano received about ten shillings a week for each. I remember these rooms as being kept in immaculate condition by young couples very proud to have their own home. As this building was due to be compulsorily purchased, these tenants eventually moved to brand new corporation houses in one of the new estates.

Anyway, I digress. The most important part of Erne Street was the old ballroom where Nano set up his marble works. I remember there were large tables built of concrete overshadowed by faded paintings on the walls.

It was in 1952 that the building was purchased by Dublin Corporation, which gave Nano a satisfactory profit and the funds to buy Cross Guns.

The old Erne Street building was demolished and today a block of flats stands in its place.

Cross Guns Bridge
Dublin Circa 1952–1953

Two men stood talking on a piece of land beside the main railway line to Galway and the West of Ireland. One was Matthew Pearse Cahill and the other was my father, Egidio Rocca, or in English, Giles Rocca. The land was the property of Pearse Cahill and the purpose of their meeting was, to agree a price on the sale of the land to my father. Eventually, they shook hands at an agreed price of £4000 which was the equivalent of a man's pay for ten years.

Once all the legal papers were completed, the land by the railway line passed into the ownership of 'E. Rocca and Sons Ltd'.

I'll pause here and give a brief history of the previous owner. Pearse Cahill was an aviator, businessman and race driver. Along with his father, Hugh Cahill, they were primary figures in Irish Aviation, setting up Ireland's first commercial airline—'Iona National Airways', 1930. They lived on Iona Road, Glasnevin and hence the name of the company.

They were major figures in the development of Collinstown Airport—now Dublin Airport. The Cahills owned the 'Iona Engineering Works' also at Cross Guns Bridge, which incidentally was to be built on the property my father had just purchased. I remember Pearse telling my father that the greatest regret of his life was rejecting the franchise offer of traffic lights.

This was a bit like 'Decca Records' rejecting the Beatles. To continue:

I remember the first morning I accompanied Nano into what we always referred to as 'Cross Guns'. The land at the front was at street level but after that it became an embankment down to the rail tracks.

The first task was to erect a very large, very long, tin roofed shed into which all the company tools and machinery were placed plus bags of marble and cement. This allowed E. Rocca & Sons Ltd to keep trading assisted by the substantial funds provided by McNaughton & Sons Ltd. The next task was to start building at the front of the property.

Corás Iompair Éireann advised and instructed how this was to be achieved and so began the big dig through hard virgin ground down to railway level. Men with picks and shovels, spent long days, including Saturdays, laboriously removing the hard black soil, which was then used as filler at the back of the property, i.e. that part which sloped down to the rail line. I assisted during holidays but two of the main workers were father and son, refugees from Yugoslavia.

The father was called Pio, and these were very cultured people, from what is now Slovenia which historically and culturally is a very Italian part of Europe. How did it happen they were refugees? Their hotels and other properties were seized by the Dictator Tito and as people in support of Italy during Second World War, they had little choice but to flee.

On request from the Red Cross, Nano agreed to employ them. Father and son were reduced to labouring whilst the females of the family were reduced to dressmaking.

Eventually, after many months, rail level was reached. I remember passengers on passing buses would stare down quizzically into what must have looked like an archaeological dig. To answer their puzzled looks, a reporter and photographer from the 'Evening Herald' came onto the building site one day and interviewed my father. The next day's edition read: 'Mystery Building Solved', accompanied with a large photograph of the deep dig.

The work continued with the construction of pillars of steel surrounded by wooden casements. After that, cement lorries arrived and poured their contents into the steel housings, which were then allowed to dry for a week or more. Once the wooden surrounds were removed, the reinforced pillars which were to support the side road and part of the building above appeared.

Then they began the construction of the cellar, which can still be seen below the building as it now stands. Slowly but surely, the building rose to street level and then we were ready to build the side road entrance. We laid long rods of heavy steel, sitting on a temporary road of wood, after which the cement lorries returned and discharged their loads, till we had a road capable of accepting the weight of heavy vehicles.

I say this now but at the time, I was sceptical as the road was only about six inches thick. "Da, are you sure this is safe?"

"Of course, it is. You could drive a tank on that," he answered in his thick Italian accent which never sounded foreign to me nor am I sure to anyone else in our family. Once the road was ready, the Finglas lorries arrived, to the mutual benefit of us and them. They carried the spoils from the new estates being built on the north side of the city.

They would reverse in over the new side road and tip their loads along the embankment, slowly reclaiming the land which rose slowly like a phoenix from the ashes. The work was hard and not helped by one of the hottest summers of the last century in 1954. As the steam trains passed, the drivers invariably blew their whistles in greeting, and by reply we would wave 'hello!' to which all the passengers smiled. As a people the great famine had reduced us from eight to two million, but we were the happy side of the island.

In parallel with land reclamation, the construction of the main building commenced. It did stop in July 1954 when Agnes, Nano, Albert and I holidayed in Italy in a new Ford Consul car. Part of the holiday included a visit and a meeting in Foggia with Padre now St Pio but this is a separate story I have in print.

By 1956, the building was complete, and part of the family took up residence in the three bedroomed apartment, above the shops. On the nights I slept there, I remember looking out at the passing traffic and the drinkers in the Brian Boru directly opposite our new building. For those who may not know, this pub was so named because the battle of Clontarf, 1014 ,was actually fought in Glasnevin. The high king himself would have walked the very ground I was then looking on.

Depression descended again on Ireland in the mid to late-1950s and despite Nano's best efforts, he could no longer keep his workers employed. There was simply no work coming in. Many, including all my brothers, had no choice but to seek employment in booming Britain.

Our leaders, including De Valera, were little Irelanders of little talent who stood at Parish pumps while the young Irish boys and girls marched by, to be greeted with open arms by booming Britain. One man, Sean Lemass, was waiting his turn to shine in the sun.

The Rocca fortunes were in decline, but there was the building with two shops and some work did eventually come, which kept Nano and his brother, Bino, going. One job I do remember was the convent school in Kilcullen, Co. Kildare, where a lot of terrazzo floors were laid. There were also the two shops of course. Nano turned one into a cake shop, which my mother managed, and the other one into a hairdresser, managed by a local girl.

It sounds like we should have been financially sound, which we were compared to most, but a major part of the family income was spent keeping my brother, Bernard, in a very expensive care home close to London. There were also my Radio College fees to be paid.

Cross Guns

1959 arrived and in the spring of that year, I painted the outside of the building a snowy white. It was so nice, I would sometimes stand outside the Brian Boru pub across the road and stare at it for maybe five or ten minutes. 1959 was also a long hot summer and I was given the task of crushing tons of marble collected from Early's Ltd.

Marble Sculptures Clanbrasil St Dublin by the Sheil brothers. The Sheil brothers were very tough men who wouldn't have been out of place at the O. K. Corral. I used to accompany them for the collections in their old open backed lorry. I remember coming down the hill past Christchurch, the driver's door swung open and Mick reached out to grab it while shouting, "Come back in, you Fu…ing bastard."

As an aside, my wife, Rita's, grandfather was one of the marble artisans working at Early's, and you can still view his church altars, etc. around Ireland, e.g. St Peter's Church Phibsborough. His father was one of the many Welsh stonemasons who came to Ireland to build churches after Catholic emancipation in 1829.

I spent weeks crushing the marble which I then graded and put into storage bins. Can I say, on reflection, this was very dangerous work, particularly as I was working alone, but safety never figured greatly in my father's world.

In that same year, an engineer from P&T arrived one day to fit a new telephone line. I remember him being up a ladder, at the right hand side of the building. He was holding a chisel in his left hand and bashing it into the wall with a large hammer using his right hand.

As the chisel was merely bouncing off the wall, instead of penetrating it, he eventually climbed down and looking at Nano and me, he said, "What in God's name is that wall made of?"

We both burst out laughing because we knew the secret of the wall.

When the original mix was being prepared to plaster the outside of the building, Nano, who loved to experiment, included a large quantity of marble dust.

When we stopped laughing, I was sent to get a heavy drill from the Nissan hut which I then handed to the engineer, and later that day, we had our new phone line. Of course, we did have a phone from 1954 with a Nissan hut unauthorised extension. As I say, safety didn't loom large in Giles world!

1960 arrived and comely maidens dancing at the crossroads had gone home to be replaced by the man who started the process of modernising Ireland namely, Sean Lemass. The emigrants started to return in small numbers including my brothers, and I qualified as a seagoing radio officer.

They came home and I joined the British Merchant Navy.

In 1961, while home on leave and after a night out at the Ambassador Cinema, I suggested to Rita that we go back to Cross Guns, and I would make her one of my special Italian style omelettes, to which she agreed.

On reaching the building, I realised I had forgotten my keys and there was no one at home as they were all away on holiday. As I had been heavily involved in building Cross Guns from day one, I knew exactly what to do. Like a cat burglar, I climbed the outside walls, eventually reaching the flat roof at the top of the building.

I was in the process of removing one of the round skylights when I heard a commotion down below. I went to the parapet on the street side and observed men in uniform shining lights up in my direction.

"What are you doing up there? Come down here now immediately."

"OK, Officer, just give me a minute please." I lowered myself into the building via the skylight, ran downstairs and opened the hall door. I could see two guards and Rita waiting to greet me.

Once I explained who I was and that I was about to entertain my girlfriend, they smiled knowingly and departed to catch real criminals.

For a while, I had vision but no sound, and then, "My mother would go mad if she knew I was going out with a total lunatic."

"Sorry. Does this mean we're not getting married?"

More silence and then, "Anyway where's this magnificent omelette you're supposed to be making?" I served it up some twenty minutes later and dessert was nice too.

Some years after this event, I suggested to Rita that I make her another of my special Italian omelettes. "Are you completely mad? That was the most horrible meal I ever had in my life."

"Sorry."

But secretly I was glad because it meant I never again had to put a pot or a frying pan onto a cooker.

In the late 1960s, my brother, Paddy, took over Cross Guns under the name of 'Rocca Tiles Ltd'.

In later years, he sold it to Des Kelly of Kelly Carpets and after them it became a bookie shop.

The year is now 2021 and the premises have become Prospect Medical Centre. I became one of its first patients some weeks ago.

On my first visit, I remarked to Doctor Kennedy how well the building looked after its recent refurbishment, but the outside needed to be repainted.

He said yes but it's hard to find a painter these days.

"If you can make me sixty years younger, I could do it."

He looked at me quizzically and I imagine he was thinking even Jesus would struggle with that that one.

"Roll up both sleeves, Donal, and I'll give the Covid-19 booster plus the Flu jab."

Less than a week later, the outside was restored to its original magnificent whiteness.

At night while walking alone, I sometimes stop outside the Brian Boru and staring across at Nano's building I remember those early years and those early people—Egidio, Agnes, Paddy, Maureen, Eda, Gus, Seamus, Anne, Albie, Ann, Linda, Seán, George, Vera ,Bernard, Pio, Rita, Me.

And as I walk on, I sometimes pause at the bridge over the Royal canal, and looking back I wonder:

What became of the people we used to be?

Italy 1947

The Roccas journey to Italy was first planned in 1938 but with the start of Second World War in 1939, the plan had to be abandoned. I guess this was a great disappointment to my father, Egidio Rocca, who looked forward to displaying his success from being a poor Italian emigrant in 1922 to a not rich, but very comfortable businessman, in the 1930s.

Nano (his family name meant little one). The story of how he was the first Italian (and Alien), to become a citizen of the Free State, is a story to be told on its own. 1947 came, and I was still an infant student at Corpus Christi school run by The Holy Faith Nuns. Even then, I wondered how God could have introduced such horrible creatures (with a few exceptions, e.g. Sister Anselm) into the lives of innocent children.

I think the strap was their God rather than Jesus. I suppose one good thing came from Corpus Christi, as my wife to be was there at the same time. Anyway, I digress. In January 1947, coming home from school to our house at 41, Home Farm Park, Drumcondra, I would do my homework, and this was usually followed by games in the street and home for tea. After that, my mother, Agnes (nee Cunningham), would bribe me to bottle feed my baby sister, Linda, born December 1946.

We had a maid, Jane, from Enniskerry and we did have a connection to Enniskerry which is a story for another day. I had a very close happy connection with Jane which was to end in some misery for me and I imagine for her. She'd encourage me to eat all my porridge saying I'd become a big boy. "Jane, am I big now?" She'd laugh and hug me.

Then we'd have fun chasing each other around the garden and up the lane at the back of the house. One day, I came running home from school shouting her name as I usually did, "Jane...Jane!" But this was met with silence. Agnes told me Jane had gone away and would not be coming back.

I later learned Jane had been sacked for a minor misdemeanour. That night, I cried myself to sleep and many more nights after that, and there was no one there to hug me. Jane had gone. January 1947 and the worst winter in living memory began with snow blizzards piling the snow so high, it almost brought Ireland to a standstill.

There was no central heating in those days, and at night, we'd huddle around a living room fire listening to BBC radio and playing cards, or brother, Albie's, compendium of games. At 10 p.m., Nano would make up a hot bottle for everyone and we'd reluctantly trundle off to our freezing cold rooms and bed. In the morning, it was hard to vacate what overnight became cosy warm beds and face another day of frost and snow.

There were very good days of course—snowball fights and building huge snowmen in the lower Home Farm ring outside Wesley Seymour's house. Nano, Paddy and Seamus built two fabulous sleighs. One was big enough for three and one for two. At the weekends, the Roccas would pile into the family car with sleighs in a small trailer behind and head for the hills of Co. Wicklow.

They were super fun days, though on reflection, probably very dangerous. As a small person, I was always jammed in the middle of the big sleigh between Nano and Paddy, and off we'd go down the steep hill, in what can only be described as very scary but very, very exciting. We were usually followed by Seamus and George or Albie on the smaller sleigh. To get some idea of what I'm talking about watch Deborah Kerr and Humphrey Bogart riding the rapids in 'The African Queen'.

21 March 1947, the Spring Equinox and the Sun moved north of the Equator. The blizzards ceased, the temperatures crept above zero and the mounds of snow slowly began to melt. By the end of March, life in Dublin was back to normal. Agnes, along with me, was able to return to her favourite Saturday morning shops in Drumcondra and Dorset Street.

On weekdays, she liked nothing better than coffee in Bewley's Cafe and then, as she was often heard to say, "A bit of business for Nano." This meant buying stationery, stamps and ribbons for his typewriter. Nano usually spent three nights a week doing Co. paperwork. The other nights were usually spent in the cinema.

One day in **May,** Agnes and I went to the Custom House (newly refurbished after being burnt by Michael Collins) and stood at a long high counter and waited for a severe looking woman to attend to us. Agnes said, "I've come to collect 5 passports please." I could tell the severe looking woman, who was probably a

1916 veteran, was disdainful of anyone going on holiday outside Ireland, but we did come away with the five passports.

Agnes decided that we should treat ourselves to a nice ice cream and with this in mind, we took ourselves to Caffolla's ice cream parlour on O'Connell Street. In the 40s and 50s, the amount of money that one was allowed to take out of Ireland was very limited, and certainly not anything near enough to fund a continental holiday.

Money in 1947—American dollars and British Pounds were acceptable on every inch of the planet. Ireland was also part of the Sterling family and no one in Dublin, Cork, Galway or wherever, batted an eyelid in exchanging the King's head mixed with an Irish Salmon. That said, if you presented a portrait of Lady Lavery in Paris or Rome, you would be met with a blank stare.

Agnes knew this and put a cunning plan in place. She put together bundles of Britannia notes and of course these had to be concealed for smuggling through customs. After consideration, the stitching on the overcoat sleeves of Sister Eda and mother were gently unpicked. The contraband currency was inserted and the sleeves expertly re-stitched. Problem solved!

The cases for travelling were purchased in Clerys and the biggest of these was a trunk so big, I could stand up in it quite comfortably. The journey began around mid-July and the five travellers—father, mother, Eda, Albie, and me, boarded the British Rail ferry, also known as the Mailboat, at Dun Laoghaire. I had never been on a ship before and I can still remember walking around the deck holding my sister's hand.

On boarding, Nano was dispatched to the pursers office where he ordered a private cabin for Agnes. Mother liked comfort. It was a roughish evening crossing and Brother Albert looked a bit greenish. We arrived in Holyhead, Wales sometime after midnight and after a British customs officer finished rooting through our carefully packed cases, and chalk marked the outside, we proceeded across the platform directly to the overnight train to London.

We were directed to one of the sleeping carriages which had layered bunks and pullover curtains. The adults had one each and the brothers shared one. The steam train travelled overnight via Chester, Stoke on Trent, Birmingham and all points south of the British Midlands, occasionally blowing its whistle till we arrived at Euston at around 8.30 a.m.

Euston Station on a July Saturday morning: There were a lot of people bustling about, some with BBC quality accents and some with accents difficult to decipher. The smell of smoke and steam filled the air as we five stood around the big trunk. Through the noise a small man in peak cap and pushing a big wooden trolley approached us.

"Take your cases, Guvnor?"

To which my father replied in his heavy Italian accent, "Yes, please, to a taxi." After the porter had loaded our cases into a London black cab and Nano paid him, we piled in and began the journey to Aunt Dotie's house in Kensal Green. Agnes, Nano and Eda sat on the main rear seat while Albie and I occupied the pull-down seats facing the rear of the taxi.

As a small person on a shiny seat, I had difficulty holding on and sometimes one of the adults would have to assist with a holding hand. We drove past many bomb-damaged buildings with armies of workmen delivering the final Coup de Grace to allow for new replacements. Agnes repeated several times, "Those poor people must have suffered terribly."

We had a present of Irish rashers, sausages and black pudding for Dotie and Albert, which was intended to give them some cheer. We passed the big roundabout at Buckingham Palace, and Agnes told us the Royal Standard was flying, which meant the king and queen were in residence. We reached number 4, Kensal Green to be met by Dotie and Albert.

Albert was a very English looking grey-haired man who drove London buses during the First World War, along with the now famous comedian, Billy Cotton. After the war, Albert got a job delivering new cars from Oxford to London. There were no car carriers in those days and each car had to be delivered by a dedicated driver. Albert's claim to fame was he once delivered a Rolls Royce.

Anyway, I digress. Dotie served breakfast, part of which included strawberry jam, a piece of which dropped from my slice onto the dining room carpet. I stayed quiet but some minutes later, there was a lot of tut tutting as Dotie tried to establish who the culprit was! After breakfast, Albert showed us a crack running the whole length of the house, caused when a German V2 rocket landed near the local railway station.

He called the V2 a doodlebug. At that time, the local cinemas in London had Saturday morning matinees for children, so Albie and I with two shillings, provided by Nano, duly attended the one at Kensal Green. The noise was deafening from hundreds of local children before the big curtains parted and silence fell. After the usual shorts and trailers, the big feature started—'Custer's last stand, starring Errol Flynn'. Toy six shooters appeared from almost every seat in the cinema.

Sunday morning and after bidding farewell to Dotie and Albert, we headed for St Pancras station in another London black cab. Having boarded the train for Dover with the assistance of another Cockney porter, we were soon trundling through the garden county of Kent, and two hours later, we could see the White Cliffs of Dover. We boarded the ferry bound for Calais. Although, normally only a short sea voyage, Agnes again enjoyed the comfort of a private cabin which opened onto the main deck.

This was probably judicious for her, as the short Dover to Calais hop turned to a nightmare sea passage when the sea was engulfed with a freak summer storm. Passengers were seasick and communal rooms with tiered sofa beds were full of people lying very still with closed eyes, which as I discovered many years later during my circumnavigations of the globe, is the best way to combat seasickness.

Albie and I strangely enough seemed fine and apart from being somewhat frightened enjoyed the adventure. I'm not sure the same could be said for the captain and deck officers, as they found it impossible to manoeuvre the ship into the safety of Calais Harbour and instead diverted the ship to Dunkirk. This was probably a happier time for this ship, as its first visit was to assist in the evacuation of 300,000 trapped British troops.

I remember us two brothers running around a huge open quay area with hardly a building in sight, as they had been levelled during the siege. On to Paris.

Dunkirk and another train boarding, this time with the aid of a French porter and we were soon on our way to Paris travelling through war torn towns, which I didn't see much of, as I was not yet six and hit the tiredness wall. I spent most of the six-hour journey sleeping with my head on my mother's lap. I awoke refreshed in Gare du Nord, Paris where we had to wait for the next train to Milano Centralo.

One incident occurred here which even today I find hard to relate, but I will. My sister, Eda, had been carrying her tennis racket, the strings of which were protected by a set. I'm not sure why she brought it as it never saw a tennis court during the entire visit.

Anyway, out of boredom, I kept trying to pull it from her grip and eventually succeeded, much to the annoyance of the adults who were also probably cranky with travel tiredness by this stage.

Wandering around the platform swinging the racket in mock play, I suddenly felt it slip from my grip and it went flying into the air. It didn't just fly into the air, it landed on the railway track. Keeping in mind all the warnings I had been given, I panicked and jumped after the racket.

I managed to recover it and placed it carefully on the platform but then found I was too small to follow. I then saw a train heading my way and heard someone screaming which in fact was me. The next thing I knew someone, Nano in fact, was dragging me up by the scruff of the neck and the safety of the platform. I can honestly say from that day to this, I became incapable of dragging something from anyone's hand.

The journey from Paris to Milan began with a meal in the dining car. I can still smell the aroma of coffee mixed with wine, French bread, cooked meats and cigars. The table was dressed with an immaculate white linen cloth, which thankfully I didn't mark with my glass of watered wine. After we finished our meal, both Albert and I went exploring by running the full length of the train probably to the irritation of the other passengers.

The steam train with clankety clank noises and regular blowing of the whistle, whizzed its way south through the French countryside and the Italian border. One part of the train running that I found nerve racking, was jumping the space between the carriages with Brother Albie saying, "Come on."

Later, we went to one of the sleeping carriages where the adults had their own bunks and we shared one. The next morning, we arrived at Milano Centralo, which in fairness to Mussolini and the Fascists, was and is a thing of beauty. As arranged, Nano's cousins were there to greet us.

Unfortunately, his mother died when he was only five, so I can only imagine what sadness he may have felt at this reunion, since he left for Ireland from this very station some twenty-five years earlier. While the adults talked, I walked around the station shouting, "Heil Hitler" (which every Dublin boy did in those days). Nano eventually caught up with me and laughing hilariously along with Gamba Longa, and his brother, Bino, etc., managed to silence me.

I wondered what all the fuss was about but I'm sure the ghost of Il Duce also enjoyed the hilarity of the scene played out before him. After another train journey from Milan to Parma, we eventually arrived at what I can only describe (possibly incorrectly) as a big farmhouse. We met Bino's wife, Aunt Linda, and her sister, Ernestina, who I found to be a very kind and caring person.

These were poor people who suffered terribly during the war, but they produced an Italian meal that could have graced the table of any rich person. Even today I can smell the freshness of the lovely after dinner fruit. One of Nano's cousins then showed me how to count Italian Lira coins. That night, I slept on what I remember as a small tent bed and tucked in by Ernestina, I soon fell unconscious probably assisted by the watered wine I'd had with dinner.

I'll continue the memories of a five, almost six year old boy, with assistance of a now, seventy-eight year old man. I awoke the next morning 100% refreshed, and having washed, dressed and eaten, I exited the farm building into a large yard and an umbrella blue sky. Once I had checked out the outbuildings and the hens clucking free range, I found myself a long seat on which I lay down and closed my eyes against the rising sun.

"Come si chiama?" I opened my eyes to see a boy about my own age staring down at me.

Not knowing what he said, I repeated back 'Comes I Chama', and he smiled at my stupidity. We were soon joined by about six boys of similar age and once they became bored trying to make sense of the new pale faced arrival, they started to run about mostly in bare feet. I followed and joined in their shouting and singing of something completely incomprehensible to me.

In later years, I discovered the 'Come si chiama' boy was my first cousin, and the following year, he stepped on a thorn and died the next day from blood poisoning. Over fifty years later in conversation with my aunt Gina, Nano's sister, her grief was still as raw as the day he died. I returned to the farmhouse where Nano was enjoying himself talking to his sister, Gina, brother, Bino, cousin, Gamba Longa, and most of all his uncle Attilio.

Agnes and Eda were engaged in their own discussion and Albie was doing his own reconnaissance outside. In 1920, it was arranged that Gina would travel to Ireland with Nano, but changed her mind at the last moment. She loved relating how when they were children, Nano would try cheating her out of her few Lira pocket money.

Great Uncle Attilio reared Nano after his mother, Carolina, died from TB when he was very young and his father, Carlo, was away with the Italian mountain troops fighting the Austrians in the Dolomites. This part of the horrendous war in the Dolomites is best explained in Ernest Hemingway's novel 'A Farewell to Arms'. Back to Attilio, and Nano said he loved practical jokes.

One night, Nano was returning home in the dark from a dance when a large white figure jumped from a bush in front of him and shouted, "Yah." Nano started to run, but then heard laughing behind him. He joined in the laughter by shouting back, "Merda, you bloody fool."

The first Sunday. It was early morning with a cloudless sky, but it was cool under the Pergola, where we all sat enjoying a continental breakfast. The conversations were interrupted, when a high sided two-toned car chugged its way into the courtyard and a man in a peaked hat stepped out. Nano and the peaked hat man then retired to the farmhouse and sometime later, Nano re-joined the Pergola group and made an announcement, "We have transport."

The first job of the high and I must say very spacious high pudding vehicle was to take us to Mass at the Fontanellato Basilica. This is a church first built in the 13th century and its most important resident is the 'Madonna del Rosario', installed during the 17th century plague period. Contrary to church teaching on Idolatry, the local residents prayed to the Madonna for sanctuary from the re-visitation of the Black Death, which killed almost two million Italians.

Their prayers were answered and since then, the Madonna has been credited with many miracles and peaceful deaths. The statue is often removed from its case of honour and paraded in the streets of Parma. Anything that gives comfort must be good.

After Mass, we walked to the nearby 'Castle Rocca Sanivitale', built by the Sanivitale family in the 13th century, and the small town of Fontanellato grew up around it. Today, it is a major tourist attraction in the area, and it contains artwork of great importance. During a visit in the late 1990s, Pierra (a family friend) arranged for Rita and I to have a private viewing of the almost completed restoration in areas not open to the general public.

One of the art restoration team explained the stories behind each of the Sanivitale family paintings, many of which are quite sad. Anyway, again I digress.

While Nano and the senior family members talked while seated on the Moat wall, Eda and Agnes checked out the local shops. Albie and I became quite bored and to relieve same, we started chasing each other around the long circular moat wall.

After the Castle visit, we were taken to the almost adjacent large red brick building which housed six hundred of the 80,000 British prisoners in Italy during the Second World War. This was a place where allied soldiers enjoyed a war of some peace and relative comfort; a place where it would be more appropriate to escape to rather than escape from. That said, the day after the 1943 armistice, the gates were opened and most of the British prisoners escaped over the Alps with the assistance of the locals and Italian Partisans.

This was at great peril, to their own safety. Some of these prisoners returned after the war to continue their love relationships including, I believe, the author Eric Newby. His novel also prompted the making of a movie, starring Peter Bowles. In the midst of all its horror, the war did instigate many Captain Corelli love affairs.

On the way home, we stopped for coffee and ice cream at a restaurant in Garibaldi Square. Agnes arranged her own brew with tea she had brought from Ireland. Nearby was the main Parma Bridge over the river Po, where Aunt Linda had a hair-raising experience.

While she and many other cyclists were crossing the bridge, they could hear the fire from a British terror Spitfire crossing the city. Abandoning their bikes, the girls squeezed in as close as they could to the bridge ramparts, and soon after Linda could see the 5cm bullets hopping their way just in front of her eyes. These visits by terror planes, to cities like Milan, Parma, Bologna, etc. were not intended so much to kill, as to demoralise the population, and speed up surrender.

With almost constant war in Europe since the fall of the Roman Empire, I suspect the peninsula had enough of invasions by the French, Austrians and God knows who else. Peace and the American Marshall plan transformed Italy completely by our next visit in 1954.

The EEC completed the transformation which is something the English Brexiteers appear to have forgotten. Sorry, Ian!

Before proceeding, I would like to revert back to Rocca Sanivitale: For those who may not know, the people of the Italian peninsula were the premier builders of castles and churches in Europe. This probably came about because Italy was made up of many independent states, all vying with each other for supremacy. Venice against Genoa, and the Papal states against everyone!

The Castell dell Angelo, and St Peter's in Rome, are prime examples. The English King Edward 1 (longshanks) built his ring of Magnificent Castles circling Wales using Italian technology and gold loans from Florence Banks. Many are still standing today providing tourist revenue to the Welsh economy.

Anyway, onward in my journey: At some stage during our stay, I met my only then living grandparent, Carlo Rocca. I say met but it was very brief, one to one, and very awkward which with the benefit of seventy-two years I can now understand. Carlo lost his wife as a young man and was then conscripted into the army, and wound up in the Dolomites fighting in a very cold and vicious war.

Even today, accelerated by global warming, bodies are emerging from the snow. Both sides in the conflict realised they could engulf their enemy in avalanches by shelling the mountains above the enemy camps and efficiently eliminate many of their opponents. The only respite Carlo and his fellow comrades would have had was an occasional withdrawal to the Liberty Hotel, Lake Garda.

During a stay there in recent years, I mentioned this connection to the travel guide, which resulted in Rita and I receiving preferential treatment. Perhaps Carlo sent this as a present from the grave!

On returning home from First World War, Carlo and many family members were victims of the pandemic Spanish flu, which killed more people in Europe than the World War. Uncle Bino survived by wearing a ring of garlic around his neck and was able to administer to the sick. Carlo then spent the next thirty years in a menial job, and they say Mr Chianti was his best friend, and I'm glad he did have one and some peace.

During the next weeks of our stay, the two tone (black and tan) car took us to Modena where, if we'd known, we could have met with the young Pavarotti.

Fidenza, where Nano was born in the house of John Bosco, located in the shadow of the famous Duomo. This small town was a resting place for Canterbury pilgrims travelling to Rome. St Dominic Savio had been a former resident of the John Bosco house. My father rarely spoke about Fidenza as I suspect the poverty and early loss of Carolina were too painful to remember.

Bologna, where Linda and Bino lived for some time! Italy is awash with famous buildings and works of art and Bologna is no exception. Possibly its most famous resident was Guglielmo Marconi, Nobel Prize winner and the father of radio. He also had an Irish mother somewhat wealthier than mine. In later years, the Marconi Company did provide me with a reasonable income and several circumnavigations of the planet.

Towards the end of our stay, Nano and Agnes travelled to Venice, for a romantic few days, leaving us in the care of Aunt Gina, Ernestina and Gamba Longa. It would be remiss not to mention the Pezzani family, close friends to the Roccas and without whom the Second World War would have been even more miserable. I often wonder, was it their farmhouse we stayed in?

Even today, the Pezzani family are close friends and no more so than Tina and Piera. Our daughter, Camille, enjoys the hospitality of both sisters, two or three times a year. My sister, Linda, has enjoyed Pezzani family hospitality going back more than sixty years.

The Farm—some memories: I heard pig noises coming from behind a locked door and spent about ten minutes communicating with the pig, on my hands and knees, via a small gap at the bottom of the door. Deciding it would be better to have a more direct conversation, I decided to open the door, but just as I was about to open the latch, a large hand grabbed mine and a 'No, no, no'.

It turned out I was probably seconds away from an encounter with a boar, from which I would have come off second best. The large hand man then took me to another animal house where he milked a large buffalo, putting the hot milk into an earthenware jug which he handed to me.

"Drink, drink," which I did and I must say, I found the warm liquid very enjoyable. The next day, I saw the same buffalo harnessed to a large round barrel.

Cousin Gamba Longa placed me on top with nothing much to hold on to and then went to the rear of the barrel, held a length of rope tied to the stopper and shouted, "Andiamo, Andiamo." The buffalo took off at some speed with me hanging on for dear life while the contents of the VAT barrel (water) irrigated the field during our flight around a large field.

On the last day, Egidio and his brother, Bino, agreed, after a long discussion, that Bino and Linda should join us in Ireland. This did happen and I can remember their Home Farm arrival in 1948. Bino became a Rocca Ltd. employee, much to my father's delight and at last, Nano had family from his own country.

I can still hear their friendly arguments and discussions which lasted for hours after Sunday lunch and drives into Wicklow. In later years, Bino got a job as a chauffeur in the Italian Embassy. As a colourful character who smoked his cigarettes in a long holder, this was a dream job for him. He could converse in any company with stories of his stay in Port Masawa (Red Sea) Abyssinia, which no doubt he related while driving ambassadors and world leaders to and from embassy functions.

In 1979, they returned to live in Collechio (the home of Parma cheese) which is a town close to Parma City. They had a very comfortable large apartment and I'm grateful they provided accommodation for my two daughters, Bernice and Camille, while they were studying in Italy. I know Linda was pleased to be back in her own country but I'm not sure about Bino, as no doubt he missed the company of the Diplomatic Glitterati.

I also feel if Linda and Bino had stayed, my father would have enjoyed his old age better in the company of his younger brother.

A sad event Linda suffered in the 1950s was to return to Italy to attend the funeral of the lovely Ernestina, who succumbed to cancer. Regarding Linda, I would say she was a good substitute for Jane.

When it was time to leave, tearful goodbyes were said and the man in the peaked cap reappeared. He drove the two-toner to Centralo Milano, where we joined the train which took us back to Gare du Nord, Paris, and then onto Calais where we boarded the ferry for Dover. This crossing was smooth and short. After another brief visit to Dotie's and the purchase of a colt six shooter for my sixth birthday, we boarded the train from Euston to Holyhead.

Here we boarded the mailboat for what was an overnight crossing, and we arrived in Dun Laoghaire around 8 a.m. and Westland Row Station about an hour later. I can remember running down the station ramp shouting Heil Hitler with no one to stop me this time! When we arrived home, Agnes insisted that we all sleep to recover from our long journey, and I remember this did not please me one bit.

However sometime later, I was released and running, while firing my prized Colt six shooter, I wondered how the 'Come si Ciamo' boy was doing.

Padre Pio

The journey to Via Reggio really begins in 1949 when my aunt Dotie from London suggested that there was something not quite right with my brother, Bernard. He looked normal and some heated words were exchanged between the two Sisters. Dotie was right and it was soon established that Bernard, although a lovely human being, was in fact what was in those days called 'retarded' (in hindsight, it was autism).

My parents, over the next few years, sought everywhere in Ireland for a cure, but of course their quest was pointless. In 1952, after a lot of household tears, Bernard was brought to a private home somewhere near London.

Sometime in 1953, my mother, Agnes (nee Cunningham), started talking about Padre Pio of Foggia, probably as a result of conversations with her brother, Patsy, who spent much of his life in Gardner street church. She read the book of Padre Pio's life, from cover to cover and although never openly said she believed, if only she could talk with Padre Pio her world would return to normal.

In the early months of 1954, my father, Egidio Rocca, known to everyone as Nano, started planning the journey from Dublin to the South of Italy. (As an aside can I tell you, Nano was one of the Italians who repaired the GPO after the 1916 rising? The story of how he became the first Alien to gain citizenship in the Free State is also worth retelling if you're interested.)

Anyway, Cooks Travel provided very comprehensive instructions with a book of maps, which became our travel Bible. You could say, it was the paper equivalent of a Garmin NUVI 205. They also provided a book of tourist petrol vouchers for use in Italy, which my father loved talking about. It ensured we always had petrol and as far as I know tax free.

In June, my father collected his new Ford Consul from Walden motors (Townsend St). He had a love affair with cars as did my older brothers. He renewed his every two years.

It was sometime after mid-July that we boarded the British rail ferry at Dun Laoghaire. The car was loaded by crane. When we piled into the Consul at Holyhead, everyone was in great form, with my father joking, as to whether or not we should allow the English flies to travel with us. I hadn't the heart to tell him we were in Wales.

One memory that stands out on our journey across England was the night we couldn't find a guest house or hotel to stay in, as so many people were on holiday. It might have been Oxford, where my father asked the local police station if we could sleep in one of their cells.

I suppose they were amused but did arrange for the four of us to share a parlour in a house nearby. The grandfather clock chimed every quarter and I remember Nano disabled the pendulum during the night.

When we looked out the following morning, we could see a big square and people were emerging from cars where they had slept all night.

One of our next stops was to visit Bernard at the private home. He seemed happy and spoke in his limited vocabulary with a very upmarket English accent.

Eventually, we reached Dover and this time drove onto the ferry. I remember Eartha Kitt was singing 'Under The Bridges Of Paris' on the radio.

With our Cooks guide, we navigated our way across France till we reached the Alps. Agnes went white and quiet, but I thought it was great looking down into the Swiss Valleys.

Onwards for stops at glamorous Monte Carlo and Nice, with views straight out of Grace Kelly's Hollywood movies! More stunning drives down the west coast to Genoa, La Spezia, and Viareggio where we stayed for a couple of days and enjoyed Pedalow rides and swims in the blue Mediterranean. After Via Reggio, we drove across country for more short stays and sightseeing tours at Pisa and Florence and then on to Rome and St Peters.

I wondered why some females were being refused entry, until Agnes told me their shoulders weren't covered! Maybe all the dead Popes would have turned in their coffins, excluding of course the Medici's! From Rome we journeyed to Castel Gandolfo, where we stood in the square and watched the Balcony appearance of Pius twelfth.

On to Naples to a small hotel where I had a perfect view of Vesuvius from my window, and prayed, it wouldn't erupt during our stay.

Onwards to Foggia and San Giovanni Rotondo! After breakfast the next morning, we drove up to the Monastery and started to queue along with throngs of others trying to gain entry. People were pushing and shoving. One of the officials seemed to notice us as some sort of exotic creatures, and after a brief conversation with my father, the cry went up, "Make way for the English."

Maybe Pio performed a miracle, because the crowds parted like the Red Sea, or in this case, black, and we were personally escorted up near the altar of what I remember as a smallish church. We all stood and eventually, Pio appeared flanked by two monks. We stayed standing throughout the Mass, during which the celebrant did stumble at times, but his two minders were on hand to help.

We were very close to the altar and at just thirteen years of age, I was afraid on two occasions I might faint, which wasn't helped by the odours of old little mountain women dressed in black. I was glad when Pio walked past me, besieged by the aforementioned females. After this, my brother, Albie, and I visited all the little stalls selling medals of the Virgin Mary and such like.

It was like the stalls of Knock had taken flight to Foggia. Albie bought scapulars believing these would guarantee his entry into Heaven. Hopefully, he's now saying 'Told you so!'

The next morning was the same as the first, with us so called English visitors occupying the same part of the chapel as on day one. Padre Pio said the mass again and when it was finished, my father, Albie and I were ushered into a small room for an audience with the great man. Much to my mother's annoyance, she was excluded as a woman and I was also told to leave so she would have company.

As a new teenager whose equipment had recently arrived, I didn't mind, and in fact was glad because I didn't want a saint to be reading my thoughts.

Agnes and I waited in the Consul with the occasional old soldier trying to engage us in conversation. One of my very few phrases was 'Siamo Irlandesi, non parlo Italiano', which came in useful.

When the privileged returned, Agnes immediately started questioning Nano, I suppose in the vain hope that my brother, Bernard, would be added to the list of miracles, which we all knew was never going to happen.

Mothers will cling to any straw. I don't remember much of the conversation, except Pio promised to pray for Bernard and the rest of the family. He also assured my father that we would have a safe journey home. I know that there were other things said, during the one hour meeting, but I can't remember them now.

After Foggia, we made our way towards home via the Eastern side of the Italian Peninsula, Pescara to Rimini and a two day stopover. Great memories of more golden sandy beaches and three of us on a large white Pedalow.

Onwards to Bologna in fading light, and the atmosphere in the car changed to sombre silence. There were whispered exchanges between Agnes and Nano, culminating in 'Ok we'll call, but only for a short visit'. It turned out Agnes only agreed to the holiday conditional on no visits to 'gabbing relatives'.

All animosity forgotten, there was great Bon Homie on the road from Bologna to Parma.

It was midnight when the Consul entered a big courtyard. We all got out and I remember it was very warm, with a full moon shining in a starry, starry night and eerily silent apart from the intermittent sound of crickets singing.

Gamba Longa (Nano's cousin, collected earlier) to a shuttered bedroom window. "Uncle, wake up and get yourself down here now," repeated several times before the shutters eventually opened and light spilled into the courtyard.

Uncle Attilio said, "What do you want, you drunken fool? Do you know what time it is?"

Gamba Longa said, "Get yourself down here now. You have a visitor."

More muttered expletives from above, including several Merdas and other things best not said. Eventually, the main door opened spilling more light onto the waiting assembly. Then, "Nano? Is it Nano? Is it Nano?"

Too choked to reply, Nephew and Uncle embraced for what seemed like an eternity.

It was the first time ever that I saw grown men cry.

(Attilio more or less reared Nano after his mother died from TB, when he was four and his father, Carlo, spent the First World War years fighting the Austrians in the Dolomites.) Albie wiped tears away and I could see Agnes had difficulty controlling her emotions. Sixty three years on and I too find it difficult to re-live.

Loud shouting followed from the house with females appearing from everywhere and throwing their arms around all of us, Nano's aunt and sister, Gina, among them. This preceded a feast with lots of talk which went on till the break of dawn.

The departure from Fontanellato the next day was full of promises to return soon, but of course these were 'dreams never to be'.

Our journey continued on towards Calais via Milan and Berne, where we stayed at a lovely small hotel where I had a wood panelled room all to myself. Albert likewise!

It was very cold, but very warm under a very large cosy duvet. I mention this because it was the first one I ever saw.

In London, we collected Dotie and in a couple of days, we were back in Dublin. The end! Omissions:

A) One night in Italy, we were unable to find a place to stay so Nano pulled into a field and blew up two Lilos, on which Albie and himself, slept under the stars while mother and I spent a very uncomfortable night sleeping in the car.

B) Another night as above was almost repeated till Nano pulled in to a farmyard and negotiated an evening meal and accommodation for himself and Agnes to sleep indoors, with brother Albert and myself sleeping in the hay barn. The farmer and his family went to a lot of trouble with the evening meal served under the Pergola, which ensured clean plates all around washed down with house wine and a couple of bottles of Chianti. The water in Italy is not great so it was normal for children like me in those times to have wine with a splash of water.

The farmer related how, when the Germans were retreating up through Italy, the male members of the family were lined up outside and told they were going to be shot. To their relief it turned out to be a German attempt at humour.

We then went to our accommodation and to this day, I can't remember having a better sleep on my bed of straw.

C) Crossing the Alps, Agnes started to say prayers and Albie asked me if I could hear the rattle of Rosary beads. Hysterical laughter and banter followed and still makes me smile even today.

D) We stopped several times at marble works where Nano loved checking out all the latest cutting machines and such like. Agnes eventually said, no more marble works visits.

E) As the Consul car was still just being run in, Nano decided to have it checked out in a garage, where the mechanic put it on a hydraulic lift. The mechanic said it looked fine and started to lower the hoist.

I noticed his right foot was over the white line but said nothing, until six inches from impact, when I tugged Nano's sleeve and he almost rugby tackled the poor man out of danger.

My Trip on the Livorno

It was early December 1960, and I was home on leave from sea duty. I was hoping not to be recalled before the Christmas holidays, so I and my girl, Rita Tomlin, could enjoy more happy days together. My thoughts were interrupted by the sound of a motorbike pulling up outside our home.

My heart sank a little because I knew before the messenger walked up the drive it was a telegram for me. *You are requested to report to the Marconi Marine Hull Office on 7/12/60 and sign on at the Mercantile Marine Office as Senior Radio Officer of the **mv Livorno**.*

The next evening, after a tearful farewell, I boarded the overnight ferry mv Leinster from Dublin to Liverpool.

Mv Leinster/EIPL, a ferry that many of our Irish members seemed to have taken overnight to travel between Dublin and Liverpool to join Marconi manned ships in the UK.

The next day, the train from Liverpool Lime Street took me over the Pennines to Hull and onwards by taxi to the Marconi Marine Office, and lots of paperwork, including sufficient logbooks, for the sea voyage to the Mediterranean. The next day, having signed on with the rest of the crew, I walked up the gangway of the

Livorno/GPWF rather nervously, as this was my first ship in charge of a radio station.

On my previous ships, I had the comfort of being only the second R.O. The second steward showed me to my cabin on the top deck and the radio room, which was adjacent. It was normal for the operator to be isolated in this way, to be available quickly if required.

Having handed me the keys, I enquired of the steward when the next meal was due to be served, only to be told, "The ship is not due to sail for the next two days and as almost everyone is local, there will be no one onboard except the loading officer, and he'll be leaving the ship at 1800 hours." This was depressing news, as I had already eaten into my limited funds. I suspect someone should have been paying me compensation for shore meals, etc., but I was too Naive to ask.

The cabin was adequate with a good size washbasin and cabinet stocked with plenty of soap. Running low on funds, I decided not to revisit the seaman's hostel where I spent my first night in Hull, but bed down in my new abode. It was cold, but there were blankets, but no bed linen as yet. I awoke the next morning feeling pretty hungry and having washed and dressed, I wondered where I might get something to eat.

Torn between wanting to check out the radio station and hunger, I decided to venture into Hull to see if I could find a cheap greasy spoon where I could get a morning fry up.

While walking through the docks complex, I noticed a large wooden building filled with men in working clothes sitting at long wooden tables, drinking mugs of tea and eating bacon sandwiches. This was the docker's break time from loading ships. Feeling very self-conscious, as I was dressed more suitably for a wedding breakfast, than a docker's canteen, I, nevertheless, entered the long wooden building, and found a small empty table, where I stupidly sat waiting for a waitress to attend to my needs.

I was aware I looked out of place as some of the patrons were staring and smiling. One of them eventually took pity on me and said in his broad Yorkshire accent, "Son, you must go up to the counter over there and one of the lasses will take care of you." I thanked him and made my way to the counter where girls young and old were busy making sandwiches and washing dishes.

"Aren't you a smart looking chap?" A girl probably a bit older than me remarked. I wasn't able to stop the blush coming into my face, but I managed to order tea and sandwiches. Having paid the cost of two shillings, I again stupidly enquired if I should wait or would it be delivered to the table.

At this stage, my blushing returned as the girls all laughed out loud, but one kind soul then said, "Go sit down, love, and I'll bring it over." Having finished my meal, I returned to my ship and started to inspect the radio equipment, some of which I had never seen before.

Fortunately, during this inspection, a company shore engineer came into the radio room and it was his job to give newly in-charge personnel a handover. Things went well till we came to a strange looking Radio Direction Finder at the corner of the office I could see he was as baffled as me, though he tried to hide it.

I knew it was something called a reactance receiver with Bellini Tosi loops (named after the two Italian scientists who developed the system) and I thought I'd have enough time to master its operation during the voyage. Unfortunately, as it proved later, this was something of a mistake.

I spent the rest of the day unpacking and going over the training notes I carried from my previous two seniors, Bewley and O'Connor. How to price telegrams sent to various countries and stations transmitting weather reports and warnings, etc.? Feeling a bit peckish by mid-afternoon, I decided to try and find a cafe somewhere in the city.

Walking past the dockers' eating house, I decided to get over my morning embarrassment and go eat there again, hoping I might not be remembered. This was a forlorn hope as I was met at the counter by a sea of smiling female faces. They were actually all very nice.

That night, I repeated my previous night's experience of sleeping with no bed linen and a couple of rough blankets with no counterpane. Next morning, I awoke to the sound of the ship coming back to life with the returning crew walking up the gangway, galley meals being prepared and the chatter of deckhands talking about things they did while on shore leave. I finished my morning ablutions and still in my dressing gown, a rap came on the door and I invited the caller to enter.

It was a steward carrying a tray of tea and toast who introduced himself. "Good morning, I'm Albert and I'll be your steward for the trip."

I replied, "Nice to meet you, Albert, and my name is Donal."

To which he hesitated but then replied, "Ok, Don, and did you sleep ok?"

"Yes, fine thank you, Albert."

He again hesitated as though he wanted to say something but instead placed the tray on the locker table and started to leave, before finally announcing that, "Lunch will be served at 1200 hours."

I spent much of the rest of the morning familiarising myself.

LIVORNO

again, with the Radio Station receiver and transmission systems. Sometime during this process, Captain West entered the radio room and enquired if everything was ok. On mature reflection and not being mature, I foolishly replied, "Yes, Sir," but I felt the station lacked a high frequency transmitter.

By the look on his face and something, he said, I regretted revealing my thoughts. This was a youngish career captain, in a high quality shipping company, Ellerman Wilson Lines, and although the *Livorno* (previous page) was one of the lesser vessels, I sensed he didn't appreciate a green blow-in like me, criticising any aspect of his ship. Photo: courtesy Iain Lovie.

The gong for lunch rang throughout the vessel so I stubbed out my cigarette and descended the two decks to the dining saloon. I could see the captain and deck officers were all seated at his table with the chief engineer (second most important man on board), and his officer engineers doing likewise at his table. I made to join the captain's table, which was the usual protocol, but was interrupted by the saloon steward directing me to a small table on my own.

I could feel the blood rushing to my face but said nothing. During the meal, I noticed the odd stare from the other two tables and recalled how similar it was to my long wooden hut encounter.

Lunch on Day One

I ordered tomato soup, roast beef with Yorkshire pudding and apple pie topped with cream. I declined the cheese tray but settled for a coffee instead. One advantage I had from my isolated position was the prompt and efficient service I received. While sipping my coffee, I contemplated how best to spend the rest of the day.

I tuned in to the conversation at one of the long tables where the captain and chief officer were discussing the loading of the vessel. The chief officer was a tallish slim man who bore a striking resemblance to my older brother, Paddy.

I thought maybe my radio room discussion with the captain hadn't gone well or perhaps it was because I was Irish. *'Thank God,'* I thought, *'they don't know the Italian connection.'* I also mused that I was the only one in that saloon who was not a company employee. I was merely a component of the Marconi Marine rental system.

I did notice one man at the captain's table dressed in civilian clothes, who seemed to look across to my table in a friendlier manner. I later learned he was one of the shore office staff being rewarded with a free trip to the Mediterranean. I finished my coffee and rose to go with a nod and smile from our passenger, who obviously had computed the situation.

I went out on deck and observed the dockers continuing their work of loading the **Livorno** with British manufactured goods which we were to deliver to Algeria, Greece and Israel. Returning to the top deck, I passed the chart room where the chief officer was working with lead weights and a scale model of the vessel. He was carrying out weight calculations of the cargo in the holds to ensure the ship was being safely loaded.

We exchanged awkward introductions after which I proceeded to my cabin. Albert had been busy, and my room now had a fresh towel and the bunk had freshly laundered linen, topped with a new blue and white counterpane. The furniture had been dusted and the cabinet mirror was nice and shiny.

Sailing day arrived. I went ashore to a telephone box where I called my girl, Rita. I returned to the ship where the deck crew were completing the battening down of the hatches. I was pleased to see they had also rigged the main and emergency radio aerials. The main aerial with heavy porcelain insulators at each end hung between the forward main mast and the after mizzen mast.

With a blast on the ship's whistle, we left the quay wall and started to steam down the Humber River. I fired up my main transmitter and contacted Humber

Radio i.e. GPWF TO GBR. I sent a TR (traffic report for use by Lloyd Insurance etc) part of which advised our next port as Dunkirk. I started my radio log entries and 500 KHz radio watch conscious that I still hadn't tried to master the DF wartime beast in the corner.

Entering the North Sea, the first early signs of fog appeared and soon as per the law of the sea, the ship's foghorn started to blow every few minutes. Its haunting sound permeated into my office. There was no fancy **GPS** positioning in those days and if the deck officers couldn't see the sun, moon, stars, lighthouses or light buoys, determining your position was by dead reckoning.

This was fine for deep sea navigation, but with an accuracy of only about 10 miles or so, it was a bit nerve racking in the coastal waters in which we were sailing.

As we approached the coast near Dunkirk, the noise from the ship's foghorn seemed to become more persistent. The door opened behind me and the second officer, whom I'll call Alister, entered in a somewhat agitated state. "We can't locate the pilot vessel and the Old Man wants you to take bearings of the port." I felt my mouth go dry but nevertheless went through the ritual of setting up the beast in the corner.

I switched it on, isolated all aerials that might interfere with its accuracy and checked what stations to use from Volume 5 of the **ALRS** books. I could feel my heart pumping in my chest and sweat on my brow. Oh God, why had I waited to learn the secrets of this Second World War technology? Eventually, with the second officer waiting patiently for a bearing or two or three, I managed to get one which showed Dunkirk roughly dead ahead.

Before I could advise Alister, the third officer entered the radio room to say the pilots had found us and the panic was over. You can nearly always rely on port pilots, through centuries of experience, to find their ships and guide them into port. When everyone had left the radio room, I lit up a Lucky Strike and nothing ever tasted sweeter.

The next day as the vessel loaded French cargo for Algeria, I spent several hours mastering the DF beast in the corner. I became so proficient I couldn't wait for the next navigational emergency and almost wished I could make it happen. As it turned out, this model of DF to my mind was every bit as good as the then modern Lodestone.

In fact, it went from being a beast to my new VBF. It was not a very restful night's sleep, possibly because my bunk held a dark secret I was not to learn for some weeks.

Leaving Dunkirk with the **Livorno** now fully loaded with a cargo of expensive British and French goods we bound for Algiers. I sent a TR report to North Foreland Radio GNF (located at the eastern end of the Thames estuary), advising our next port as Algiers. After a pause, my shore counterpart wished us a safe passage and safe visit to Algiers! I had no life experience to speak of, so his second good wishes passed over my head.

The fog had been replaced by blue umbrella skies as we steamed at the magnificent speed of 10 knots, which is about 11.5 miles per hour, down past Calais, Guernsey, Brest and into the Bay of Biscay. Life on board settled into a daily routine, meals at my lonely table, watch keeping and sleeping in a bunk whose dark secret was still to be revealed to me.

My weather reports to the bridge, apart from the usual ones everyone is familiar with from BBC/RTE Radio, Sole, Fastnet, Plymouth, etc. also included much more detailed Atlantic Ocean weather reports, which I copied from Portishead radio/GKL and Washington Radio NSS (USA).

Sometimes I could hear Captain West and his Navigation Officer Alister discussing in low voices the contents of my reports. As was normal, most ships had a hatch between the radio and chart rooms. After a number of days with charts rustling, I heard, "Ok, I'll ask him," after which the captain entered my office and asked, "can you explain where these Atlantic weather areas are please, because we can't locate them."

Feeling somewhat pleased at knowledge they didn't possess, I took down from the bookcase, my copy of ALRS List Volume 3. I went to the pages where it listed the Atlantic areas North and South Central, West and East Central which I explained to the captain in latitude and longitude language. I was surprised the deck staff were not aware of these areas which I sailed through in 1960 during my previous voyages from Manchester/Dublin to ports in Canada and the USA.

I looked on myself as a new boy in the company of experienced mariners, but these men were employees of a company which only traded to the Baltic Ocean and Mediterranean Sea. The Atlantic, Indian and Pacific Oceans were only names to most of them. As a new boy, I also didn't realise that I was feeding them with too much information. He thanked me in a slightly friendlier manner and returned to impart the new knowledge to his fellow officers.

Passing the Southern end of the Bay with La Coruna and Santiago de Compostela on our port side, I decided I had better switch areas for navigation and weather reports. The choice was Monsanto Radio also known as gentle Jesus. Why Gentle Jesus? Well mariners assumed weather reports were compiled by monks in the local monastery and even if it was blowing gale force winds off the Peninsular coast, it would always have sentences which read, "There will be gentle breezes today in sea areas west of Lisbon, etc." If there are any old mariners still alive when you read this, please ask them if they ever heard of 'Gentle Jesus', and it's almost certain you'll get a big smile and 'yes!'

Onwards we went towards Lisbon, then Cape Trafalgar and Cadiz, towards the Pillars of Hercules.

The Pillars of Hercules

21 December and as we approached the Straits of Gibraltar, the number of ships in our immediate vicinity increased dramatically. Passing the Rock of Gibraltar, I transferred to operating via the British Naval base in Valletta Malta. Captain West handed in a telegram which I sent to the Ship's Agent in Algiers, advising our ETA and requesting our berth details. I copied the reply to him which came back via an Algerian coast radio station.

We continued our journey along the North African coast and the night before our arrival, as I sat on my late night watch, the whole radio room lit up like the sun had suddenly reappeared. A voice with a French accent boomed out, via a long range loudspeaker, "Ship on our port side, reduce to quarter speed now." Sweet Jesus, what's this all about? Peering through one of my portholes, I could see a small French warship with marines on deck aiming heavy calibre machine guns in our direction.

These ensured that a speedy response from the *Livorno* engineering staff, who reduced our speed to a crawl. After a few more heart-stopping minutes under the glare of powerful searchlights, the booming voice called out again. "Thank you, British ship *Livorno,* please proceed to your destination. Safe sailing." The French navy patrol vessels were there to intercept the arms smugglers from Morocco and elsewhere feeding guns and bombs to the Algerian liberation army.

The next morning, the pilot clambered up our Jacobs ladder in fairly choppy seas, and began the process of bringing us into port. The narrow port entrance had heavy round pillars on each side, and I marvelled at his skill in avoiding a collision, in such rough weather. I thought a trip ashore might be a good idea to sample the delights of the Algiers Casbah district, but Albert dissuaded me from this idea saying, I might end up hanging from a lamp post.

Hanging from a lamp post? Albert was a seasoned visitor to Algiers, and I had only a vague idea of the independence war. He told me how half a million French soldiers, including the savage French Foreign Legion, were ruthlessly fighting the freedom fighters. After our little chat, I decided to content myself with a short stroll along the quays.

That night, we could hear the sound of rifle fire, and machine gun noise, interspersed with French military helicopters ferrying soldiers to scenes of the heaviest fighting. I thanked God at least one lamp post was deprived of its victim.

Christmas Eve 1960

Leaving Algiers behind, I sent our TR message to Malta Radio GYR. 'QTO Algiers bound for Piraeus'. I copied the Malta weather report and handed it in to the bridge. As usual I was probably copying more than was necessary and had been doing so since we passed Gibraltar. This time, after muttered conversations emanating from the chart room via the hatch, the second officer, Alister, entered the radio room holding my latest report.

"Your weather reports are referring to sea conditions in the Ligurian Sea? Are you sure you're not making some of this stuff up, because we've been sailing these waters for many years and we never heard of the Ligurian Sea? Our charts show no such place exists."

I hesitated and considered my answer, "I'm sorry, Alister, but that's what I'm copying." After a further pause, "My father used to stop the car on the way to our holidays in Tuscany, and my brother and I swam in the Ligurian Sea which is located in the bay of Genoa, north of Corsica." I immediately regretted revealing my Italian connection as it might now mean me having my round table relocated to the after deck.

Alister left somewhat flummoxed by my revelation. I could hear more shuffling of charts and shortly afterwards, Alister returned. "Sorry, Sparks, we found it."

Christmas Eve Continued

Travelling down the North African coast towards the Bizerte headland in Tunisia, I entered the dining saloon for dinner at 1730 hours. The chatter from

47

the other tables went momentarily quiet and I noticed the chief engineer smiling in my direction. He was a heavily built Scotsman called Andrew.

Having finished my meal, I rose to leave the saloon aware of stares from the captain's table. Our passenger, Clive, was smiling. Entering my cabin, I remembered the Christmas cake my mother, Agnes, had given me. I laid the cake on my table along with a knife I had borrowed from the galley.

After finishing watch and switching on the type M Auto Alarm, I decided to visit the chart room and make myself tea and eat my sandwich from the bridge tray. It wasn't very appetising, but then I remembered I had a Christmas cake. At that moment, the third officer, Mason, came into the chartroom to have his supper.

He was a young man about my own age and typically English with fair hair and blue eyes. We had only ever spoken formally but then I had what I thought was a light bulb moment. "Mason, would you like some of my Christmas cake?"

"No, thank you, Sparks, there's heavy traffic about and I had better return to the wheelhouse."

Christmas Morning 1960

I drew the curtains from my portholes and saw it was a nice sunny morning with a calm sea still covered with lots of ships, flying flags from all over the globe. The coast of Tunisia lay plain to see on our starboard side. Albert knocked in his usual style and entered immediately without permission. Placing my morning tea and toast on the dressing table, Albert wished me a happy Christmas and asked in his now quizzical way if I had slept ok?

I reciprocated his good wish and from the look on his face said, "What is it, Albert? Have you something to say to me?"

After a long pause, he said, "Well yes, Don, but maybe you won't want to hear it."

At this stage, he had my full attention. "And why is that, Albert?" After a long pause and an intake of breath, he proceeded to tell me the dark secret of the mattress.

"Last trip, your predecessor, who was a nice chap was much too fond of his best friend, Johnny Walker. He never seemed drunk, but every night before retiring, he filled a glass with the liquid provided by his best friend and left it beside his bunk—that bunk, for consumption when he woke up."

There was another long pause. "And yes, Albert, what?"

"We were sailing among the islands off the Greek coast that morning when I entered the cabin and I noticed the whisky glass was still full." Another long pause.

"Albert, please tell me!"

"Sparks didn't wake up that morning."

"You mean he was dead?"

"Well in Cockney rhyme Brown Bread."

"My God, and you're only telling me now. Who else knows?"

"Well everyone, possibly excluding the new cabin boy, but I'm sure he must also know by now." I asked Albert to continue. "Well, I informed the officer of the watch who called the chief steward on the intercom, and he appeared pretty sharpish in the company of the captain. We, respectfully, removed the body to the cold storage room, because obviously, there had to be a post mortem, which subsequently took place when we reached Salonika the next day."

"We did lose a day from our schedule waiting for a replacement operator. He insisted on transferring to the pilot's cabin on the captain's deck."

"Is that it, Albert? I've been sleeping in a dead man's bunk, and incidentally, Albert, that's the crappiest Christmas present anyone has ever given me."

"Oh, it's no problem, Don. There was a bit of leakage which we cleaned with Dettol and the pillow is new."

"The pillow is new! Is that meant to make me feel better?"

"Sorry, Sparks, I must fly, the captain is waiting on his morning tea."

"Thanks, Albert, see you later."

Christmas Day 1960 continued.

With Albert's revelations still buzzing around my brain, I descended to the captain's deck who was exiting his day room. "Happy Christmas, Sparks."

I absentmindedly replied, "Oh yes, thanks and same to you." My reply didn't go down well as I subsequently heard him complain to those at his table that I was reluctant to reciprocate his good wish. After the usual breakfast, I went out on deck for a breath of fresh air. After a short while, I became aware of someone standing close to me.

"Hello, I'm Clive."

It was our passenger and I replied, "Oh hello, I'm Donal but you can call me Don."

"Isn't it a beautiful Christmas morning?"

"Well, Clive, I must go on watch, but talk to you again soon."

"Actually, old boy, I wanted to ask you, if you'd like to join me for a drink in my cabin later tonight."

"Yes, Clive, that would be very acceptable and I'll see you when I finish my last watch." Christmas dinner wasn't much different to the usual dinners, except it was enhanced with Christmas pudding, topped with heavy duty custard followed by mince pies.

The rest of the day's watches were quieter than usual with only the odd Morse exchange between vessels. That afternoon, Albert brought my afternoon tea tray into the radio room decorated with another couple of mince pies. He asked with a smile, "Ok now, Don?"

"Yes, Albert, but I'm not relishing the thoughts of sleeping tonight." With that, he left, obviously still highly amused. After dinner and my last watch of the day, I knocked on Clive's door.

"Come in, old boy, and make yourself comfortable," he said pointing to a large comfortable armchair. He handed me a glass of beer and we started talking about run of the mill things such as the latest films and TV programmes. He told me about his young days in the Army and his adventures in Palestine in 1948 during the Arab Israeli war of independence.

I didn't think to ask what position he held in the company but I assumed maybe an accountant or maybe he really was one of the directors which would tie in with the respect shown to him by Captain West and his deck staff.

At some stage and after a few more beers, Clive smiled and said, "I hear you found a new sea no one was aware of, Don."

Bolstered by my fill of beer I replied, "Yes, Clive, but I was surprised our deck colleagues weren't aware of the Ligurian Sea, seeing as how our ship the *Livorno* shares the same name as the Port of Livorno situated in the middle of the Ligurian Sea." Clive started to double up with laughter, so sensing I was on a roll, I continued, "And it's only a stone's throw from Pisa. Galileo probably saw it every day while carrying out his experiments on the Leaning Tower."

Once Clive had composed himself, he asked, "How do you know all this stuff, old boy?"

I hesitated but the beer made me continue. "Well, the clue is in my surname Rocca, which of course is Italian, and every year my father loves spending three or four weeks in Tuscany and all roads south. He found the pasta in Pisa particularly tasty." There was a silence, and I thought our little soiree might come to an abrupt end.

"I say, old boy, that's very posh. Let's finish off with another can and tell me more about yourself." I told him about Albert's revelations, but I suspect he knew already. We bid each other good night and I climbed slowly up to my lonely room. That night I slept with the overhead light on.

St Stephen's Day, 26 December 1960, and Beyond

I looked out of my starboard porthole and the sea was still a lovely shade of blue with small diamond studded waves matching a cloudless sky. The *Livorno* was now set on a course to take us to the Southern tip of Sicily. While finishing my breakfast, I was surprised to see Second Officer Alister come and sit on the opposite side of my table.

My heart started to pump faster thinking he might have overheard my Ligurian jokes with passenger Clive. "We'll be taking noon sights today, Sparks, so when you come up to the bridge, can we get a time check on the ships chronometer please?" He didn't have to ask in such a polite way as it was part of my job.

"Of course, Alister I'll be there shortly." Returning to the bridge, I tuned into Rugby Radio which was a long wave station transmitting on 16 kHz. With Alister standing by the chronometer, I listened to the transmission from Rugby and on the minute shouted, 'now' via the hatch into the chartroom. The error was logged into a book for future use.

The next few days at sea followed, more or less uneventfully, with occasional visits to my new friend, Clive, during one of which I confided that I wasn't very popular with the captain and deck staff. "Oh, I'm sure that's not the case, old boy." Unfortunately, during my next visit, he confirmed my assessment as correct which I didn't particularly want to hear.

I still went to bed at night with the light on and the hope that I wouldn't receive a visit from my predecessor. Some three days from Cape Bizerte, we entered Piraeus, the port of Athens.

Piraeus, Greece, Early January 1961

The *Livorno* was docked alongside multiple flagged ships including Greek island ferries. We could see millionaire's yachts berthed across the harbour, one possibly carrying Onassis and Maria Callas? The mail from home arrived and the chief steward took the letters I had written at sea for posting. I read Rita's letters with pleasure several times.

That night at dinner, I noticed a number of my colleagues, dressed in civilian clothes. After dinner while passing the wardroom, those dressed in civilian clothes were congregated discussing how they would travel into Athens. I enquired if I might accompany them. Eventually, the chief officer answered, "Ok but we're leaving shortly."

I hurried to my cabin and donned my best suit, white shirt and tie, etc., and hurried back to the wardroom which I found empty. Thinking they might be waiting for me at the end of the gangway, I ran down only to see they had left and were now exiting the dock gates. I hung around till I was sure they had gone and walked out to the main road.

I had about £4 pounds in drachmas which I had subbed from my monthly pay and didn't want to blow any of it, as I thought, on an expensive taxi, so I enquired from a passer-by where I might get a bus into Athens. We communicated in sign language and broken English, and I eventually got the information I needed. I alighted from the bus in Athens happy that the fare had eaten very little from my shore stash.

I wandered around for several hours taking in the sights and smells of the city. The smells, apart from the drains, included the aroma of Greek cigarettes, Turkish coffee and fresh fruit. Albert told me I should visit the Parthenon, but I knew it was too late for that.

Thinking I might return to the ship, I passed a bar called the Delphi, which seemed to be full of young people having a good time with many English speakers among them. I was just about to pass on when someone shouted, "In here, Sparks, come and join us." I was confused and couldn't make out who the caller was but eventually one of the *Livorno's* crew came to my rescue.

"We're at that table over there and you're welcome to join us." The table he referred to had a mixture of *Livorno* deck and engine room crew, sitting around a large table. They made room for me, and I sat down a little self-consciously. They continued talking among themselves and I said I would go to the bar for a beer.

"No need, Sparks, Anna will bring it over." Anna was a youngish girl with typical Latin good looks whom those at the table obviously knew from their many previous trips to Piraeus. They made laddish but not unkind remarks about Anna. She accepted their banter as a compliment which I know most girls today would reject as insulting. Anna brought my drink and departed with a smile. "You're in there, Sparks!"

At some point in the evening, one of my new-found friends enquired, "Are you sleeping ok, Don?"

"Yes, thank you, Michael." At which point, everyone burst into laughter. Anna came over and admonished them in her lovely Greek accent.

"Stop it, boys, he's lovely and he has lovely skin." At which point, she rubbed her hand along my cheek. I couldn't stop the blood rushing to my face, which only added fuel to the table's laughter.

One Welsh lad said, "You really are in there, Boyo!"

The rest of the evening progressed with the boys relating all their female conquests and such like, many of which I suspect were heavily exaggerated. We also got into conversation with the crew from another British ship at a table close to us. One of them was the radio officer older and much more travelled than me.

When he heard we would be going to Haifa, he advised me to be very careful. With the tension between Jews and Arabs, the port was full of agents gathering information from crews of visiting ships. I told him I couldn't see me adding much to their knowledge.

"Just be careful and don't try calling any Egyptian stations, because the *Livorno* is bound to be blacklisted and they won't answer you." I thanked him and returned to my new friends who had moved on to bantering each other. Anna kept the table well stocked with Pils beers, and sometime around one in the morning, we were all ready to return home.

The lovely Anna bid us all good night with a wink and a smile. It took three taxis to get us back and I think my share wasn't much more than the bus fare I had paid earlier. Walking up the gangway, my new-found friends told me I was welcome to join them again the following night.

Athens, Day Two, Early January 1961

Entering the saloon for breakfast that morning, I noticed that my table had a second set of cutlery, and the chief engineer was smiling at me, in some sort of knowing way. The Judas brigade at the captain's table were staring down at their plates not making a sound. '*What's this,*' I thought, as the Third Engineer Branok sat down opposite me and Andrew had a look of satisfaction on his face.

Third Engineer Branok was a senior officer on board equivalent in rank to Alister. We started up a conversation and he told me he was from Fowey in

Cornwall and had served his apprenticeship in Ellerman and Wilson Line, so I estimated that he was probably about twenty-five years of age. He enjoyed talking about different ship's engines and suchlike. Breakfast over, I wished Branok a good watch and returned to my office.

I wrote another letter to Rita and then brought my paperwork up to date. As part of my £40 salary, I had to submit accounts at the end of each voyage, including submissions of completed logs to the Master of the Mercantile Marine Office. In 1961, accounts were in pounds, shillings and pence and sometimes trying to find a missing penny on a spread sheet could be a nightmare. And then when you did find the missing penny, it would be a great mystery as to how you could have kept making the same mistake over and over.

After dinner, I went on deck to suck on a Lucky. I wondered if I should ask Branok if we could go ashore together but thought better of it. Anyway, I had told my new friends I'd see them in the Delphi. I boarded the blue bus for Athens with my remaining drachmas and a fresh pack of Luckies.

Repeating my walk around the centre of Athens, which didn't include a visit up the Acropolis, I ended up outside the Delphi. I could see Anna serving the customers but none of them were from the *Livorno.* Not having the confidence to go in alone I was about to walk on when I heard a familiar Welsh voice from the pavement. "Where are you going, boyo, come and join us."

I didn't need to be asked twice and soon we were all seated at the same table we had occupied the previous evening. Anna came and took our order and I had to endure more banter how they thought she liked me. This wasn't helped by her stroking my cheek again, when she returned with a fully laden tray.

The next day, our Athens' cargo fully discharged, we singled up and I sent a TR to the local and indeed worldwide station SVA, reporting our ship's name and next port of call, Salonika.

Aegean Sea, Early January 1961

We wound our way through multiple Greek islands on a northerly course for Salonika. Radio communication became a bit difficult due to the incessant bursts of static in my headphones. The weather report from SVA said, there were heavy thunderstorms over Bulgaria, due to reach the Aegean shortly.

I handed in my report to the Bridge and an instruction was sent to the Bosun to make sure all hatches were properly secured. The arrival of the storm was heralded by a frightening burst of lightning, followed by a tremendous roar of thunder. The sea whipped itself into a frenzy and the *Livorno* started to roll, well beyond 'Gentle Jesus' levels.

The wheelhouse Quo Vadis radar became almost unusable, due to sea clutter and the impenetrable walls of heavy rain. I received a request from the captain to take radio bearings. Glad to use my new-found skills and my very best friend in the corner, I started to take bearings, hampered by the rolling ship and constant bursts of static but eventually managed the task.

I handed Mason my figures, not wholly confident of their accuracy, which as it turned out were satisfactory. The storm lasted much of the day but almost miraculously disappeared in the afternoon. The sea calmed and blue skies reappeared. The Quo Vadis radar came back into its own.

Sometime in the middle of the night, we berthed alongside in Salonika. The next morning, we discharged what little cargo we had for this Northern area of Greece, and by noon we were on our way to Haifa.

The days at sea were spent listening to radio exchanges between Alexandria Radio and those heading for the Suez Canal. I think I was Clive's only evening visitor despite his proximity to the captain's cabin and he seemed genuinely to enjoy my company. On day two, we were south of Cyprus heading towards the Lebanese coast. Nearing Haifa, we received a message from 4XO to go to an anchorage as the berths were all full.

Haifa, Mid-January 1961

I could see the aerials of marine radio station 4XO on the hills above the city. I sent a TR report for onward Telex transmission to England. I also sent several telegrams via 4XO, from Captain West to the ship's agent saying, when are we going to be allowed to berth? In fact, I sent so many I think the 4XO operators were getting fed up with me, and it didn't help that the captain kept asking if there was a reply.

The first reply said that all the berths were still occupied, and we would be advised when one became available. There was no reply other than this.

After a few more boring days swinging on the anchor, I went down for breakfast one morning during which it became noticeable that the *Livorno* **seemed** to have developed more movement than normal. By the time I returned to my office, this movement was increasing steadily and within the hour, the ship was being buffeted by heavy seas. The Chief Officer was up forward with the

Bosun, and some of my friends from the Delphi bar feeding out extra chain, in an effort, to stop the anchor dragging.

They struggled to hear each other above the din of the storm. Suddenly, the ship took a big swing to starboard. The anchor chain had broken, which left us drifting towards the harbour wall, until the engineers were able to start the main engine, and with all hands on deck, we ploughed in heavy seas towards the shore. The captain, in something of an agitated state, scribbled a note detailing our plight which I sent to the shore agent.

This time we got an immediate reply, telling us to put the Jacobs ladder over the side and a pilot would attempt to board us within the hour. Forty minutes later, a man dressed in a white uniform made what I thought was a suicide leap onto our Jacobs ladder. I suppose it helped that the ladder was named Jacob, because shortly after he appeared in the wheelhouse with a big smile on his face, to be met by Captain West who was also smiling.

The pilot skilfully navigated the harbour entrance and we were soon alongside. The storm passed and all was quiet again.

'While out on the top deck, I saw the ship beyond was flying the Danish flag and what a beautiful ship,' I thought. It looked much bigger than the **Livorno** and its perfect paintwork meant it was probably on its maiden voyage. That night as I walked down alone again with the equivalent of £5 in Shekels, I got into conversation with three of the crew from the Danish ship.

"Nice ship you have men," I said to which they replied.

"Thank you. It's one of three new ships recently commissioned by our company." We talked till we reached the dock gates, where I bid them farewell and walked on.

One of them followed me and said, "We are going to a bar up the road and you're welcome to join us."

I hesitated, wondering if I had enough Shekels in my wallet but then said, "Yes, thank you."

We entered a bar halfway up the hill to be welcomed by a table attendant who remembered my new friends from their previous visits to Haifa. At some stage while we were talking and supping our Gold star beer, a girl asked if she could join us. This was strange I thought but the Danes seemed more than happy to agree.

Her name was Ophira and she lived in Jerusalem. She had completed her army national service and was now studying fashion with aspirations to join a

London fashion house. At about 11 p.m., I felt ready to return to the *Livorno* when Ophira suggested we all go to another bar situated on the hills overlooking the city. I said I didn't think I'd go, but everyone else, buoyed up with Gold star, insisted I join in.

Haifa seemed to be awash with taxis and we five piled into one which took us to a location with a stunning view over the city. I reached into my wallet to pay my share of the taxi but the oldest of the Danes said, "No, no everyone, keep your money. I'll pay."

I thanked him and one of the others said, "Thank you, Kapitan."

We entered the late-night bar, located at the top of the hill, overlooking Haifa city. It was a seriously big barn of a place, absolutely full of people, none of whom looked more than twenty-five. What settled for tables were long wooden affairs with long wooden benches seating up to 12 people either side. The tables were adorned with dozens of bottles of Goldstar beer which accounted for the great humour everyone was in.

Everyone seemed to know Ophira and as this place had zero formality, some of her friends made room for us at one of the long tables. I ordered the second round and was very happy the price was so cheap, that it didn't strain my stash of Shekels. Every so often, one of the tables would burst into a rendition of Hava Nagila (let us rejoice), while other boys and girls would dance joyously on their tables. As I said, there was no formality and if there was any management it was invisible.

The dawn was breaking when we left the big barn and piled into one of the waiting taxis. On the way down, Ophira suggested we finish off with a morning coffee and ordered the taxi driver to stop at some place, whose name now escapes me. This was almost a mirror image of the place we had just left, except it was very quiet and full of very old men smoking strong cigarettes and talking quietly.

This was another weird experience and I asked Ophira, why are they here and not at home? "They cannot sleep." At the docks, the senior Dane insisted on paying the taxi again, including extra to take Ophira on to wherever she was going. Reaching the *Livorno* gangway, we all bid farewell with handshakes.

Entering my cabin, I didn't feel tired or drunk but decided to skip breakfast and get some sleep. During the rest of that day, the dockers finished unloading whatever cargo we had for Israel and we departed empty for the port of Jaffa.

Jaffa, Mid-January 1960

Having left Haifa, we sailed down the coast past Israel's second city, Tel Aviv, arriving off Jaffa on a nice sunny morning. As Jaffa was only suitable for yachts and fishing boats, we had to anchor off the port to facilitate loading.

No shore leave was possible, so we had to content ourselves with views of the city and the bustle of harbour activity. The first of the barges arrived a few hours later and the *Livorno's* derricks were soon loading crates of large oranges into our holds. The barges kept arriving in a constant stream, and by noon the next day, with hatches battened down, the Bosun and his crew lifted the anchor.

The chief engineer ordered his staff to increase the engine revs to maximum and we started our 12-knot dash across the 3500 miles, to the Pillars of Hercules.

Why all the hurry? Our cargo had to arrive at its destination in prime condition. The chief officer in conjunction with the captain and chief engineer, discussed how best to maintain hold temperatures by setting the flow of air via the ventilation system. I could see he was carrying a lot of burden on his shoulder because there'd be no sale for overripe oranges.

I reported our next port to 4XO as Ceuta, the Spanish city on the North African coast's most western end. Soon we were past Malta and abreast of Bizerte. We passed down by Algiers but this time there was no French Navy to greet us. The captain handed in a telegram for the Ceuta agent detailing our bunker and water requirements, plus a priority turn around as we were carrying a perishable cargo.

We arrived in Ceuta ten days after leaving Jaffa. The captain's request for a priority turnaround was granted and six hours later, with fresh oil and water, we left Ceuta, destination unknown. This was to change when we re-entered the Atlantic and I copied a message from London Head Office.

Atlantic Ocean, January 1961

Just as we changed to a northerly course at Cape St Vincent, on the southern tip of Portugal, our ship's name and callsign *GPWF* burst from the speaker of my main receiver. It was Portishead Radio GKL with a message for Captain West. "Proceed to Dublin for full cargo discharge, Marine Superintendent Ellerman Wilson Lines."

I typed the message using my portable, put it in a Marconi envelope and brought it down to the captain's cabin, where I found him sitting at his desk doing ship's paperwork. He read the message and repeated several times 'Dublin?

Dublin?' He looked at me and said, the *Livorno* has never been to Dublin. I asked him if he would like it to be confirmed but I suspect he thought doing so might put him in a bad light with the Super, so he said, "No, Sparks, thanks."

Returning to my office, I wondered if he thought I was pulling the wool over his eyes and being young, started to have doubts myself. With about nine days to go, we headed up the Portuguese coast past Gentle Jesus, Lisbon, Porto, Santiago de Compostela and into the Bay of Biscay.

During lunch one day, my table companion, Branok, asked me how many of the seven seas had I sailed? "Well, Branok, so far I've only sailed the North Atlantic several times to such places as New York, Boston, Philadelphia, etc. I've also sailed up the Great Lakes to Chicago, Toronto and Duluth etc. and was on ships where we had to avoid icebergs and batter our way through ice fields."

The two big tables went silent and knew I had an audience, probably realising they hadn't been showing adequate respect to their young radio officer. They, as I said previously, were Baltic and Mediterranean seamen. On a roll and warming to my task, I went on to tell Branok that I had not, as yet, sailed any of the seven seas. "What do you mean, Don? You already told me you sailed the North Atlantic?"

Yes, but that's an ocean and not a sea. Without looking, I knew I had the occupants of the long tables riveted with curiosity, so I continued, armed with the education I had received from previous shipmates. "The seven seas are located North of Australia, south of Papua New Guinea and Indonesia. Some of these seas are named Timor, Yellow, Solomon, Banda, etc."

Looking at me, he says, "That's impressive, Don, anything to add?"

I said, "Absolutely," and paused a little, to tease the silent brigade. "In the 18th and 19th centuries, the seven seas were very dangerous because it wasn't possible for the Admiralty to survey every reef and small island. Some ships did risk it to save time, but this was a decision that many Masters regretted, as they are now asleep in the deep. As a result of the losses, Lloyd's of London would not agree to insure vessels entering these dangerous waters."

Onwards to Dublin, Last Week of January 1961

The shipping lanes became much busier as we started to cross the Western end of the English Channel. The airwaves became a cacophony of radio messages being sent to Amsterdam, Rotterdam, Hamburg and all places beyond. During one of my watches, a knock came to the door and Clive entered. It was his first visit to my office, and he apologised for any interruption. "Don't be silly, Clive, come and sit down."

"I enjoyed listening to your seven seas conversation yesterday."

"Thanks." He looked around at the benches of equipment. "Do you understand how to operate all this stuff, Don, with so many knobs, meters and dials? And all that stuff coming through the speakers?"

"Well yes, Clive, it's why I'm here."

"I must say I'm really impressed and had no idea you were so important. Anyway, old man, I better let you get on with your work but you're welcome to join me for a nightcap this evening." That evening as I entered Clive's cabin, I could see the lights of Penzance and St Ives through one of his starboard portholes.

Clive poured a couple of beers and we talked about where we'd been and the night of the big light off the coast of Algiers. "And now we're going to Dublin, Don. I don't think the Old Man is too impressed."

"I know, Clive, but if he doesn't enjoy Dublin then someone better tell him not to go to Heaven."

"Please tell me more, old boy."

Enjoying my audience of one, I elaborated on the cinemas and cafes of O'Connell Street, Clerys' store and dance hall, the Metropole and its dance hall. Listen to Noel Purcell in song telling you Dublin can be heaven with coffee at eleven and a stroll round Stephen's Green. And for coffee go to Bewleys and when you emerge onto Grafton Street and an absolute wonderland of European class shops.

"Go into Brown Thomas' and you may not want to come out."

"You make it sound absolutely wonderful, Don."

"Well, it's not London, but it's a bloody good copy." The next morning with Wexford off our port side, Albert entered with the morning tray.

As he was leaving, he said, "Sparks, some of the crew asked me to ask you if Dublin would have shops and buses and things like we have at home?"

Remembering last night's conversation with Clive, this left me somewhat deflated, but I replied, "Of course, Albert." As he was about to leave, I remembered to add, "If you and the rest of the gang don't enjoy Dublin and Ireland, don't bother going to Heaven." That evening at dinner, coming abreast of Bray, Captain West started to make insulting remarks about the Irish coast line.

"Doesn't it look a wild and dreary place." Seeing the look on my face, he had the good manners to shut up. I was glad to see the Dublin Pilot climb up the Jacobs ladder and soon we were alongside an Alexandra Basin berth.

Dublin, Late January 1961

After breakfast the next morning, I dressed in civilian clothes and walked up to May St Drumcondra and a reunion with my girl, Rita. She knew the ship was due and managed to take two days of annual leave from the Department of Lands. That morning, we walked into town chatting and holding hands. When we reached Dublin and Ireland's most famous landmark, 'Nelson's Pillar', we started to cross.

On the pavement at the bottom of the Pillar, there were street traders selling flowers and fruit from wooden tables. "Are your oranges fresh?" I asked.

"Fresh off the boat this morning, son." I ordered two, handed over a florin and receive a bob as change. "Your girl is lovely, son."

"I know," I replied as I handed my lovely girl a Jaffa.

The last of the *Livorno's* cargo left the ship around 1700 hours and I re-joined after another lovely day spent with my girl. Exiting Dublin, I transmitted some ship business telegrams to the owners via Anglesey Radio GLV and a TR message next port Hull. Albert entered my cabin with the morning tea tray and a big beam on his face.

"Sparks, we all had a great time and I think one of the lads may have fallen in love, because he can't wait to get back."

"Glad to hear that, Albert, and I hope you found the buses to your liking."

"Ha ha, Don."

At breakfast with the Bristol Channel on our port side, Clive sat down opposite me on Branok's empty chair. "I say, old boy, your wonderful description of Dublin still didn't do it justice," and looking towards the Captain's table added, "and I'm not alone in thinking that."

"Thanks, Clive, I'm pleased you enjoyed my city." A few days later having sailed our way through the English Channel past Hastings and Great Yarmouth, we were near the end of our journey. I prepared my end of voyage paperwork for signing by the captain. He invited me to take a seat.

"May I offer you a drink, Donald?"

"Thank you, Sir. A mineral water please." He was so nice, he reminded me of Scrooge on a Christmas morning! Papers signed, I returned to my cabin and a final sleep in the bunk I wished Albert hadn't told me about.

The next day in Hull, we all signed off Articles at the Mercantile Marine office, after which, I handed in my paperwork to the Hull Marconi Marine Office, and in a way, it was nice to be among my own kind again. Armed with packed suitcases and a wallet full of back pay, I made my way back over the Pennines and the *mv Leinster* to Dublin.

My girl and I spent two more happy weeks together, then one morning in late February 1961, a motorbike man, message in hand, called again. "Please report to Newcastle Office where arrangements have been made for you to sign on *mv Arctic.*"

My Voyages on the Arctic

Newcastle upon Tyne, February 1961

It was raining as I walked up the outside steps and into the large Victorian built building, which was the Newcastle upon Tyne Marconi Marine offices.

I was glad to be out of the rain as I ascended with my cases up the large wide staircase to the main offices. There I was met by one of the clerks who directed me into the radio officer's waiting room, where I nodded to about six of my contemporaries already seated in green coloured leather armchairs. I removed my wet, navy blue coat, and joined them in one of the four remaining seats.

After a period of silence, one of the waiting six started up a conversation to which we all joined in. The primary topic of conversation was what ship each of us would be assigned and where would it go.

It wasn't long before the first of our party was summoned to the main office via a large loudspeaker located above our heads. He returned sometime later holding a folio of papers and a cup of tea which he finished while telling us the details of his new ship and where it was going. Memory fails me on the details, but it could have been anywhere from Canada to New Zealand or even Japan.

Eventually my turn came. "Mr Rocca, go to the inspector's office please." I was pleased my caller pronounced my name properly. I was invited to take a seat opposite the Inspector who informed me I was to join the tanker *Arctic* which would be leaving in a few days for the US Gulf. He probably detected my confusion as he repeated, "US Gulf, Gulf of Mexico."

I lied as I said, "Yes, of course thank you." Once all the paperwork was complete, I bid my new friends goodbye, gathered my cases and started to exit the building.

Going down the outside steps to a waiting taxi, I looked up and could see the famous Tyne Arch Bridge towering above us. "Where to, son?"

"Wallsend Shipyard driver, please."

63

The taxi pulled up in a small street adjacent to the shipyard with small red brick houses on either side. These were yard worker's houses and there were thousands more in neighbouring streets, because this yard like many more in Britain employed thousands of workers building and repairing by far the biggest Merchant Navy in the world. I passed through the security gate with a warning from one of the guards. "Be careful of the cranes, son."

"Thanks I will."

John I Jacobs tanker *ss **Hollywood/MLP** (note: Built 1951, renamed **Arctic** in 1960, renamed **Dealbrook** 1962, scrapped 1964, kept same call sign throughout. TS)*

The *Arctic* was undergoing repairs and painting in one of the large dry docks and it had to be large to accommodate this huge vessel. At least, it was large to me, in those days. It was built in Sunderland in 1951 and originally named **Hollywood.**

As I walked through the ship's centre castle, there were two men in deep discussion. I could see both had chief officers braid, so I introduced myself and asked for directions to the chief steward's cabin. "We're finished here, Sparks, so give me one of your cases and I'll take you up." On the way, he advised me he was going on leave and was giving the new chief officer a handover. Based on my accent, he told me how to get to the local Catholic church for Sunday Mass and his wife and himself would accompany me, if I so wished.

*The only photo of **Arctic! MLPJ** we can find, is this poor quality image from the internet, probably because she only held this name for a short period.*

The *Arctic* had two sets of accommodation, one centre ship and one aft. The centre accommodated deck officers, the chief steward and his catering staff plus me. The aft accommodation was for the engineer officers, oilers and donkey men. The *Arctic* was such a big ship with the engine room located aft, this was the only way the accommodation could be laid out.

Each area had its own mess room, but the main dining saloon was in the midship's accommodation. The chief steward briefed me on mealtimes, etc., and then asked the Second Steward Wally to show me to my cabin.

As I say, the *Arctic* was a big ship and to fill the space, the cabins also had to be big. Everyone, including me, had very large cabins, though the more senior officers had extra-large bunks and furniture. My cabin was on the starboard side with one large porthole. On the same side were the second and third officers.

The chief officer and chief steward were on the port side. The catering staff were on the deck below and Captain Hort was on the next deck up and beyond him the bridge deck. I emptied my cases into a wardrobe and drawers while Wally made up my bunk with fresh linen and a company monogrammed counterpane. "Dinner will be served shortly, Sparks."

The Evening of Day One

The saloon steward showed me to my chair in the dining saloon. This was at a round table, covered in a crisp white tablecloth, monogrammed company serviettes and silverware. The most senior man at this table was the chief officer whose name I forget, but I'll call him George because he looked like Captain Mainwaring from the TV show, 'Dad's Army'.

Next to George was the second officer and he asked us to simply call him Buckley. He was a man, probably in his late forties, with dark hair parted in the centre, and he wore no braid but did have a white handkerchief protruding from the lapel pocket of his black mohair uniform. He spoke in a posh English accent and on reflection, my best description of him would be a clone of the actor Sir Noel Coward.

I did wonder how a man in his late forties who wore no braid was still only a second mate. This mystery was revealed in full detail later in the voyage.

The third officer was about my age. He was tall with fair hair and blue eyes. A lot of Britain's East coast population have this Nordic look. Again, as I can't remember his name, even though we became good friends, I'll call him Alan.

He had just finished his apprenticeship and joined the *Arctic* with his newly acquired second mate's ticket. Another man at the table was the fourth officer and his cabin was opposite mine on the port side. He was probably a couple of years older than Alan and I, and tended to dominate the conversation. I'll call him Jack.

It should be noted that most of the personnel on board were not direct employees of Oil and Molasses Tankers Ltd., London, but recruited from what was called the Pool. This meant many were reduced to the Pool for reasons which will become apparent as I proceed with my tale. One exception at our table was Fourth Officer Jack, who revelled in the fact that he was directly employed by the company and appeared disdainful of those who weren't, even though everyone else at the table was senior to him.

After a while, George enquired of Jack exactly how long he had been a permanent staff member. "Three weeks," came the reply which elicited suppressed laughter.

Seated at the other tables were Captain Hort, his wife, and the chief engineer. The last table had the second engineer from Glasgow and his number two from Liverpool. Also seated at this table were the third and fourth engineers. Two of the men at this table were later to show why they were Pool registered officers. Wally was one of those serving and he and the captain's wife engaged in some very racy and entertaining conversation.

After dinner, I went to inspect the radio room which housed the standard radio equipment. It also had a Dynatron radio which connected to various locations around the ship for the entertainment of all on board. Apart from a small library usually managed by the third mate, the Dynatron radio was the height of shipboard entertainment. Some ships did carry a cine projector and half a dozen old movies but not the *Arctic.*

The radar was a Marconi Radio locator Mk 4 and as it proved troublesome during the trip, it was probably the primary reason I attended a radar course at Kevin Street in 1962. The bridge equipment had a Marconi MF/HF radiotelephone which Captain Hort liked using to make calls home, range permitting. These calls which I logged in my returns were expensive.

During the last week of February 1961, the drydock filled with water and when the big gates opened onto the Tyne, the *Arctic* slid gracefully into the river and entering the North Sea, we set a course due south towards the English Channel.

The North Sea, Late February 1961

I fired up the long range Oceanspan 7 transmitter and contacted Humber Radio/GBR. I sent my TR message, "*Arctic MLPJ* QTO Newcastle bound for US Gulf." We were only about an hour out when I heard the ship's foghorn sending out its haunting warning for other ships to stay clear. I went to the bridge where Buckley was on watch.

The fog was so thick it was difficult to even see the focsle head. The watch had been tripled to include one AB up for'd and one on the Monkey Island. Their job was to report the sight or sound of any other ship nearing the *Arctic.* They had zero chance of seeing and if they heard any, it would have been too late.

Their presence complied with insurance regulations, and the Mk 4 fifty kilowatt radar made sure, we could see any vessel that might come too close. The deck staff had taken the wise precaution of steaming a bit further off the English East Coast to avoid encountering the hundreds of colliers feeding London's power stations and large factories.

Sometime later, the captain came to see me with instructions to take DF bearings. The ship had been navigating by 'Dead Reckoning' which was fine, but he wanted to know our exact position. I switched on the Lodestone DF and isolated any of the antennae that might interfere with it. I took radio bearings from three stations with as much of an obtuse angle from us as possible.

I handed in my findings to the chartroom which was dimly lit by orange coloured lights. Buckley leaned over the North Sea Admiralty chart and using a large parallel rule, marked out in pencil the bearings I had taken. The result was a very small cocked hat indicating our exact position. Captain Hort looked very pleased and relieved, and I felt I had made a good start with my new shipmates.

The next morning after the usual breakfast, I went out on deck and lit up a Senior Service. Alan joined me and together we stared across a clear North Sea filled with ships either bringing or taking goods to every corner of planet Earth. Our ship was completely empty which meant we were riding high but also meant we would roll like a bucking bronco when inevitably we would hit our first storm.

Being empty also meant our huge tanks would have to be cleaned to accommodate the cargo waiting for us at a Southern United States port, yet to be advised. We sailed down past Flamborough Head and down into the English Channel. Once we reached Brest on the north coast of France, we altered to a Southwest course which would take us North of the Azores and onward to Miami.

I started to copy the Atlantic weather reports from Portishead Radio. Also, at this stage, the Chief Officer George arranged for the deck crew to start cleaning the cargo tanks with the use of high pressure hoses. Captain Hort told me to expect a message from New York advising our loading port.

I contacted Chatham Radio/WCC Massachusetts and gave the operator our ship's name, destination and advised we would monitor his traffic lists. He wished us bon voyage.

The *Arctic* was a designated OBS ship which meant we were fitted with weather monitoring equipment. Four times a day, the officer on watch would take air and sea temperatures, check cloud formations and note the barometric pressure. He would then add the ship's position and deliver the completed form to me. I would then transmit the information to radio stations in the UK and the USA, or one of the four Atlantic weather ships permanently stationed in a line from Land's End to Newfoundland.

These reports from OBS ships would then be relayed to meteorological offices around the world where the experts would join them all together. In 1963, I did receive an award from the British Met Office with a scripted address for my valuable work at sea. As it's the only recognition I ever received, I might have it mounted on my going away box.

We progressed towards the Azores at a speed of about 12 knots and if there's one ocean that's rarely calm it's the North Atlantic. We rolled in heavy seas and sitting in my office chair sometimes I was looking at the sky and next minute directly into the deep ocean. When we left Newcastle, it was cold and wet but every day that passed now we were 350 miles further south and the Spring Equinox was only weeks away. With the passing of each day, the temperature rose towards summer levels and we also had blue skies and seas.

The pay wasn't great, but at least we had sunshine and of course the BBC Light programme on 200 kHz via the Dynatron radio. In those days, the Light programme sent out a huge powerful signal which could be heard equally as clear in Galway or Achill as London or Berlin. During breakfast one morning, Buckley whispered he would like to discuss a private matter with me later.

North Atlantic Ocean, 1 March 1961

We continued our 14-day journey towards Miami, at a speed of 12 knots. I wondered what Buckley's secret whisper meant and when I could expect him to visit. That day, our afternoon watches finished, and we descended to our cabins together.

"See you shortly, Donal." Buckley entered my cabin holding two bottles of Gordon's gin, which he put on the day table before seating himself down on the settee.

He paused and said, "Before I begin, old boy, I want to relate some of my life to you. I was born in Fowey Cornwall where I still have a nice house overlooking the sea." Buckley continued to tell me how, after his public school education, he joined one of the UK's more prestigious shipping lines carrying passengers to the Far East.

Having served his four years as an officer cadet, plus further years of study at sea and the Plymouth Nautical College, he acquired his deep sea masters certificate. He climbed the ladder to become chief officer and within a few more years might have made captain.

Unfortunately, he and many of those serving on passenger vessels fell to the lure of on-board socialising. Nights of entertaining passengers attired in dress uniforms, attracting the attention of female company, mixed with glasses of champagne and gin, was a honey trap that sent many young men staring into the bottom of empty glasses wishing they could turn the clock back. Buckley was one such young man and his ruin came when he fell asleep while on watch in the South China Sea.

The company couldn't risk the same thing happening again, possibly with the loss of a thousand passengers, so it was suggested Buckley might consider resigning! He did have some good luck because his final downfall began whilst in the company of one of the passengers sailing on that trip. This turned out to be a senior executive in one of the large British oil companies. Feeling somewhat responsible for Buckley's misfortune, he said, "Don't worry, old man, I'll fix you up with a good position."

This good position turned out to be a large office overlooking the Thames and every so often someone would come in with graphics and other things to be agreed and initialled. Continuing to relate his story, he said, "Things went fine for about six months, though I hadn't a bloody clue what I was supposed to be doing. The large salary cheque at the end of each month was very welcome and allowed me to continue a very comfortable lifestyle."

Unfortunately, one day someone said, "What exactly is that man doing on the top floor?" The answer resulted in Buckley vacating his large office clasping a golden lifeboat cheque.

Buckley knew his days of sailing on premier division ships were over, so he joined the ranks of those on the Pool. As already said, these were men who could be classed as Freelance. When Buckley finished, I knew why his only uniform adornment was a white handkerchief. As a gentleman mariner, he wasn't prepared to highlight his humiliation to a reduced rank.

He further related how his position on the *Arctic* was conditional on him accepting the purchase of only two bottles of spirits a week. It must have taken courage to open up his heart to me and I'll never know why. Pointing to his two precious bottles, he said, "I want you to be the keeper and twice a day, once in the morning and once in the evening, pour me a glass topped with Schweppes tonic."

"Ok, Buckley, and when would you like to start?"

"Now old boy, now." I complied and secured the remains of his precious liquid into my book case.

"You're quite sure, Second, you wouldn't prefer to keep them in your own cabin?"

"I would, Donal, if I could be sure they'd still be there tomorrow morning." And with that he left.

North Atlantic, Early March 1961

Each day followed as the one before. I made sure I tuned in the Dynatron radio before some crew member called to complain there was no music or whatever. I kept copying the traffic lists from Portishead UK and Chatham Radio USA. I placed an entry in my Radio Logbook every ten minutes.

Copied the Atlantic weather and sent our OBS reports which I sometimes copied to Horta in the Azores. Buckley would visit twice a day for his gin fix after which I'd mark out the next measure.

One morning after breakfast, I was sitting in the chief steward's office having a smoke, and talking about nothing in particular, when the chief cook came in holding a menu card. This was a daily ritual where the two men discussed what meals should be served the next day. I offered to leave but the chief steward said no and as a matter of fact we both want to ask you a question.

"We were wondering if you might agree to help Wally on Bond Night."

"Ok, what would I have to do?"

He handed me a book and said, "It's quite simple. You join Wally behind the counter, in the centre castle store room, where the Slop Chest (bond) is located. He'll hand out the cigarettes, drink and whatever else anyone wants, and you enter it in the book. You return the book to me and the captain deducts payments from each man's pay at the end of the voyage."

"No problem, Chief, I'd be delighted to do something different."

The bond was a privilege given to seamen. A carton of two hundred cigarettes cost ten shillings, 50 pence in today's money, and a bottle of spirits seven shilling and sixpence, equal to 35 pence. There were also other bits of cheap clothing and suchlike. The bond was opened several evenings a week though goods were available on request.

The first night of my new (unpaid) job, Wally and I stood behind a largish table and the crew queued in a line in front of us. The accents were mainly Geordie with lots of 'Wy Aye' and 'Champion'. I became aware that our customers were looking at me with lots of smiling faces. Someone remarked, "I didn't know you were light on your feet, Sparks," which provoked lots of laughter!

"Stop it, boys, he's not one of us."

The line became more orderly till one sailor came to the table and ordered toilet rolls. "How much will I put in the book for that, Wally?"

"No, Don, we don't charge for toilet paper," and before he could finish the sentence the whole assembly burst into hysterical laughter.

"Sparks is going to charge us to go to the toilet now lads!" This was one of those moments in life I'd rather forget. On my way up to return the chief steward's ledger, my crew mates were still smiling, and I've no doubt the little incident was probably recalled a thousand times in the pubs and clubs of Newcastle and Middlesbrough. Still, it was a little break in the monotony of a long sea voyage. I did have to endure more, gay and toilet jokes for several more bond nights.

As we edged ever closer to the American coast, we started to pick up music from the American stations and what fabulous music it was. The Everly Brothers, Roy Orbison, Elvis Presley and many more. I had to make sure to keep everyone on board happy by ensuring the Dynatron never went off tune.

The charter stated that we should be advised of our final destination before coming abreast of **Miami,** but we got closer and closer with only silence from New York. I was getting worried that I might have missed something, and my anxiety wasn't helped by visits from Captain Hort enquiring, "Why were we not being informed?" Just when we had almost reached the designated latitude, the Atalanta receiver speaker spat out our callsign MLPJ from WCC QTC 1.

This meant there was one telegram for us which I copied and delivered to the captain's cabin.

Please proceed to baton rouge to load molasses for European port to be advised.

I returned to the wheelhouse and borrowed the bridge binoculars which I focussed on **Miami** Beach to see how rich people spent their leisure time.

Florida Keys, March 1961

We edged down the Florida Keys still listening to the best music ever made and blissfully unaware that we were probably in the company of Russian ships bound for Cuba with weapons of mass destruction. With the Bahamas on our port side and Cuba a stone's throw south of us, we entered the Gulf of Mexico. We continued our journey towards Louisiana, and three days later entered the port of New Orleans.

New Orleans, Early March 1961

We tied up at a lay-by berth and waited for a health inspector to check that our tanks were suitable to accept the cargo of molasses. Unfortunately, we were too late for the Mardi Gras festival, but at least we were in New Orleans. Anyway, shortly after tie up, Alan and I were sharing morning tea and a smoke along with the chief steward in his day room when Wally called in to say the second engineer wanted a thousand cigarettes and two bottles of Johnny Walker.

The second never did things by half. The chief handed over the storeroom keys and shortly after Wally returned with the goods. Having little to do, I volunteered to make the delivery and with smoko over, Alan and I made our way down the catwalk joining the midships and after accommodation. Before reaching the second's cabin, we could hear a noisy party in full swing. "Come in, gentlemen, and grab yourselves a beer."

The party already had the third and fourth engineers present plus a few donkey men and I could see everyone was in very good humour. I handed over the cigarettes and whisky, and not wishing to appear unfriendly, both Alan and I sat down. As it was only mid-morning and neither of us were more that social drinkers, we asked if we could have a soft drink. This produced howls of laughter, and, "Don't be daft, lads, this party is beer and spirits only."

We both accepted a can of beer. Can I say at this point, I can't now remember the names of the two most senior engineer officers, which is probably just as well, because of what was later to happen in Baton Rouge. Meaning no disrespect, I will refer to them as Glasgow Gorbals and Liverpool Toxteth. The party continued and with a few more beers, Alan and I became full participants.

A singsong started and several times the uncensored version of 'Maggie May' was sung along with 'I belong to Glasgow' and 'The Blaydon Races'. The party broke up shortly after the lunch gong rang out and we all made our way to the saloon. I can still remember trying to be normal with amused stares from George and Buckley.

After lunch, I went for a few hours' sleep, after which I had a nice cold shower, dressed in my best, and joined Alan for a night out in New Orleans. We walked the streets and drank in the sights and smells of what could easily have been a French city, with its fussy veranda ironwork and exotic music coming from a thousand bars. We wound up in one bar which was very dimly lit and ordered two Tom Collins.

At times, the black bar attendants looked at us strangely as did the patrons who were also all black. After a few more Tom Collins, we thought no more of it but at the end of the night, we did look into a room at the end of the bar which we hadn't noticed before. There was jazz music and lots of couples dancing in a very sensual fashion.

It was late so we decided we had better return to the *Arctic* as the trip up the Mississippi was scheduled to start mid-morning. I often wonder about that bar and whether as white guys, we strayed into territory we shouldn't have?

On schedule, the large ropes holding the *Arctic* alongside were released and our journey to Baton Rouge commenced.

New Orleans to Baton Rouge, Early March 1961

We made our way slowly up the mighty Mississippi and I could hear the river pilot call out the course corrections to our helmsman, "Right a bit," "Left a bit," which was the American way rather than port and starboard. I decided to visit the wheelhouse and see what was going on in the Big Muddy. Maybe a showboat might pass, and I could imagine Paul Robeson belting out, "Old Man River," or Huckleberry Finn running along the river bank. "Would you like a coffee, Pilot?"

He removed a half-smoked cigar from the side of his mouth. "Yes, young man, black with no sugar." I took him the coffee along with one for myself and listened to his river tales, which he told with some enthusiasm while the *Arctic* slid its way along the Big Muddy. That evening, we arrived in Baton Rouge and everything looked new as the port had only opened a few short years earlier. I remember we were berthed close to a big iron bridge spanning the river.

After dinner, Captain Hort invited a few of us to his cabin for a drink. Buckley was there and I was nervous he might succumb to temptation even though he had his two large measures of Gordons and Schweppes. I needn't have worried because he was happy with ginger ale, and cigarettes which he smoked using a long black holder.

Things went well until a few hours later, one of the Able Seamen knocked on the cabin door to report there was trouble on the main deck. The captain and George went to investigate leaving us with instructions to remain where we were.

Sometime later, both men returned looking a bit shocked. Glasgow and Liverpool, it seemed, had not paused in their drinking session from the day before and were now harassing anyone who came near them, even to the point of fisticuffs. George, the chief officer, assured the captain that his little talk with them would have the right effect and soon they'd be asleep in their bunks. I'm not sure why the chief engineer hadn't intervened?

I'm afraid George's reassurance was not to be as a few minutes later, we heard Glasgow and Liverpool shouting up the stairs, "Come down here now, you f...ing bastard, and we'll sort you out."

We all assembled on the captain's landing and tried to reason with the two very drunk men. This only seemed to make them worse and left with no choice, the captain told me to call the police using the bridge radio telephone. Alan came with me and I could see he was as frightened as me. Once the Marconi transmitter valves reached operating temperature, I tuned in to 2182 kHz and called the local Marine Station.

The operator patched me through to the local police station and I advised the desk sergeant our ships name, location and said two of our crew had gone berserk. "Ok, Sir, please hold." After what seemed like an eternity, during which time Alan locked all the wheelhouse doors, the reply came, "Ok, Captain, help is on its way."

A few minutes later, we could hear the police sirens screaming to our aid and soon officers from two squad cars were running up the main deck, some of them with guns drawn. This would have been great excitement if we'd been in a cinema, but this was real life and though everyone was scared, we all pretended not to be. Alan and I went to the bridge wing where we saw Glasgow and Liverpool being dragged down the gangway with their hands cuffed behind their backs.

After a discussion with the captain and senior officers, the police left in a much quieter fashion than when they arrived. We re-joined the group in the captain's cabin where large brandies were waiting for us. Some of the men in that room were seasoned mariners and even served in the Second World War, but all agreed that what had just happened was unique.

We all knew there was friction between Captain Hort and two of his senior engineers, but I'll let the details lie in the past. I didn't sleep very well that night and even to this day wonder why two men who spent years studying against all odds, would so stupidly throw it away, because there was no way this was going to have a happy ending.

Baton Rouge, March 1961

I was still asleep when Wally called with my morning tea and toast. "Good morning, Sparks, great excitement last night, though some of the crew are nursing black eyes and bloody noses."

"Yes, Wally, and I feel like I've been awake all night."

"Will I pull the curtains, Donal."

"Yes, Wally, thanks," and when he did, I could see that we had shifted to a berth full of large round silver tanks from which umbilical type hoses were feeding molasses into the *Arctic's* holds. When I opened the cabin window, a sweet hot sugary smell entered the cabin. Breakfast that morning was full of talk about gun toting cops running madly about our decks.

With breakfast over, I decided to catch up on my paperwork, but I hadn't got very far when Wally called to say the captain wanted to see me in his cabin. Entering his cabin, I could see a large man dressed in American style clothes and smoking a large cigar seated in front of the captain's desk. The captain introduced him as the Ship's Agent, whom I'll call Walter.

It was explained to me that Liverpool and Glasgow were still in the local caboose with no way of them being allowed back on board. Walter had already booked flights for them back to London. I wondered why I was being fed this information, but I didn't have to wait long for an answer.

The captain explained that all the deck staff were busy loading the ship but as I was free, he would like me to do a little job for him. "Please, Sparks."

I was hardly likely to refuse and said, "Of course, Sir." The little task was for me to visit Liverpool and Glasgow in prison and deliver their discharge books and other items, including cigarettes, which the agent said they specifically requested. The cigar smoking agent handed me a note with the station address which meant I wasn't going to ride in his big Cadillac car parked at the end of the gangway.

I walked up the quay wall in my new suit, provided by Bests of O'Connell Street, which I purchased during my last leave. I was very proud of the hand stitched lapels. Either Captain Hort forgot, or just didn't bother, to give me taxi or bus fare, so as it was a nice morning, I decided to walk and with directions from local pedestrians, I arrived at the police station, about forty five minutes later.

Entering the station, I walked up to the counter and a big man dressed in a black police uniform with various insignia and a gun strapped to his hip came over and said, "What can I do for you, sonny?" I didn't think this was a great start, but I explained I was there to see the two prisoners they had arrested the night before. The big man looked amused and shouted across the office to another man wearing sergeant's stripes.

"Hey, Rick, this Irish Kid wants to see those two Limeys." This was going from bad to worse, but Rick came to the counter and I explained again that I was from the *Arctic* and wanted to see my two shipmates.

"Those two guys have been entertaining my officers all night with jokes and stories. Have you got any identification?" I produced my seaman's passport which seemed to satisfy him and asked, "What do you do on board?"

"I'm the ships radio officer in charge of the ship's radio station, Sergeant."

"Did you make the call to me last night?"

"Yes, Sergeant, that was me." My answer seemed to work some kind of magic, because everyone looked at me in a different light, and Rick escorted me into the interview room, where Liverpool and Glasgow were already seated. One of the officers brought in a tray containing three cups and a large pot of coffee. I was a bit nervous but Liverpool tossed my hair and said, "Don't worry, Sparky, we won't eat you."

I passed over the goods I was carrying and both men immediately lit up a Senior Service, which they inhaled deeply before taking a large slug of the Maxwell House.

They asked me to pass on their apologies to anyone they had harmed or offended and then added, "We had enough and anyway tomorrow we'll be back home and away from that b…"

"But what about your careers?"

Both men laughed, and Glasgow said, "You know how when you're finished a beer you bend the can in two?"

"Yes."

"Well where we come from, they do that with dust bins! Don't worry we'll be back at sea within the month." I wished them well and Rick escorted me back to the main office. As I left the building, there was a chorus of 'See you, Don' and 'Thanks'.

I made my way back to the *Arctic* again on foot too late for lunch, but Wally told me to take a seat and he would bring me a cold plate. While I was eating, Captain Hort joined me and enquired how the meeting had gone. I gave him an edited version. That afternoon, I continued with my paperwork and that evening Alan, Jack and I made our way into the centre of Baton Rouge.

We had one drink in what I think the Americans call a Tavern where we decided to take in a film and what a film! *Psycho,* starring Anthony Perkins and Janet Leigh.

You'd think we would have had enough drama for one day, but we enjoyed being frightened by Anthony with his big knife pulling back the shower curtain and Janet screaming her head off. The cinema was air conditioned which meant, when we stepped outside, the heat of the night wrapped itself around us like an electric blanket on a cold winter's night. We finished off back in the Tavern and two Tom Collins before making our way home.

I had just entered my cabin when Captain Hort called down the stairs for Alan and I to come and see him. When we got to the top, we could see that Walter, the cigar smoking agent, was there along with the captain and he was particularly sozzled. "Can you lads help the agent to his car please?"

With great difficulty and extra assistance from Jack, we eventually managed to get the very drunk man to the end of the gangway, and his big two tone Cadillac. Despite everyone suggesting he should sleep on board till the morning, he insisted he'd be ok once he got into the driving seat. This took us several attempts to achieve but eventually we managed it. The Caddy burst into life and the last we saw of it was the big tail fins and large rear red lights weaving its way down the pier.

The next day, with our belly full of molasses, we commenced our journey back down the mighty Mississippi towards New Orleans.

Mississippi River, March 1961

With Baton Rouge astern of us, we made our way slowly down the mighty Mississippi passing river boats, yachts and ships flying flags of almost every nation on Earth. We arrived in New Orleans and after a brief stopover to take on two new engineers, oil, fresh water and food we made our way back into the Gulf of Mexico.

Using the big Dynatron radio, I tuned in to the best of the many US Gulf Stations, and soon had the *Arctic* rocking to the sounds of Elvis, Roy Orbison, The Everly Brothers and many, many more.

I contacted Halifax Radio Canada, and advised, our next port would be known when we reached 40 degrees north. Our cargo of molasses would be traded on European stock markets several times, before our final destination was known. We set a southeast course for Key West and three days later, we arrived off Key Largo.

In common with the Spanish and Portuguese explorers, we edged our way into the Gulf Stream which pushed our speed up from 12 to 14 knots. We knew we were in the stream because of all the kelp riding along with us. We changed course to Northeast towards the Azores and the English Channel beyond.

It was night-time when we entered the Bermuda Triangle and after a warm shower before bedtime, I sat out in the cool night air and lit up a Lucky. There was little or no noise save the gentle lapping of water against the ship's hull. The full moon danced on a calm sea and my best description would be from the poem, *The stag at eve had drunk his fill, where DANCED the Moon on Monan's Rill.*

A few mornings later, Alan came into my cabin and said come up to the bridge Sparks and prepare to be amazed. I entered the wheelhouse and remember saying, "Sweet Jesus, what have we here." Captain Hort made no comment as he had probably seen it all before. We had entered the Sargasso Sea and the water was a light blue covered in brown seaweed as far as the eye could see.

Alan and I stood on the starboard bridge wing for maybe twenty minutes mesmerised by the experience. There was no time to dally as watches had to be kept and by evening, the sea had returned to its usual grey and normal North Atlantic swell.

That evening, I copied the weather forecast from NSS Washington Radio and handed it in to the bridge. We were heading into an area of low pressure. The next morning, we were south of Bermuda when the storm hit.

Fortunately, it was not hurricane season but we started to roll and pitch and even though the *Arctic* was a big ship, the storm tossed us about like a cork in a swimming pool and huge waves broke over our for'd deck, which became invisible until the *Arctic* appeared again out of the water like a breaching whale. The wind howled like a banshee on a Mayo winter's night. The storm stayed with us till we were north of the Azores and an area of high pressure.

Azores, North Atlantic, Late March 1961

We reached 40 degrees north and the days were becoming noticeably cooler. My main station was now Portishead Radio, and Captain Hort was becoming anxious, as there was still no word from London, re our final destination. This may have caused the friction between himself and Buckley, which had become a regular occurrence and resulted in Buckley visiting me one afternoon just after 1600 hours. "Get the Gordons down, Donal."

"But, you're hours too early, Buckley!"

"Never mind all that. I can't take much more of that man, and I need something now." Buckley, as I intimated earlier in the story, was a gentleman mariner more used to dealing with people of a similar ilk.

While Buckley sat down on my settee and lit a Senior Service, located at the end of his long cigarette holder, I poured a generous measure of gin topped with a splash of Schweppes and handed it to him. Soon all animosity between himself and Captain Hort was forgotten, and Buckley started to regale me with more of his encounters sailing on passenger ships in the Far East.

Towards the end of his visit he said, "You know, old boy, I probably wouldn't be here today if it wasn't for your country and an Irish doctor." He went on to explain that he got very sick when he was a young man and could do no more than lie in bed all day, getting thinner and thinner and weaker and weaker. His mother never left his side but could do no more than hold his head over a sick basin. No matter what he ate, it came straight back up.

"So, what happened, Buckley?"

"Well, old boy, one day a new doctor came to visit, and I could tell by his accent that he was Irish." After the usual examination and discussion with Mother, he recommended I go on a diet of Guinness mixed with milk." He went on to explain that it didn't sound very promising but from the first glass of the magic mixture he started to feel better and within weeks, he was almost back to normal. Mother was ever grateful to Ireland.

During the evening watch, our call sign MLPJ was on GKL's traffic list and when I copied the message addressed to Captain Hort, it gave instructions for the *Arctic* to proceed to Antwerp for full discharge. Soon our cargo of molasses would be used in the making of Belgian chocolate to be enjoyed by those of a more discerning taste! Towards the end of my watch, the captain, who was now in great form, handed me a Marconigram addressed to Mrs Hort Taunton Somerset.

"ETA Antwerp end of March, bring the girls and I'll have accommodation ready, Love."

I sent it off immediately along with our latest weather observations and an acknowledgment of instructions to the London owners. I felt a little sad, because I knew I couldn't invite my girl to visit, even if I could afford it, which of course

I couldn't. We ploughed our way through more bad weather with the Dynatron now tuned to the staid emissions from the BBC Light programme, and finally reached Antwerp at the end of March 1961.

Antwerp, Late March 1961

Arriving at the Scheldt Estuary, the pilot vessel came alongside, and our pilot ascended the Jacobs ladder. He soon navigated us, safely up the River Scheldt and , and alongside a pier with large round stainless steel tanks waiting to accept our cargo of molasses. We could see the docks were within a reasonable walking distance of Antwerp city centre.

By the time the Captain's wife and daughters were walking up the gangway, the dockers had already inserted big suction pipes into the belly of the *Arctic.* The chief officer's wife was also a new arrival. I had visitors from Radio Holland who came on board to service the Mk4 Radar.

That morning I was in Alan's cabin enjoying a morning coffee, when I noticed the photograph of his girlfriend which he displayed on his desk. She had a look of Kim Novak whom she obviously modelled herself on, but the thing I noticed was the frame because my photo of Rita, which stood on my desk, had none.

It wasn't much of a plan, but coffee break over, I donned my suit with the hand stitched lapels, put my Belgian Francs in my wallet and headed up town on my own. I walked around the city enjoying the sights till eventually I found a shop selling photograph frames. I settled on one with soft white plastic framing the glass. It didn't cost very much but I thought it was magnificent and couldn't wait to give it a home, which I did, soon after returning to the *Arctic* for lunch.

That evening, George and his wife suggested we go on a visit to the local bars and enjoy a few scoops of Stella Artois. I must say even today I can remember it going down very easily. Another attraction that night, the long-stemmed glasses, the beer was served in.

Some were engraved with coloured portraits of sailing ships. George's wife couldn't resist liberating a few into her handbag which I found uncomfortable. My discomfort increased with a visit from the head barman who delivered a whispered message into the culprit's ear, resulting in the stolen goods being placed back on the table.

The second day passed uneventfully and late that evening, after a successful passage back down the Scheldt, we entered the North Sea. I powered up the

Oceanspan 7 and advised Portishead Radio that our next destination was Montreal and the Canadian Great Lakes beyond. We sailed down the English Channel and a day later, we were south of the Scilly Islands, where we set course for an Atlantic voyage towards Cape Race at the southern end of Newfoundland.

The second morning of our voyage with Ireland's south coast on our starboard side, I decided to tune in the Dynatron to 562 kHz Radio Eireann. Transmissions didn't start in those days till the Angelus was played at noon. It rang out, loud and clear in every smoke room of the *Arctic,* and I fully expected a visit from the crew complaining that they wanted music, not prayers.

None came and from memory after the Angelus came hospital requests. The Kennedy's of Castleross, IMCO Cleaners with sponsored music of Frank Sinatra, Burl Ives, etc., which would have been very much to everyone's taste. By late afternoon, the signal weakened to the point where I had to switch back to the BBC Light programme.

That evening, I joined Wally in the centre castle bond room. One of the Geordie lads cried out, "Hey, Sparks, don't be putting any more toilet paper against my tab." Laughter followed.

"Ok and did you enjoy the mid-day entertainment?"

"Aye, it were champion, but my gran would turn in her grave if she knew I was listening to Catholic prayers and Taig music."

Wally intervened. "Your gran would spin in her grave if she saw the tarts you were sneaking on board every night in Baton Rouge, Tommy, so let's have more respect for the officer please."

Several of the men signing for their cigarettes, beer and whisky remarked, "It was champion, Sparky, and don't mind Tommy."

I returned to my cabin with Buckley's weekly Gordons and placed it in the book cabinet above Rita's new home. Our journey continued due west to the edge of the Porcupine Bank, where the depth falls from a few hundred fathoms to thousands of fathoms.

Manchester Merchant! MGZQ

We reached 30 degrees west and I knew from my four previous Atlantic voyages on the *ss Manchester Merchant* and *mv Irish Oak* that it was near time to start copying the ice reports compiled by US and Canadian meteorologists. Captain Hort, who as a veteran voyager to the Labrador coast and Hudson Bay, also reminded me that these reports would soon be required.

Irish Oak/EIQD

The days and nights became noticeably colder, and George increased the lookouts with one well muffled sailor on the focsle head and another on the monkey island. Their job was to report any sightings of growlers, ice fields or icebergs. They scanned the horizon with powerful binoculars. It was also known that approaching within a couple of miles of a berg, the air temperature would dramatically drop but this information was only useful in poor visibility.

Buckley and Captain Hort marked out the charts with the berg and ice field locations as per my reports. We also had the Marconi 48 nautical mile MK 4 radar. This sent out a very narrow vertical shaped beam at approx. 9.5 GHz from an orange peel scanner. When the beam hits its target, it dislodges some of the electrons surrounding the atomic nucleus and these electrons release their energy to form 3 cm waves of electromagnetic radiation that travels back towards the orange peel antenna.

This works fine on ship targets, whose iron atoms have many electrons spinning around the nucleus, but H20 is a different matter, as this molecule possesses much fewer electrons. This means that ice makes a very poor reflector, so for example an iceberg might only paint on the screen once or twice every ten scans. When it does paint, it's very ghostly, so the radar operator has to be very observant.

The situation improved dramatically when the scientists increased the frequency/wavelength from 3.5 to 10 cms or S Band as it is known.

We were beyond 40 degrees west when I heard Alan shout out, "Iceberg target at 8 miles, Sir, fine on the Port bow." The lookouts were informed, and it wasn't long before the white monster came into view. It was magnificent, and in the moonlight, it was like looking into the face of God.

On instructions from the bridge, I reported the position of the beautiful berg to CFH Halifax Radio. We gave it a wide berth not wishing to repeat the Titanic disaster.

The next day, we had to reduce speed to avoid colliding with the many growlers (mini bergs) occupying large areas of the sea around us. A growler, while not particularly dangerous, could if hit hard enough, loosen one of the ship's plates.

For the next day or two, the ever-present Newfoundland bank fog, enveloped the *Arctic,* causing us to reduce speed further. It also meant, the foghorn sent out its haunting sound, to warn other ships of our presence. Occasionally, we could hear warnings to us from other vessels in a similar dilemma.

Due to the fog it was not possible for Buckley to plot our position any better than dead reckoning. I was instructed to get a radio bearing from Cape Race Radio which from memory was a paid service! Once I had the Lodestone DF prepared, I requested my counterpart in Cape Race to start transmitting.

This lasted twenty seconds and once it was over, I handed Buckley the bearing which he plotted on the chart. We were smack on course to round the southern end of Newfoundland and enter the Gulf of St Lawrence.

South Coast of Newfoundland, 1 April 1961

We continued our passage into the Gulf of St Lawrence and when we reached the tiny French Islands of St Pierre and Miquelon, we set a course northwest towards the island of Anticosti. For those who may not know, I'll pause and tell you about these islands and who knows maybe someday, if you're on a quiz show, it might come up as a million Euro question.

These tiny islands over four thousand kilometres from Paris are part of France and the European Union and are restricted to French citizens. The currency is the euro, and apparently, if you go as a tourist, it's similar to visiting any small town or city in France.

We passed the north end of Anticosti and altered to a south-westerly course, which took us into the St Lawrence River, where we were boarded by the River Pilot at Father's Point. I sent a Marconigram from the captain assuring the Canadian authorities all the crew were disease free and we were granted Pratique.

Passing the city of Quebec, the Chateau Frontenac towered above us. I had been to this port twice and walked along the Boulevard in front of the Chateau. I knew for the most part those speaking anything but French, were not particularly welcome. I also knew that Elizabeth II was and is the Queen of Canada but excluding public buildings, her portrait would be as rare as that of the Pope in East Belfast.

We arrived in the city of Montreal and went to a lay-by berth where we received fresh food, water and oil. This city is a bit less French than Quebec. That night, Alan, Jack and I made our way with our subs of Canadian Dollars, to some of the local taverns. I remember you could buy a glass of Molson's beer for ten cents, which didn't taste great but once your taste buds were anaesthetised with the first few sips it wasn't bad.

There was a price to pay though, particularly for a casual drinker like me, and the next morning, I had to ask the chief steward tor some pain killers. I swore in future to buy the proper 25 cent beer, but this was a promise I wasn't to keep. I mean, when your salary is £624 a year (admittedly plus keep), you have to watch your outgoings!

The next morning, with our first Great Lakes Pilot on board, we commenced our long journey towards Duluth. For those who might not know, the Great Lakes project began in the 1950s. It was one of the greatest engineering feats of the 20th century, built by the USA and Canada. It was inaugurated by President Eisenhower and Prime Minister Diefenbaker in 1959.

We continued down the St Lawrence along with many ships on a similar mission until we entered Lake Ontario, near the Canadian city of Kingston. In Lake Ontario, for the first time we encountered the Lakers which I was familiar with, from previous voyages. These are very long, strange looking, flat bottomed ships designed to carry thousands of tons of cargo such as grain, coal, salt and other bulk cargoes.

Being flat bottomed, they are not suitable for deep sea voyages and if a bad storm blows up when they are crossing any of the Great Lakes, they have to make a hasty retreat to the nearest harbour. The Ontario Pilot recounted stories of past great storms that sent many of them to their doom.

Lake Ontario, April 1961

The sun shone and it seemed sort of weird to be on a large ocean-going vessel on a freshwater lake, sliding our way towards Niagara Falls City. Radio communications was now voice only and the Marconi radio-telephone was located on the bridge, which is where I now spent most of my day, passing and receiving messages to the various radio stations located in ports around the Lakes.

To relieve the deck crew a bit from the task of sailing the *Arctic* in such enclosed waters, I agreed to take a turn at manning the wheel plus sometimes the ships telegraph. It sounds important, but steering the ship in open waters, was a skill I learnt on previous voyages. As for the telegraph, this too was easy enough so long as you repeated the commands given by the pilot or deck officer.

For example, 'Half Ahead' and you repeated 'Half Ahead' while simultaneously turning the big brass handle to register 'Half Ahead' or whatever it might be. This command was then acknowledged by the engineers before they proceeded to turn silver wheels and shift gear levers. Having crossed Lake Ontario, we tied up near the entrance to the Niagara River, and next morning with the Lake Erie pilot on board, we started the multiple lock passage through the Welland Canal.

These are not, Royal or Grand Canal locks. These are mega locks that elevate ships up almost like a passenger lift. The view from the bottom lock was like staring up a small mountain and when we reached Lock 8 at the top of the mountain it was like looking down into a valley.

At each lock, the walls were lined with tourists. Bear in mind, this miracle of engineering was new and many American and Canadian inland dwellers, only ever saw pictures of ships, so we were something of a novelty. Most of the tourists were there primarily to visit the Niagara Falls, which was only a short drive away.

As we traversed each lock, the tourists who stood only a few feet from us, would ask questions as to where we were from and where we were going. Captain Hort said we were carrying trout and salmon for release into Lake Superior. Some of the young boys and girls said, "Really!" while their parents gave a wry smile.

At one lock, a couple with teenage girls asked if I would like to join them on a visit to the Falls and they would have me back on board before we reached the entrance to Lake Erie. I suspect my uniform might have been part of the reason for the invitation, which I had to politely refuse unfortunately. We did eventually reach Lock 8, and as I already said, the view back down was something to behold. The next morning, we entered Lake Erie.

Lake Erie and Lake Huron, April 1961

Our passage across Lake Erie was much the same as Lake Ontario and in less than a day, we entered the Detroit River and continued our journey past Detroit City, in the State of Michigan, eventually tying up overnight near Port Huron. We knew from all the tourists we had seen, and the towns and cities we passed, this was a seriously wealthy part of planet Earth.

Rested and fed, our journey across Lake Huron commenced under the control of a new pilot. I found it interesting listening to their stories which they loved to relate, in the same way as London black cab drivers. We arrived at Sault Ste Marie and again tied up for the night.

The next morning, we commenced our journey through Sault locks, again to be met with many tourists, interested to know, who we were and where had we come from. Happy with all the attention, we made sure to look our smartest and entertain them with enhanced stories of our encounters with hurricanes, icebergs and whales. They probably suspected we were exaggerating a little bit, but still couldn't get enough of our lies, and again two bars of gold, and a star on a twenty year old really, really helped.

Our passage across Lake Superior was the longest of all and it was well into April 1961 when we reached our destination Duluth in the State of Minnesota.

Duluth, Minnesota, Late April 1961

Duluth, where we were to load fifteen thousand tons of grain for Europe, was where, about two years earlier, Buddy Holly and other prominent rock and roll stars were there to entertain. This was their last gig, and all died in a plane crash soon after in what is known as, 'The Day The Music Died'.

We berthed at a long open quay with cathedral size silos. Normally bulk cargoes such as grain are carried by ships with big open hatches into which small JCB excavators can be lowered. The excavators are used to trim the grain to an even level. We were an oil tanker and in sixty years I've never known another tanker to carry grain.

It was not possible to lower a JCB into our tanks, but we could lower men with shovels, and this is what we did. As the grain entered, those men trimmed it smooth, and when each tank was almost full, we could see the grain spilling out from the top of the four foot round hatch, with the men still underneath it.

I thought, "Bloody hell they'll suffocate," but after what seemed like an eternity, the grain slowly sank like sand in an egg timer, and smiling sweaty bodies would emerge to fill their lungs with fresh air. This method of loading was slow, so our stay in Duluth was going to be a long one.

As already said, our main source of entertainment was the Dynatron radio and a small library located in the wardroom. One of Alan's jobs was chief librarian. Soon after we tied up, a man from the local phone company came on board and connected us to a landline. Someone suggested we should club together and get a rental TV.

The ship's agent supplied the phone number for a local shop, and within hours, a seventeen inch, black and white TV was up and running in the ward room. The rest of the crew followed our example. Bear in mind, in 1961, TV was still new so to us this was a real luxury. During the day, we could watch old Westerns and at night, shows like 'I love Lucy, Bonanza, Batman and Robin'.

At night, we'd go ashore to the local cinema followed by a trip to one of the many diners for hamburgers and Cokes. We'd feed the jukebox, smoke our

Luckies or Pall Mall seated on red mock leather seats and imagine we were James Dean or Marlon Brando.

Duluth, Early May 1961

Week two and the grain kept filling the tanks of the *Arctic.*

More curious visitors came on board every day. Many of these Americans had never been outside their own country nor had they ever seen the Atlantic or Pacific Oceans. In a vast rich country like the USA, they had little or no incentive to do so.

We were flattered by all the attention. The engineers were proud to show off their engine room, the deck staff, the bridge, with its state-of-the-art radar, and hydro acoustic equipment, the chief steward and his staff, the saloon, wardroom and galley, and last me. I showed them my radio station and explained how I could send and receive messages across oceans.

And sometimes asked, "Are you actually Irish?" I was never sure how to respond. Many on board enjoyed American hospitality with drives along the lake shore and evening meals in their homes.

The night before sailing, Captain Hort invited the ship's agent and his wife to join him for drinks in his day room. I, along with others, was also invited to attend. I should point out that the captain's accommodation was considerable in size. Buckley only had soft drinks that day in order that he might participate more fully in the evening entertainment. He in fact was the premier entertainer with stories of his time spent on passenger ships in the Pacific and South China seas.

The Farewell

The morning of our departure the air was cooler as a cold wind blew down from Hudson Bay and the Lake was covered in a light mist. With all hands on board except one, George and four sailors manned the for'd windlass, in readiness for the release of the large ropes, holding what was now thirty thousand tons of shipping. Buckley was in charge of the after deck, doing a similar job.

The captain, Alan and Jack were controlling the bridge along of course with the pilot. I had my now usual job of manning the engine room telegraph. "Are we ready to go, Cap'n?" The pilot enquired.

"Just a few minutes more, Pilot, please," he replied as he walked out to the starboard bridge wing.

Looking back, he signalled for Alan and me to join him which we did. On the quay wall below us, was the missing sailor embracing a young girl in a white summer dress. Captain Hort raised five fingers to two seamen, waiting to raise the gangway, who nodded in reply. Alan was instructed to give two blasts on the ship's whistle. "Time to go, Cap'n," the pilot called out again.

"Just a few more minutes, Pilot, please." The lovers unlocked and with a final kiss, Jamie walked slowly up the gangway to be met with pats on the shoulder/from his two shipmates. I could see the girl in the white dress was trying hard not to cry but eventually, tears flowed freely down her cheeks.

Using a megaphone, Hort gave the command, "Let go for'd, let go aft," and two tugs pulled us slowly from the quay wall. This had the effect of allowing a gentle breeze access to the quay wall. The white dress swayed gently from side to side in a wave of goodbye. As we eased our way further into the Lake, she still stood there motionless.

Captain Hort gave a long farewell blast on the ships horn and she replied with a wave before finally fading into the morning mist.

Lake Superior, May 1961

As we steamed across the lake towards Sault Ste. Marie, I recalled how on my last visit as second R/0 aboard the *mv Irish Oak* we had to make an emergency exit to avoid being iced in for the winter. It was November 1960 and winter came early that year, with blizzards roaring down on the Great Lakes via Hudson Bay. All ships were advised to leave immediately, as soon the Lakes would freeze making passage impossible.

The chief engineer burned all his extra fuel, for extra speed, there were no overnight stops, and just in time we reached Montreal. Some of our companion ships failed to make it in time, and had to wait till spring arrived, plus assistance from ice breakers.

As we made our way through the many locks of Superior, Huron, Erie and Ottawa, the tourists seemed to arrive in even greater numbers asking us the same questions which we were glad to answer. Eventually, we reached Lake Ontario and just south of Toronto, we altered course for Wolfe Island and the St Lawrence River. We had an overnight stop in Montreal before proceeding down the river past the Chateau Frontenac, and onward this time to the North of Newfoundland and the Belle Isle Strait.

A fast-flowing tide astern of the *Arctic* propelled us at high speed back into the North Atlantic.

North Atlantic, June 1961

I had established contact with Halifax Radio informing them that we had left Montreal and our next port was Antwerp. It was still iceberg season and George again increased the lookout watch. Fortunately, and unusually, the sea was calm, and visibility was good, which encouraged Captain Hort to edge up closely to a number of the larger bergs we encountered. At night, we had a ringside seat to view the Northern Lights and the weather remained kind.

One night while I was on watch, I heard the door opening slowly behind me, but I wasn't able to look around, as I was copying the Washington weather report. I thought no more of it and with my watch over, I activated the Type M Auto Alarm, when I heard giggling coming from the chartroom and I could see Alan and Hort through the gold coloured grill.

"What's that all about I thought, and what's that funny fishy smell?" The laughter continued at a greater level and almost hysterical when I discovered a bird sitting on one of the office desks.

I burst out, "WHAT THE FU...HELL?"

The poor creature had collided with our spinning radar scanner and fell with a thump onto the monkey island. The wheelhouse comedians thought a visit to my office would be funny, which of course it was. Once our friend had recovered, we released it back over the ship's side.

The next day, the westerly gales returned along with the normal service of heavy rolling and pitching. Persistent rolling in heavy seas has the effect of making everyone a bit cranky due to interrupted sleep. As we edged closer to the Continental shelf and Ireland the signals from Valentia Radio/EJK became stronger and stronger.

We were nearing home and then one day, Radio Eireann came in loud and clear, so I gave the crew another listen to hospital requests, and the Kennedys of Castleross.

We were soon in the English Channel and then back alongside the docks in Antwerp. Big pipes started sucking the Duluth grain from the innards of the *Arctic*. I believe, its final destination was for the brewing of Belgian beer, possibly Stella Artois.

Many new crew members arrived but there was none for me. In those days, even the thousands of operators were insufficient to meet the need of British shipping. Just as I was beginning to despair, my relief arrived. He was about my age and hailed from Malta.

The next day, I signed off along with George and a few others at the Belgian British Embassy. I wished Captain Hort goodbye and that afternoon, Buckley, Alan, George and I boarded the Hook of Holland to Harwich overnight ferry.

The next morning, I wished my Board of Trade companions farewell and boarded a train for London and the Marconi East Ham Offices, where I handed in my papers and collected my pay.

The rest of that day I spent crossing England to Holyhead via Crewe. The next morning, I left the B&I ferry in Dublin and that afternoon, a happy reunion with my girl, Rita.

Polamhall

Polamhall 1

London, early June 1961. The taxi pulled up at the Royal Albert Docks and having paid the driver, I got out and saw the *Polamhall* for the first time. It was a large cargo ship built in 1950.

POLAMHALL

It had just returned from Lagos, Nigeria, and my first impression was, that the hull could do with a good clean. The ship was empty which meant the gangway was close to vertical, so I had to struggle to reach the boarding deck with my two cases. Once on board, I introduced myself to the Chief Steward Tom, who arranged for the cabin steward, a young man in his early twenties called Bryson, to show me to my cabin and office.

Normally, the operator's cabin would be located on the bridge deck, but on this ship, it was halfway down the midship's alleyway on the starboard side. The first cabin we passed was the chief officer's, followed by the second and third officer's, then me followed by our only deck cadet.

While settling in to my new home, my neighbours called to introduce themselves. Chief Officer James, a Scotsman in his seventies, who came out of retirement possibly due to boredom. James who was born in the 1880s and had served for many years himself as a ship's captain.

Second Officer Steve, a man of about thirty, and later in the voyage he told me how he had served in Strick Line which was a very upmarket Co. Unfortunately, Steve had succumbed to a bit of cargo pilfering which resulted in a bad discharge, and he was now reduced to sailing on lesser vessels like the *Polamhall*.

Third Officer John, from Wexford, was aged about twenty three. John's career with Irish Shipping ended, when he was involved in a car accident and was advised never to go to sea again. I suspect he never revealed this information to the ship's owner, 'West Hartlepool Steam Navigation Co.'

My last visitor that day was Ian, the ship's only deck cadet. Ian had two years of his apprenticeship served so I'd say he was about nineteen. I liked my new home because it meant I had someone to talk to every day rather than being isolated and alone on the bridge deck.

At 1700 hours, the bell for dinner rang and we all repaired to the dining saloon. There were two long tables decorated in the usual British Merchant navy fashion—crisp white linen tablecloths adorned with silverware cutlery and monogrammed serviettes. One table was set for the captain, chief engineer, chief officer and second engineer.

The second table had Steve, John, Ian, Third Engineer Malcolm and me. I was the new kid on the block as everyone else had been sailing together on this ship for the past year or more. They all made me feel that I was one of the gang. The captain shouted across, "Welcome aboard, Sparks."

"Thank you, Sir." Captain Armstrong was a man in his fifties who spent much of the voyage alone in his cabin. I say alone but he did have the company of his cat, Benny, plus I suspect Johnny Walker.

My curiosity was aroused when I heard the senior personnel discussing how the on-board problem was to be resolved. My curiosity evaporated that evening!

Polamhall 2

After dinner on the first day, we all met for coffee and a Lucky Strike in the wardroom, where I was introduced to the Fourth Engineer Derek, who had just come off watch. Derek from Liverpool was the same age as me. That evening, I checked out the radio equipment housed in a much larger office than my previous vessels. Satisfied that all was in order and that my main transmitter was High Frequency, which meant I could communicate over thousands of miles, I decided to check out the Bridge Electronics for which I was also responsible.

Everything went well till I reached the Marconi Mk 4 fifty kilowatt Radar installation. The transceiver unit was a large cabinet, about five feet high, and three feet wide, and I could hear funny noises emanating from it. That's odd I thought as I pulled out the lower tray to be met with a couple of large rats staring straight at me.

I froze thinking my saloon curiosity was now solved. I left the chartroom in something of a hurry and descended the stairs three at a time till I reached the wardroom, where the Third Engineer Gerry was seated in one of the large green leather sofa chairs reading a book. "What's wrong, Sparks? You look a bit pale."

I babbled out my chartroom encounter and he suggested we should go together and sort it out. "Go together," I thought, "are you mad?" Not wishing to appear a wus, I followed Gerry back up to the bridge, and stood nervously at the chartroom door. He suggested I close the door and he would carry out a cull on his own. I readily agreed.

For the next fifteen minutes, I could hear frightening noises as Gerry seemed to go through his task with some relish. "Everything ok in there?"

"Why aye. Two have escaped into the rolled-up chartroom carpet, but I'll soon sort that out." There were more noises accompanied with Geordie expletives and eventually Gerry emerged with a rosie half full, with the bodies of our unwelcome friends. I thanked him and returned to my office and lit up a lucky.

When my nerves had settled, I returned to the task of checking out the MK 4 Radar. It should be noted that in the 1960s, and before, radars were hugely expensive and probably the equivalent of £100,000 in today's money, so any rat damage to cable looms or whatever, would have been a serious problem. I opened the lower tray again, only to be met this time with the charred remains of two more unwelcome house guests.

I found Gerry re-seated in the wardroom, and sheepishly asked if he could help again please. "You'll have to get used to this sort of thing, Sparks, because the ship is infested."

"Are you serious, Gerry?"

"Yes, Sparks, and you had better rap on your cabin door before entering tonight." Sweet Jesus, take me out of here! "Come on, Sparks, I'll sort you out and don't worry, fumigation will take place in the next couple of weeks."

A couple of weeks…sweet Jesus!

Gerry seemed to enjoy the task of lifting the corpses out by their tails, over the side from the starboard bridge wing. I followed his advice and rapped on my cabin door that night before entering. I don't remember sleeping very well imagining every noise to be a visit from the relatives of the wheelhouse dead.

Polamhall 3

Day two: Royal Albert Docks near Poplar East End of London located where 'Call the Midwife' is filmed, and coincidently, precisely set in the time our vessel was there. Note in those days, a ship of our size took as long as ten days to load and involved as many as fifty dockers. The cargo had to be carefully stowed so as not to shift in bad weather and located sequentially if intended for various ports.

Mixed cargoes had to be separated to avoid possible fires, i.e. jute bales might combust with constant rubbing on a rolling ship.

Anyway, as I passed the 3/0's cabin on the way to breakfast, I was stopped in my tracks by the noise of a squawking bird. I pulled back the curtain and saw John talking to his pet parrot which he had brought back from the west coast of Africa. "Come in, Donal, and meet my friend Beaky."

Beaky was a magnificent young Grey parrot perched in a large cage at the end of John's settee. Why Beaky? Because he had beaks that could cut through hazel nuts as quick as a hot knife could cut through butter. John would allow him out of the cage once or twice a day but only behind closed doors because Beaky was still wild.

He could only be handled with safety gloves unless you had grown tired of your fingers. I was informed by John that we would be going ashore after breakfast to find a pet shop and food for Beaky. I assumed we would be using public transport, but as we stepped off the end of the gangway, I noticed a Norton motorbike sitting close by.

John started it up and told me to join him. To this day, I'll never know how he managed to acquire a motorbike, but he was an excellent talker and on reflection I imagine, he managed to come to a deal with one of the dockers loading the *Polamhall*. We zoomed around God only knows where in London, with me nervously located on the back seat. Thinking about John's recent car crash didn't help but it hadn't fazed him as we sped past slow moving traffic and zoomed around roundabouts.

At some stage, a pedestrian advised us where we could find a suitable pet shop where John bought a seriously large bag of birdseed. This was to last Beaky for six months. I had to hold it in one hand for the homeward journey while holding onto John with the second. Dear God, in less than twenty four hours, I was fit for the nut house.

Later that day on the phone to Rita, I gave her all the news omitting the chartroom adventure. The following days were spent in paperwork preparation and on some afternoons Ian, Derek and I would walk around the East End and sometimes Leicester Square, etc. talking and checking out the clothes shops. At night, we often went to the Poplar 'Flying Angel' Seamen's mission for a few drinks and a game of snooker.

The missions were not-for-profit organisations run by either the Anglican or Catholic church and strictly for seamen. They were originally set up to cater for distressed seamen who has missed their ship, either through drunkenness, or staying too long with ladies of the night. The mission usually managed to arrange their repatriation through another ship. Over the years the missions expanded to cater for all seamen.

On several nights, there would be dances, usually Rock and Roll and approved female hostesses would attend. These were girls normally middle class, who volunteered to meet and partner seamen from all over the world. This was a tradition first started during the Second World War as something of a respite to merchant seamen who perished in their thousands at the hands of the German U boats.

It was absolutely made clear that the hostesses went home alone at night and anyone breaking this rule was barred. The reason of course was obvious as too many moonlight kisses cooled in the morning Sun, and when girls were giving birth, their love partner was probably sailing off Valparaiso or Capri. Departure day eventually arrived, and we sailed down the Thames and entered the North Sea. I fired up my Oceanspan 7 and advised Northforeland Radio GNF our next Port as Hamburg. "BV 0.M," came the reply.

Polamhall 4

London to Hamburg:

The *Polamhall* passed Southend on sea at the easternmost end of the Thames and altered direction to a northeast course. Even with the fifty-kilowatt Mk 4 Radar, spitting its 9ghz beam to a distance of up to 48 miles, it was necessary for lookouts to be placed on the Monkey Island and Poop deck, as the traffic increased dramatically and particularly as dusk was falling. The lookouts became more imperative the next morning as we ran into North sea fog.

The bridge watch put the ship's horn on auto and every few minutes I could hear its haunting sound entering through my open port hole. I put my main receiver on external loudspeaker, so I could keep my distress and call watch while I had a mug of tea in the wheelhouse. Captain Armstrong was there with John—Beaky's daddy! The fog seemed to get thicker and we could hear fog warnings from distant vessels.

We were heading towards the area of the Dutch and German coasts still seeded with numerous mine fields from Second World War. The captain explained that it would probably take forty to fifty years to clear those minefields completely, so it was very important not to stray from the lanes which had been made safe. Christ almighty rats, suicide ride on a motorbike, and now heavily mined seas. If only I could be back in the Savoy with Rita.

The captain, sensing he had an audience in me, left John in charge and brought me into the chartroom where he rolled out a large Admiralty chart showing the shaded no go minefield areas. Hitler and his admirals had done an admirable job!

The bridge staff were confident of our position, but just to be certain, I was asked to take radio bearings from some of the Dutch and German DF stations, which confirmed our position as good. The next day, the fog had lifted as we neared the entrance to the River Elbe. The captain handed in messages for the Hamburg Agent, which I sent via Norddeich Radio, Callsign **DAN.**

The passage up the river towards Hamburg was very, very pleasant. These days, tourists pay serious money to cruise on the Elbe and for us it was free! We entered mighty Hamburg, one of the world's greatest ports, which received major attention from the Allies during the war, causing firestorms and killing many thousands of civilians. German efficiency over the previous fifteen years had restored the city to its former glory, and apart from the occasional bomb site, it looked normal.

We entered the docks area where the famous German battleships Bismarck, Graf Spee and Tirpitz were built. We tied up and the dockers immediately started to open the hatches and commenced discharging the cargo using large cranes mounted on the quay wall. I saw my first German words 'Fumar Verboten' 'smoking is forbidden'.

Over the next few days, men in overalls invaded every nook and cranny of the ship, resulting in many of our unwelcome guests, exiting the vessel, in long cylindrical, stainless steel containers.

In order to get from our berth to the city proper, we had to travel in small river ferries where everyone, mainly seamen, had to stand shoulder to shoulder below decks. Very claustrophobic! I pause here to say I've been warned not to talk about the Reeperbahn...SO I WILL. Every evening, John, Derek, Ian and I would take the claustrophobic ferry across the river to the St Pauli district of the city.

Bryson, the second steward, and his pals were doing likewise. On my first visit to the Reeperbahn, I could hardly believe my eyes. This red-light district, about a mile long, was lined with topless bars and state approved brothels. I saw young men negotiating prices with ladies of the night via street level windows. Music was blaring out of every bar.

I wondered if McQuaid or any of his army could envisage such a place, but then again and with the benefit of hindsight, maybe some of them did a detour on their way home from Rome. As Rod Stewart might say, the Reeperbahn was every schoolboy's dream. Once we became bored with people watching, we would repair to one of the local bars and schooners of the world renowned, German beer and free floor shows.

One night we went to a local theatre. There were families with children and the stage entertainment was very adult, similar to the Moulin Rouge. I found returning to the ship at night a trial, because the ferry seemed even more crowded and with almost everyone smoking it was like being caught in a nicotine fog. With the ship fully empty, we sailed down the Elbe again, exiting near the Kiel Canal and into the North Sea.

I called Norddeich Radio Dan and informed him that our next port was Liverpool. The reply came, "QSLBV."

Sometime before we reached the English Channel, Captain Armstrong entered the radio room, holding a large book labelled confidential. He sat down in the spare chair and started up a conversation about the war and his admiration for Churchill. With the benefit of hindsight, I'd say the captain was one of the many who suffered during the battle of the Atlantic, probably spending days in lifeboats before being eventually rescued.

He said he would want me to send a birthday greeting telegram to Winnie in November. I didn't ask him if he'd like also to send one to our wartime leader De Valera. His parting gift was to hand me the confidential book with sections marked out for me to study—'What to do in case of war or conflict'.

We were scheduled to transit the Suez Canal, where a year or two before there was a major conflict between Nasser and the British/French Alliance, which ended when President Eisenhower intervened, so maybe he had this in mind. Anyway, over the next day, while steaming down the English Channel, past the Isle of Wight, on a course set for Penzance, I did as I was instructed, and read my section of the big black book.

What stations and frequencies to use, codes, sea area to remain silent and all sorts of other boring stuff. By the time I finished reading, I wished Captain Armstrong had handed me a horse tranquilliser along with the big black book. Rounding Anglesey Island, we exchanged messages with the Liverpool Agent via Holyhead Radio GLV.

On a warm sunny day in early July 1961, we entered the mighty Mersey and berthed alongside in Canada docks. A second fumigation of the ship had been arranged to clear the vessel of any remaining vermin, including cockroaches.

This meant the ship had to be vacated to allow the fumigation team to proceed with their grisly task. The crew options were to go home for a few days or stay in Anchor house. Either option was good, but I chose to surprise Rita, and that evening, I boarded the B & I *mv Leinster* for the overnight voyage to Dublin.

Polamhall 5

Liverpool to Port Said and the Suez Canal:

My stay in Dublin with Rita lasted about three days and then it was time to get the *mv Leinster* back to Liverpool. It must be understood that, we had an unspoken agreement best summed up in our song 'Save the last dance for me'. This was probably the theme song for many deep sea mariners as nobody expected their partners to socially isolate over long periods apart.

When I got back on board, the ship was fully cleansed, and Bryson had all the cabins freshened with clean bed linen and fresh towels. Even Beaky seemed in a very chirpy mood. Within a few days, the *Polamhall* was fully loaded with goods for the Persian Gulf, and we were soon steaming down the North Welsh coast and Anglesey, where the pilot wished us bon voyage as he descended down our Jacobs ladder and on to the deck of the pilot vessel anchored offshore.

I reported our next port to GLV as Port Said and the reply came, "QSL TKS OM."

For the next fourteen days, we made our way past Land's End, Brest, the Bay of Biscay, Gentle Jesus, Gibraltar, Bizerte, Malta, Tripoli, Alexandria and finally late one night, Port Said, where we dropped the anchor to await our turn to enter the Suez Canal.

During our voyage, Second Officer Steve would recall his trips to the Gulf and educated us all on the correct etiquette in dealing with Moslem men and women. John regaled us with stories of his adventures to the White Man's graveyard on the West African coast. Beaky entertained us by finding a way out of his cage and flying up and down the alleyways, much to the annoyance of Benny, the captain's cat. I went to bed unaware of the surprise which was to greet me when I awoke the following morning.

Polamhall 6

Port Said, Egypt, September 1961:

I awoke the next morning to sounds of laughter coming from the starboard alleyway. I opened my eyes, blinked several times and said, "What the fucking hell?" This had the effect of increasing the laughter to hysterical levels.

I blinked again but no it was still there—several lines of string running the full length of my cabin adorned with small white souvenir camels, leather writing cases inscribed with Egyptian hieroglyphics, boxes of Turkish delight, khaki coloured tropical shirts and shorts, Port Said bibles and other things I can't remember.

A little man, I'll call Ali, dressed in a long white Arab style dress seeing the look of incredulity on my face said, "Don't worry, Sir, I got permission from your friends and I will give you a nice present when I leave this afternoon." My friends Steve, John and Ian were now standing in the doorway somewhat more composed with just big grinning faces. It turned out the goods in my cabin were for display only, as Ali's shop was actually a bum-boat tied up alongside the Polamhall.

This was one of the bum-boats in Port Said selling to crews from thousands of ships which annually waited at anchor to traverse the Canal going south into

103

the Red Sea. During breakfast, the merriment died to the occasional burst of laughter, and the Chief Officer James intervening with 'Like bloody children'. After breakfast, I joined Steve on the bridge to take in a panoramic view of the city.

On deck, Ali and his workers had set up tables with goods from the bumboat laid out for sale. We could see deck and engine room crew bargaining somewhat loudly with Ali. I suggested to Steve that we should join them. "No, no, Sparks. What we do is wait until they're finished their next prayer session when with Allah still present in their heads, they'll be more amenable not to cheat."

"Ok fine, Steve, thanks." When morning prayers facing Mecca were over, we descended to Ali's shop. Steve negotiated my purchase of Khaki shirts suitable for Epaulets, shorts and a box of Turkish delight. That afternoon as the Egyptian pilot was boarding, Ali handed me my present of two small white soft plastic Camels and I also bought one of the leather writing cases.

John said the camels were normally stuffed with medical waste from one of the local hospitals, which was information I never gave Agnes on my return home. I have memories of looking at them in the Ballymun sitting room for many years after that.

With the pilot on board, we received a message from Ismailia to proceed to the Canal Entrance. The chief officer oversaw the lifting of the anchor and we could see many ships in our vicinity doing likewise. We all proceeded in Convoy like an Elephant Line as instructed.

Polamhall 7

Port Said to Aden and beyond:

The Suez Canal, continuing the Emperor Napoleon's dream, the French commenced cutting through the Sinai desert in 1859. A few years later in something of a panic, the British requested to join them and the French accepted. The world-famous Canal was opened with great fanfare in 1869, reducing the sea journey from Europe to the Far East by up to six weeks, by bypassing the Cape of Good Hope.

The *Polamhall* made its way slowly through the desert past Ismailia, the Great Bitter Lake, finally entering the North end of the Red Sea at the spot where Moses crossed, leading the tribes of Israelites into the promised land. The sea was smooth and crystal clear.

Soon after we passed the port of Jeddah, I received a request from a ship full of pilgrims heading for Mecca, asking if we could assist by giving a bearing to the Moslem shrine Port. *'Steve checked the chart, a bit reluctantly,'* I thought, but armed with the information I passed it on. "Thank you and may Allah guide your way, AR."

We continued our journey past Port Masawa in Eritrea where Bino served with the Italian army during Second World War. It's surrounded by sandy hills and as Bino often said, it was like living in an oven. Seven days after exiting the Canal, we entered the Port of Aden. It was a dry red Mars like place and Captain Armstrong said it hadn't rained there for the past hundred years.

Aden was a place where nearly all ships entering and leaving the Red Sea stopped for bunkers (oil), water and other provisions.

Chief Steward Tom arranged for fresh food and replenished the ship's Bond with alcohol and cigarettes, etc. All ships carried a Bond which was customs sealed in port and not opened till the vessel was 3 miles from land. The goods were sold to the crew at minimum profit and zero duty.

A 200 Carton of cigarettes could be bought for about ten shillings and a bottle of spirits, for even less. This was one of the small concessions given to all mariners. Another one today is the Neptune Ward in Guys and St Thomas' Hospital London, where mariners are treated free of charge.

Anyway, fully replenished we left Aden and I called Ceylon Radio to send a TR message, but I received an answer from the British base in Mauritius instead. I passed my message for Lloyds, next port Das Island Persian Gulf. We continued our voyage up the Arabian Sea past Muscat the Gulf of Hormuz and into the Persian Gulf six days after leaving Aden.

Polamhall 8

Persian Gulf 1961:

We sailed through the Straits of Hormuz, the narrow stretch of water between Dubai and Iran. We converged with hundreds of ships from every corner of the planet, most of which were tankers, coming to drink their fill of the liquid black gold which was powering a world boom. I say world boom, but countries like mine were still being run by men of limited vision, standing at parish pumps on Sunday mornings, while legions of young Irishmen marched past them on their way to work on the rebuilding of England and the new intercity motorways.

The straits were peaceful unlike today, where ships are likely to be boarded by Iranian or American Special Forces. By lunchtime, we were in the Gulf proper and new additions to the dining tables were salt tablets and lime juice. To avoid heat stroke and scurvy, all crew members were required by the law of the sea to take the tablets and drink the lime juice every day. I too became a Limey!

The captain had a right to fine anyone not complying. As we approached Das Island, the temperature soared into the mid-thirties. Das Island was a dot of land 1.5 miles long by 0.75 miles wide, and a turtles paradise for probably hundreds of thousands of years. In 1961, it was just being developed for what is today one of the major ports exporting gas and oil. It now supports six thousand oil workers.

John insisted on me asking the small radio station, if there was any night life that we could participate in. The operator said there was a small club for the site workers, but this was now off limits to us, as the previous week the crew of a ship ran amok causing serious damage to furniture, etc. It was probably caused by an on-board argument spilling ashore.

Anyway, there would have been little time to go ashore as the pumps and whatever else we had was soon landed into barges as we lay anchored offshore. On to Mina Al Ahmadi! This too was a recently built city accommodating what even then was a major oil port in Kuwait. We lay alongside close to Strick Line ships which were fully air conditioned with sweeping staircases and almost Michelin star food.

As an ex- employee, Steve explained these standards were required to entice crews to sail in the stifling heat of the Persian Gulf. The *Polamhall* was actually on charter to Strick line as their fleet, big as it was, couldn't cope with the boom.

The rust on the hull and superstructure of our ship had worsened since leaving Liverpool, so the ship's agent arranged for a large team of migrant workers from Pakistan to start a major clean up. The chip hammers started at about 8 a.m. every morning and didn't stop until late at night. The black paint rollers followed up on the chippers and by the time we departed the *Polamhall* looked almost respectable.

To escape daytime noise and when not on duty, John, Ian, Derek and I would take a taxi into the city and just walk around as there wasn't much else to do. Being young men, we would admire the girls who walked past us. Sometimes we would get a stern look from a male walking behind them. I wondered about this, until I remembered Steve's course on Arab etiquette.

The men were probably fathers or husbands, and even our innocent glances, were absolutely taboo. At night, we tried sleeping on deck to escape the heat, but I found this didn't work for me so I would return to my cabin. Our ship was one of the very few that didn't have air conditioning, and in fact this was a ship more suitable for sailing in the Arctic rather than the stifling heat of the Gulf. The shushing noise from the cabin blowers only added to my discomfort.

Sometimes I could lie half awake, until 4 a.m. before falling into a coma like sleep. At 8 a.m., when Beaky would start squawking and Bryson would call with morning tea, I wasn't able to open my eyes as they were glued together with sticky emissions. I would go blindly to the sink and bathe them with water and even then, the sticky stuff would persist until I painfully prised my eyelids open.

And now for something that has given me nightmares for the last almost sixty years. The noise from the hammer brigade was less loud in my office, so one day I decided to shine up my radio equipment with Pride, polish provided by Tom the chief steward. After several hours of hard rubbing, I sat back and admired my handiwork. I then decided to catch up on my paperwork, because if it was left too long it could get out of hand.

When I finished, I stubbed out the Lucky I'd been smoking, locked the office, and descended for the afternoon tea. For this, we normally congregated in the galley and exchanged lies about past adventures we had had on our ships. When the lies and banter were finished, I climbed the stairs back to the bridge but before I got to the top, I could smell smoke. In something of a panic, I opened the doors into the bridge and chartroom which were smoke free.

I ran back and opened the radio room door to be met with smoke impossible to see through. "Oh Jesus, Oh Jesus," I heard myself saying aloud, while at the same time grabbing the fire extinguisher. "Oh Mary, mother of God, help me," and maybe she did, because I could see flames coming from the rosie into which I had emptied the ash tray earlier.

I grabbed the rosie and ran through the wheelhouse like a madman repeating, "Sweet Jesus, help me. Sweet Jesus, help me." When I reached the outside bridge toilet, I emptied the rosie contents into the bowl and pushed the handle. Immediately, there was a loud bang, and I had to check that someone hadn't shot me, until I realised, the red hot Pride bottle that I had put in the bin earlier had exploded.

After a few more intercessions, I ran back into the radio room which was still full of smoke. I pulled back the curtains and opened up the two big radio room windows (not portholes). I recovered the still hot rosie, returned to my office and put the blowers on full blast. I then went to the Port bridge wing and observed the large clouds of smoke exiting the radio room.

It should be noted that Mina Al Ahmadi was possibly the world's largest oil port and anyone of authority witnessing what was playing out before me would immediately have put the port into lockdown. Oil flows would have been stopped and fire brigades, along with fire-fighting tugs, would have been summoned. I might have wound up as a guest of the Kuwaiti Royal family.

I waited for someone to start shouting blue murder, but nobody did. When the smoke had cleared, I returned to the radio room and propeller fanned the air with a towel, but the smell just wouldn't go away. I removed the window curtains and hastily washed them in the officers' bathroom. I re-hung them before they were fully dry, but the smell still prevailed.

I stayed silent and for the rest of the voyage, not a single word was spoken about something that can still wake me up at night. After several days more, our cargo for Kuwait was fully off-loaded, and we set off for the Shatt Al Arab. I signalled Portishead Radio in the Bristol Channel our position and next port, Abadan in Iran.

Polamhall 9

Kuwait to Abadan Iran:

We entered the Shatt al Arab and made our way slowly up the Tigris towards Abadan. Lots of other ships were doing likewise and it looked like they were floating across the desert sands because it wasn't possible to see the water unless you were in the wheelhouse or looking over the side. As we progressed up the Tigris we passed the Iran/ Iraq marshlands and exchanged greetings with some of the Marsh inhabitants who were busy fishing from small boats.

The weather got even hotter and it was difficult to keep the thirst at bay. John, the third officer, came up with a solution by handing out Arab clay pots he had bought from a seller in Mina Al Ahmadi. The clay part was important because what you did was fill it full of water and hang it up normally overnight and the next morning you had it half full of ice cool water. The lost half seeped out producing the cooling effect.

No doubt this was a trick dating back to the prophet's time or before. Beaky and Benny couldn't get enough of the liquid heaven. John also learnt another trick which I helped him put into practice. He got a wooden box supplied by the ship's carpenter about three feet high by two feet wide. He placed a large can in the centre of the box and surrounded it with sawdust also supplied by the chief petty officer.

He then filled a sack with more sawdust which he secured to a wooden lid and placed it on top of the box. Once that was done, the chief steward provided ice from the cold room, which went into the can with about twelve cans of Pepsi Cola from the Bond room. John was like a child waiting for the Cola to freeze and when it did—guggle...guggle...guggle.

"Lovely and cold, enough to knock the teeth out of your head." The homemade fridge could last a full day before requiring more ice.

We reached Abadan city and tied up alongside.

Polamhall 10

Abadan Iran, September 1961:

We tied up close to a very large oil refinery circled with palm trees. The smell of methane filled the air and don't think me mad or weird, but I didn't find it unpleasant. It seemed to reawaken a congenital memory from a time when we all started our human journey in a chemical swamp millions of years ago. At breakfast on the first morning, there was a new face at the captain's table. He was a man dressed in an Iranian uniform.

As I was leaving the saloon, the captain requested I see him in his cabin in about ten minutes' time. I went out on deck and thought what excuse can I make about the rosie episode. Ten minutes later, I was in the captain's cabin along with the uniformed man and Benny who was stretched out on the day room settee. Heart pounding, I was waiting for the axe to fall.

"Sparks, this man wants to inspect the radio room and then seal it while we're in Port. Can you take him up please?" I was about to blurt out an apology for almost burning down the Kuwaiti Oil Terminal, but before I could say anything, the military man introduced himself and suggested we start the inspection.

I entered the radio room expecting him to question me about the fire, but all he said was 'That's fine, Sir, thank you', as he removed a long orange coloured cardboard strip from a briefcase he was carrying. In Arabic and English, it said, something like—It is an offence to **break this seal**.

As we left the office, he stapled the seal between the door and bulkhead and bid me a pleasant day in Abadan. I went to my cabin, lit a Lucky and thanked God for my good fortune.

I spent the rest of that morning in John's cabin trying to teach Beaky to say, "Who's a cheeky boy then," while visitors from both alleyways came and went. Ian reminded me that he and I had bought Airfix models during our Liverpool visit. Mine was the passenger ship *United States and Oriana*, while Ian's was a *BP and Shell Tanker*.

At one stage, we had a visit from a local trader selling Hubbly Bubblys and I bought one, which I immediately set up with water in the jar and tobacco in the top receptacle.

I sucked on the pipe for about ten minutes before deciding it wasn't for me. It's probably still sitting now gathering dust in the attic of Home Farm Park. During lunch, Second Officer Steve passed on his knowledge of the city and of particular interest was the Mariners Club and its swimming pool.

That evening, dressed in some of my Port Said purchases, I boarded the shuttle bus to the Mariner's club along with many more of the crew. We all had our swimming trunks rolled in one of Polamhall's towels. After a short ride, we entered the club and immediately found vacant tables in a large area surrounding a big blue pool. There were crew members already there from many other ships and soon the sound of many different languages filled the air.

It wasn't long before some of my shipmates were splashing about in the water, and in the heat of the evening, I found joining them to be irresistible. It was pure heaven. Occasionally, we would leave the water for a cold beer or Pepsi and a smoke before plunging into the cool water again.

I noticed one of the Able Seaman, whose name now escapes me so I'll call him Craig, and he was sitting at the bottom of the pool in a Budda like position. When he surfaced, I tried to imitate his Budda trick, but I couldn't sink more than a foot. Craig laughed at my effort and then proceeded to show me how it's done. "Hold your nose, Sparks, and let yourself sink by expelling the air from your lungs via partly pursed lips."

After several attempts, I descended to the bottom where I sat for about ten seconds before rising for breath and a few repeats of my new-found skill. I got to know Craig during our voyage down the Red Sea. He was one of the sailors who manned the wheel. With permission from the officer of the watch, he showed me how to steer the ship using the magnetic compass, and how in bad weather to anticipate the bow movement by applying counter rudder before the head swung past dead ahead.

Every ship today has an autopilot, and as I still work…YES! I supply and fit several every year as well of course as a full range of marine electronics, radars, radios, hydroacoustics.

Polamhall 11

Abadan, September 1961:

Over breakfast, Ian and I decided to start assembling our Liverpool purchased Airfixes. My radio station was sealed so this seemed a good way to start the day. After my usual NON conversation with Beaky, where again I avoided losing a finger, I went to my cabin and laid out the components of the SS United States.

Following Ian's advice, I masked the hull and started painting all the bits and pieces, i.e. lifeboats, for'd deck winch, radar mast, etc. At some stage, Bryson came in to make up the cabin. "Looks good, Sparks." And by time the lunch bell rang, I fully agreed with his observation. Sometime during lunch, the captain and chief engineer returned from a shore meeting with the ship's agent.

Both men looked a bit agitated and the captain looked in my direction. I thought, '*Sweet Jesus, I'm still not free of the Kuwait incident.*' Lunch finished, I started to leave the saloon and return to my building project.

"Donal, can you call in to my cabin later please." I thought, that sounds friendly enough and he never called me by my name before.

"Yes, Sir, of course." I could see that everyone else in the saloon were wondering 'what's all this about'. Sometime later, I knocked on the captain's door and received permission to enter. Benny as usual was curled up on the day settee and the captain was behind his desk with the chief engineer facing him. I could see that both men had been compiling a Marconigram.

I was invited to sit down on the empty chair beside the chief, which I did. "Sparks, we want you to send this message to head office." Thank God I thought but then remembered the station was closed. Captain Armstrong anticipated my next question by saying, "I know, Donal, but we've decided to remove the seal." My mind went into a bit of a spin thinking, how would I survive an Iranian hell hole?

Then I thought, '*Well, I'm of no great importance and after all the decision was being made by the ship's two most senior officers.*' Then I thought why can't the Marconigram be sent via the agent's office? After all, Iran was not some backwater. Again, Captain Armstrong interrupted my thoughts by saying the chief engineer is experiencing engine problems and needs advice from the Marine Shore superintendent and the engine manufacturers.

Without him saying it, I knew it was best if the charterers were not made aware of any problems, as this charter was particularly profitable to the *Polamhall* owners. As I left the captain's office holding the Marconigram, the chief said, "Thanks, Sparks." I nodded. After carefully removing the bulkhead end of the orange seal, I nervously entered the radio room and switched on the Atalanta receiver, so named after one of Marconi's daughters.

I knew the two senior men would like the lengthy message containing all sorts of technical data and measurements, etc. to reach the marine superintendent as soon as possible. I also knew radio waves travel more easily over water than land which meant the 4000 miles of land (Syria, Turkey, Romania and Germany) between Iran and Portishead Radio in the Bristol Channel might prove challenging. I tried tuning in to GKL 8 MHz, GKS 12 MHz, GKM 16 MHz but all to no avail.

I thought I'd have to abandon a direct route and use one of the other British overseas stations such as Malta, Colombo, or Vizagapatam, but then I thought I'd try Portishead's highest frequency GKI 22 MHz; I tuned up the Oceanspan 7 and tapped out QTC1. My signal bounced instantaneously across the European continent using the Kennelly E gas layer 120 miles above the earth and I immediately received a reply. I tapped out the chief's lengthy message and received a QSL from GKI.

I informed the captain and said I would check for a reply during the next Traffic list. I returned to my building work but found it hard to concentrate. Over the next days, we exchanged messages with head office and advice that Engine spares would be available on our arrival at Durban later in the voyage.

I could see that the engineer officers struggled to keep the main engine operational, and at one stage, the second engineer had to be assisted from the engine room suffering from heat stroke. After a couple of day's rest plus extra salt tablets, he was back to normal.

The Abadan nights were the best as we repeated our visits to the Mariners' Club and the luxurious blue pool. By the time sailing day arrived, I finished the SS United States and sat it proudly on the desk-top for all to admire, and they did. Ian's BP Tanker looked equally as good. I also resealed the radio room as best I could.

Before sailing on the fifth day, the Iranian Officer returned and removed the seal with a 'humph' and a smile. After breakfast, we departed for Khorramshahr and Basrah.

Polamhall 12

The Tigris River, October 1961:

We left Abadan and set off up the Tigris towards Basrah stopping briefly at Khorramshahr City to offload about a dozen wooden crates.

On our journey towards the Iraqi port, large tankers with flags from many nations passed us, their bellies full of oil, which in a few weeks would be powering cars travelling down new European motorways and planes taking tourists to the new holiday resorts in Spain and Portugal. We berthed alongside the docks of Basrah, the port where the fictional 'Sinbad, the Sailor' set off on his adventures, as told in the tales of '1001 Arabian nights'.

As the dockers started to offload what remained of our cargo, everyone was summoned to the wardroom, where a doctor and nurse waited with trays of needles.

As we were scheduled to go to Africa, all on board had to be vaccinated against the yellow fever virus. After each injection, the nurse would stamp our vaccination passports which every seaman was required to carry. These books were proof of vaccination against smallpox, yellow fever and other diseases I can't remember.

Without these, ships could be refused Free Pratique entry to port. The world had learnt that it wasn't only rats that ships carried but diseases that could wipe out complete populations.

Based on Second Officer Steve's knowledge, we all departed by coach that evening for a club a few miles distant into the city. This was not exclusively for mariners but a club for the many overseas oil workers now resident in Iraq. It was a bit more upmarket than the one in Abadan but with a similar pool. Alcohol was freely available, which was unusual for a Moslem country, but of course all that changed with the arrival of Saddam Hussein some years later.

During the day, Ian and I would continue our ship building projects, mine being the passenger vessel *Oriana* and Ian's large Shell tanker. My work was occasionally interrupted by a request to visit Captain Armstrong's office to be handed Marconigrams with Hartlepool and London addresses. It was totally illegal for ships to transmit in Port, but he had become addicted to the comfort of having his own personal communications network, and it also gave him more time with Benny and his second best friend, 'Johnny Walker'.

I was young and in no way inclined to go against the master's wishes. Of course, it was very foolish and dangerous to transmit in Port, particularly close to an oil terminal and air full of combustible gas. A little corona discharge from the antenna could potentially have sent half of Basrah into orbit.

Of course, these were different times and from experience, I know it couldn't happen today. On leaving the club one night with John, we decided to walk back to the ship. On our way, we passed a large open area full of single seats facing a large screen showing a film of some Arab story.

As access seemed free, we sat down on two seats at the back of the open-air cinema. Obviously, the dialogue was in Arabic with men on camels travelling through the Saudi Arabian desert. We persisted in watching for a while sucking on a couple of Senior Service cigarettes. Before reaching our boredom threshold, a large single light appeared above the desert travellers and a booming voice from heaven, descended down on them.

The watching audience immediately went into a frenzy of screaming joy and crying while standing on chairs and shouting something like Al Shaddai or whatever. I'm not sure even today what provoked such an outpouring of joy, but perhaps, it was some message being sent by God to Mohammad? Anyway, as we were the only Christians present to nail to the nearest door, we made a discreet retreat.

Similar days followed with the extreme heat, only relieved with ice cold Pepsi's from John's fridge. One night, John and I decided to leave the club early, probably 9 p.m., and walk back to the *Polamhall*. At some stage in our journey, we started to pass what looked like a posh club. The gardens were a lush green with manicured grass and flower beds.

Lights of white and green bathed a ring of palm trees. Standing guard in front of a Mahogany door was a large man dressed in Moroccan style clothes including red Fez. "Donal, let's go in here." I started to feel panic as I knew my few remaining Rials wouldn't go very far in what looked like a place for millionaires,

114

but John being John from Wexford, insisted on approaching the man with the Fez.

"Oh no, Sir, only members are allowed to enter." Breathing a sigh of relief, I turned to leave but my anxiety immediately returned when I heard a man with an American accent, dressed in clothes that would have devoured a year's pay for me and what looked like a solid gold watch on his wrist. "It's ok, Mohammad, I'll sign these young men in." John couldn't hide his pleasure and I didn't know whether to run or cry.

We entered the club and I wondered how I was going to buy a round of drinks. John seemed oblivious to the fact that the club we entered was for the American and British directors/upper management of the various **oil** companies such as BP and Shell, etc. Men were sitting around in large leather chairs, brandy glasses in one hand and large Cuban style cigars in the other. There were a few women in designer clothes present, presumably executives' wives.

Occasionally, some of the members would gaze across at us dressed in our cheap Port Said attire, which only made me feel more self-conscious. The bar staff were dressed, similar to the big man guarding the entrance and our American host, whom I'll call George, called out to one, "Mustafa, my usual please and two large Carlsbergs for my guests."

Mustafa delivered the beverages, one of which was a large brandy for George who sensing my nervousness pointed John and I to two large bar stools and said, "Don't worry, Don, the drinks are on me." It turned out every member signed a chit for their drinks which were then paid for on a monthly basis, so my few remaining Rials were safe and I began to feel more relaxed particularly with the arrival of more Carlsbergs.

The drinks continued to arrive, and John was in his element. George seemed interested in our sea adventures, particularly when John related his stories of disreputable places he had visited in Ghana and Nigeria. I often wonder now who George was but I'm sure someone important from the way the other members, both male and female, showed him such great respect.

We thanked our host and left the air-conditioned club to be met with the comfort of the warm late evening air. Our walk back was somewhat staggered. The following evening after another pleasant visit including an hour in the pool of the oil workers club, we returned by coach to the Basrah docks.

There was Gerry 3/E, Derek 4/E, Ian, cadet and me. We met some of the crew from a Swedish vessel berthed close by and they invited us on board for a coffee. We gathered in the saloon which was somewhat more palatial than ours as was the whole ship in fact.

A night steward brought in pots of coffee which he poured into white porcelain cups before handing them to us. The air conditioning complemented the luxury of the fresh coffee. As we left, we thanked our hosts and I was glad to hear they were due to sail the following morning as I thought a reciprocal invitation from us might not be a good idea. A few days later, the *Polamhall* fully empty left Basra in ballast bound for Bahrain.

Polamhall 13

Late October 1961, Tagus River to Durban via Bahrain:

We re-entered the Persian Gulf and commenced our three days voyage to Bahrain. As usual traffic was heavy with many Arab Dhows plying their trade in a way that hadn't changed for a thousand years or more. The food from the ship's larder was starting to show its age. The boiled eggs were getting greener by the day and the breakfast cereals were becoming infested with weevils.

We solved this problem by drowning them in milk and scooping the dead bodies into a saucer before continuing to eat. We usually finished breakfast with salt tablets and a glass of lime juice. The heat was relentless and sometimes we would stand out on the open deck, simply to cool down, in the 10 knot breeze generated, as the *Polamhall* ploughed through the silky sea.

One day just as lunch was over with only Ian, the chief officer, and me still present, Ian blurted out, "Why did the Irish not help us during the war and why did you supply the U-boats on Ireland's West coast?" This was quite out of character for Ian and to this day, I wonder what prompted it.

Before I could answer, a loud Scottish voice filled the saloon. "Don't dare talk like that, young man. Many thousands of brave Irishmen fought and died for this country and I'll hear no more of it." Ian's face flushed red and he said no more. The incident was never referred to again, though I did thank the chief officer for coming to my defence.

In actual fact, Ian's remarks, which he had probably picked up in the British gutter press, did have a grain of truth. I mean neither the Aran Islands or Achill Island had an oil refinery or an ammunitions factory, but they did have fresh fish. It was not uncommon for U-boats or indeed British destroyers to barter cigarettes and Schnapps for fish with the west coast fleets.

We arrived at anchor in Bahrain and a tanker commenced the business of filling our empty domestic tanks with fresh water. The ship's agent climbed aboard followed by a local doctor to check out some pains the captain was having. The doctor was shown into the chief steward's office to wait while the agent went to see the captain.

The meeting with the Agent was going on longer than expected so I was asked if I would pass a message to the chief steward to entertain the doctor a bit longer. This didn't go down well as this was a man used to dealing with the royal family and not the captain of an old cargo ship. We left Bahrain six hours later for Durban and a mini disaster.

Polamhall 14

The Straits of Hurmuz to Durban:

We made our way at 10 knots from Bahrain to the Straits of Hurmuz and entered the Arabian Sea to be met with cooling winds from the Indian Ocean. Soon after passing Muscat on our starboard side, we reached the Northeast of Oman and the small city of Al Had, where we changed course to 180 degrees. It was early November 1961 as we progressed down the Arabian Sea towards the Island of Socotra, the Horn of Africa and northern most part of Somalia.

Before reaching Socotra at the eastern end of the Gulf of Aden, Bryson entered the radio room to advise me on the mini crisis. "Sparks, one of the Engineers pumped all the fresh water over the side." The engineers were still having problems with the main engine and out of tiredness one of them had turned a wrong valve and dispensed our expensively bought water into the Indian Ocean.

Realising his mistake, he managed to save some, which was enough for drinking and cooking. Other than that, the toilets had to be flushed with seawater and we had to wash with saltwater soap which proved almost useless. Fortunately, we still had enough milk to drown the weevils.

It was also fortunate we didn't have to visit Mogadishu in Somalia where Second Officer Steve said it was not a place mariners should go voluntarily, unless they got tired of carrying their heads around on their shoulders. The engineers managed to keep the engine going past Somalia until we reached the coast of Kenya. It was almost midnight and I was about to switch off my bunk light when the ship went eerily quiet.

The main engine had stopped. I pulled on my dressing gown and made my way to the bridge where James, the chief officer, had just started his watch. "Doesn't look good, Donal," he remarked. We were soon joined on the bridge by Captain Armstrong and Malcolm, the chief engineer. They retired to the chartroom to discuss the situation while James and I went for a smoke on the starboard bridge wing.

Fortunately, the sea, which was lit by a full Moon, was calm and I remember that the stars couldn't have shone any brighter. The two most senior men joined us a short time later. The helmsman was dispatched to the Bosuns cabin with instructions for him to hoist the two black balls to the top of the main mast. These were to warn other ships that we are not under command, to keep clear.

I was instructed to send a TTT message, warning other ships of our dilemma. It indicated we were drifting with no power but not in distress or in need of urgent assistance, but to be aware that our situation might deteriorate to that level. I decided not to activate the Auto Alarms of ships within a 600-mile radius, as my radio officer compatriots might not appreciate being awakened from their slumbers.

The captain also agreed it wasn't yet necessary to do so. The C/E returned to the engine room where his staff were working hard to get us up and running. The C/O told me to get some sleep and he would call me if there were any developments. Some hours later and just before dawn, the *Polamhall* roared back into life.

I washed in so far as was possible with saltwater and once I was dressed, made my way again to the bridge. The captain and chief engineer were in conference and Steve, the Second Officer, was on watch. The chief looked exhausted and his normally crisp white overalls were covered in black oil.

The Bosun was instructed to remove the NUC balls and I was instructed to send a TTT message advising ships in our vicinity that we were again under way. We continued our journey passing Mombasa, Zanzibar Island and Dar Es Salaam on the African East coast before reaching the Comoros Islands. It was dark and John asked me to come and look at the radar picture which showed tiny bright targets about 10 miles ahead of us.

We agreed it was a large cluster of fishing vessels and it would be best if the captain was called to take charge of navigation. With Benny strolling his way around the wheelhouse, the helmsman was instructed to apply Starboard ten degrees, etc. until the bright radar targets were astern of us. Benny and his daddy returned to the lower deck. With Madagascar on our Port side and Mozambique on our Starboard, we sailed down the Mozambique Channel past Beira and Lourenco Marques (now Maputo).

Lourenco Marques, named after a famous Portuguese explorer, had a radio station transmitting addictive rock and roll music which was equivalent to Radio Luxembourg and **WYNNS WYNNS** 1010 New York.

Our long sea voyage from Bahrain to Durban ended on 25 November 1961 as we tied up alongside in the Windy city, as it is known.

Polamhall 15

Durban, South Africa, Late November 1961:

The fresh water and food supplies came on board followed by new main engine pistons and other parts. It was the first time in weeks we could all have warm showers with proper soap and shampoo. We all sat down for the chief cook's dinner special of roast beef, Yorkshire pudding and roast potatoes.

The desert was jelly and custard followed by cheese and biscuits for those who could manage it. Coffee and a Senior Service completed a meal we hadn't enjoyed since Basrah.

Durban being South Africa's premier holiday resort meant we had a choice of evening entertainments.

John, Ian, Steve, Derek and I headed for one of the bars recommended by Able Seaman Craig (My Abadan swimming instructor). I drew £5 in Rands as a sub. We decided against a taxi in favour of a more sensible option of public transport. When two half full buses failed to stop, we wondered 'What the Hell is going on here?'

It was Steve who first noticed the bus sign saying 'Non- Europeans only' or some such in English and Dutch. This was our first encounter with the Apartheid system. Steve said, to hell with this, and we all piled into the next passing taxi.

We entered the bar recommended by Able Seaman Craig and found a table with room for all. Derek went to the bar and returned with a tray of glasses and five Castle beers.

We settled in with everyone taking it in turn to replenish the table with more of the Castles. The Craic, as we now say, was good and at one stage, John started imitating the Cinema Muslims of Basra. One of the staff told him standing on chairs was not allowed.

At a table close by, there were three girls unaccompanied which I think was unusual for South Africa. They were very easy to look at and Wexford John tried engaging them in conversation but with no success. These seemed like upper class girls who were probably warned never to let a sailor lad an inch above their knee.

Undeterred, Wexford John said he had a cunning plan. "And what's that?" Ian enquired.

"Never you mind but watch an expert at work." He just sat there which had us all intrigued. Sometime later, he went to the Gents and emerged about five minutes later along with one of the *Polamhall's* deck crew. He re-joined us with a smug look on his face.

What's going on here, we all thought but we didn't have to wait long for the answer. The heavily muscled AB from John's toilet encounter appeared at our table and saluting smartly addressed John. "Excuse me, Captain, but some of us were wondering if we might have tomorrow afternoon off so we can go to the beach?"

"That should be fine, Oliver, so long as the work on the Mizen mast is completed by noon."

"Thank you, Sir, I'll inform the Bosun." With that, Oliver saluted smartly again and returned to his friends.

I noticed on John's next round a double whiskey appeared in front of Oliver.

After a brief period, John enquired of the uptown girls if they were local and received information that they were studying at the local university. "Care to join us for a drink, girls?" After passing looks between themselves, they agreed. John whispered, "That's how it's done, boys."

I must say his performance was impressive. That said it didn't yield much profit other than having the pleasure of female company for a few hours. Just before last orders, the three girls stood up and informed the table that they had better get back to the campus before it closed. We wished them well with their studies and ordered another round of Castles.

After further banter about the Mizen mast fairy tale, we finished our drinks and boarded a taxi back to the docks. The dockers commenced loading the vessel early next morning—iron ore for Middlesbrough, where the Teesside mills would turn it into steel for the production of British cars, White goods, bridges and many more things besides. It would probably also turn it into Parish pumps where our political dwarves would still stand and watch our best, marching past them.

Steve, whose job it was to oversee the loading, explained it should be complete by the end of the day. He also cheered us up by explaining how dangerous a cargo of iron ore can be, because if it shifted in bad weather the ship could roll over. The roll over part was brought home to us very clearly during the next leg of the voyage. Loading was actually finished earlier than expected, but the engine repairs were still ongoing, so we had another night out at AB Craig's bar.

John was disappointed that the uptown girls were not there. At breakfast the next morning, we heard Malcolm, the chief engineer, inform the captain that the main engine was now running, and fingers crossed, all should be well for our return to the UK. Unfortunately, this was not to be.

With hatches battened down, two tugs under the direction of the local pilot pulled us off the quay wall and we headed for the open sea after the pilot climbed down our Jacobs ladder and onto the deck of the waiting pilot vessel. I fired up the radio station and advised Durban ZSD and Mauritius Naval base GYR— *Polamhall* QTO Durban, next port Middlesbrough, England.

Polamhall 16

Durban, Indian Ocean to Atlantic Ocean, Late November 1961:

We continued our voyage down the Southeast African coast. It was the start of the Southern Hemisphere summer. We listened to the Rock and Roll music being belted out by Lourenco Marques Radio which even Beaky enjoyed, judging by his constant squawking. The sea was millpond smooth though there were signs of things to come as signalled by the start of the Cape Rollers.

The sun shining from an umbrella blue sky decorated the peaks of the Rollers with diamonds. The *Polamhall* was a big ship with only forty men on board so there was plenty of room for everyone to sunbathe and hopefully become eye candy for our homecoming. Even the Dolphins, who were our constant companions since leaving the Horn, seemed to be jumping higher.

We sailed down past the cities of East London and Port Elizabeth where we altered course due west for the Cape of Good Hope. Sometimes at night, Third Officer John would come into my office for a brief visit, and read out a song he had just written. Even today I can remember some of the lines which are not repeatable here.

We reached the Cape, which as you'll all know, was first discovered by the Portuguese Explorer, Vasco Da Gama, in the late 15th century. We altered to a Northwest course, and could soon see Table-Top Mountain, and the city of Capetown. It was early December 1961 and as we progressed north, the Cape Rollers with their long slow swells became even bigger and the *Polamhall* started to roll forty degrees to Port and then forty degrees to starboard.

Lots of Galley crockery went crashing to the deck. The chief steward ordered the dining room chairs to be anchored and the table linen to be dampened. This was to stop soup dishes, etc. sliding onto our laps. Gazing out over the sea we could see the largest animals ever to have existed on planet Earth. Pods of Blue Whales seemed curious as they came over to see who we were.

I contacted the British Naval base at Simonstown and advised the duty officer of our position and destination 'Middlesbrough'. This proved not to be! I fitted the sideboard to my bunk and eventually managed to nod off even though the *Polamhall* was now rolling violently. Sometime around 5 a.m. just as the sun was rising, I was elevated from my bunk and flung across the cabin on to the heaving deck.

"Sweet Jesus what the fuck is this?" As I clambered to my feet. The silence was deafening; the main engine had stopped. I grabbed my dressing gown and hurried into the wheelhouse. Steve, the second officer, was on watch.

"The bloody engine has packed in again, Sparks." The helmsman was struggling without much success to keep the ship's head into the swell, but with only the rudder to work with this was a pointless task. With the sea now beam on, the *Polamhall* started to roll even more violently.

I went to my cabin and dressed, splashed some water on my face and went back to the bridge. The captain, chief engineer, and Steve were in conference. Tom, the chief steward, was instructed to get all hands out of their bunks. The Bosun was instructed to hoist the NUC black balls to the top of the Main mast. I was told to open the radio station and the captain would join me shortly.

The dawn had broken, and the skies were still blue, and there was little or no wind to speak of, but boy were we rolling. Sometimes the ship would come around with the sea on our stern and as it ran ahead of us, it was like looking up a blue mountain.

The captain came in with a Marconigram both he and chief had composed for head office. It was agreed I should send out another TTT message first. Captain Armstrong was considering upgrading this to an XXX (urgent) but decided against it in case deep sea tugs were dispatched to our aid and the ship might have been forfeited as salvage.

This time I did send the Auto Alarm signal of three four second dashes with one second intervals and waited for ships in the area to open their stations. I sent the TIT which warned we had an engine breakdown and are now 'not under command'. Some ships acknowledged receipt as did Capetown Radio.

I imagine some of the ships were a bit annoyed as normally activating the Auto Alarm is for XXX or **SOS.** I felt we were borderline, particularly, as I was having difficulty staying in my chair and trying to Morse Code at the same time.

I contacted **ZSL** Capetown and transmitted the captain's Marconigram addressed to the Hartlepool marine superintendent detailing our latest dilemma. My colleague at the other end acknowledged receipt and hoped our engineers could soon get us up and running. The Chief Steward Tom arranged an early breakfast for everyone, which was accompanied by lots of 'Stay steady, you rolling bastard', which of course was kindly meant. Everyone had their own thoughts, and mine as second last man, to abandon a ship in distress was the hope that my courage wouldn't fail at the last moment. I knew Captain Armstrong would not fail in his duty.

Polamhall 17

December 1961, Adrift in the South Atlantic, 150 miles west of the African coast:

After breakfast, I returned to the bridge. The *Polamhall* was still rolling heavily but almost in slow motion. Like everyone else on board and keeping in mind Steve's message of doom, I hoped the thousands of tons of iron ore we were carrying would not take a sudden shift to Port or starboard. If it did, we would soon be swimming with the fishes and beyond any hope of rescue.

On the next traffic list from ZSC Capetown, our Callsign was listed. These traffic lists contained telegrams for maybe a hundred ships and the messages were sent uninterrupted, after which each recipient would send a **QSL** acknowledgement. I awaited my turn and copied a message addressed to the captain and chief engineer.

"If possible, to get under way, proceed to Walvis Bay where spares will be waiting along with Marine Superintendent Chapman." The message also contained some technical advice, and if possible, avoid losing the ship to salvage.

I sent a QSL and went to the captain's cabin. The chief engineer was handed the telegram which he read slowly.

"OK let's see if we can do something but my crew are already pretty exhausted." The captain suggested some of the deck crew might help with any heavy lifting and the chief thought this was a very good idea. The chief officer's approval was sought and given.

Over the next day or so, the engineering staff laboured in sweltering heat to do whatever they were doing, with chain pulleys strung from beams at the top of the engine room lifting pistons and other heavy metal parts. This looked highly dangerous and with only Donkey engine supplying the ship's power, it was not possible to run the large fans, which usually cools engine rooms to levels fit for humans to work in.

The weather was pleasant and those of us with time on our hands could stand on deck and be entertained by the dolphins, flying fish, whales and the occasional albatross. Lourenco Marques Radio was still coming in loud and clear. Occasionally, the main engine would turn over and everyone would hold their breath hoping it would keep going but it didn't. It was a bit like Stewart Grainger starting the aeroplane engine during the last scenes in the film 'Flight Of The Phoenix'.

While sitting in the radio room in the afternoon of the third day, I heard the now familiar cough from the main engine but this time it stayed going, with black smoke belching from the funnel. Everyone held their breath and after about five minutes, a great cheer could be heard coming from the engine room skylights.

Sometime later everyone assembled on the bridge. The chief and his staff were covered in sweat and black grime. The assisting deck crew were similarly covered in dirt and sweat. That didn't matter because everyone was smiling and sucking on Senior Service cigarettes.

The chief was the first to address us with the good news and then the bad news. "The engine is running but only on low revs. If we increase the revs, it's probable the engine will stop again and this time maybe for good." Captain Armstrong took over thanking everyone and promising those who had worked hardest a bottle of rum or a drink of their choice in appreciation. This elicited further smiles and fresh Senior Services.

"We'll get under way shortly for Walvis Bay, Southwest Africa. As the chief engineer has indicated men, we'll have to proceed at a reduced speed of about 4 knots." We knew this would increase a normally two and a half day journey, up to the best part of a week. Did we care, did we hell! We were safe and alive.

Everyone thanked the engineers and crew for their heroic work. The Bosun removed the Black Balls and I advised ZSC TTT ended and *Polamhall* now bound for Walvis Bay at reduced speed.

As we got closer and closer to the African coast, the sea became calmer and the Cape Rollers melted away. As we neared the port of Walvis Bay, Pelicans started to appear overhead. We weren't paid much, but the entertainment was good! Captain Armstrong, still worried about salvage, wouldn't allow the tugs to take our ropes until the pilot was on board.

We entered Port and everyone breathed a great sigh of relief. The exhausted engine room heroes retired early for a 12-hour sleep.

Polamhall 18

Walvis Bay South West Africa early December 1961:

After breakfast, I went to the radio room and decided to polish the equipment with Pride provided by Tom, the chief steward. I could see the rosie with its brown burn marks staring at me. "Do not repeat Mina al Ahmadi!" It seemed to scream!

Around mid-morning, Bryson came in with my mid-morning tray, and in a hushed tone said, "The Marine Superintendent has arrived, Sparks." To most mariners, superintendents have the status of demigods.

Sometime later while taking a breather on the bridge wing, I noticed a big open backed lorry arrive with the eagerly awaited main engine spares. The *Polamhall* deck crew started the task of offloading the precious cargo with ropes and one of the deck winches. The engine room skylights had already been dismantled to facilitate the lowering of the heavy load.

At lunch that day, the senior table had a new face—The Demigod, Mr Chapman, who at one stage raised a hand in greeting to the fun table. "Hello, everyone."

He received a chorus of replies, "Hello, Sir." He returned to continue a deep conversation with the four most senior personnel while we planned our night ashore.

Walvis Bay, a small city in Southwest Africa (now Namibia), part of the German Empire till it was put in the care of South Africa, following the Treaty of Versailles at the end of First World War. That evening after dinner, I dressed in some of my Port Said best and went to the wardroom where John, Ian and Derek were waiting for me. The agent had suggested a local bar was a good place to go, so we descended to the quay wall, not knowing if we'd need a taxi and how would we get it.

Many of the rest of the crew were also gathering on the quay and one of them answered the question. We walk, and maybe thirty of us started to walk but this was not just a normal walk. No, it was a walk across a mini desert of soft sand and dunes to the outskirts of the city where we entered a large barn of a pub. There were many big cheap tables and plastic chairs where crews from other ships had already started their night's entertainment.

We sat about eight to a table and agreed we stick with rounds in our own tight group. The bar owner, a large well-built man, with fair hair and a Dutch accent, came to take our order of Castle beers. I say Dutch accent, but it might have been German and maybe he was from a German family who never went home after First World War.

His wife carried two large trays filled with Castles and with an accent mirroring her husbands, "Now, gentlemen, who's first?"

Wexford John, never one to miss the opportunity of talking to a female said, "Over here, Bella Donna." She laid the trays down for everyone to help themselves and collected payment in African Rands.

Before returning to the bar, she smacked John's head in a playful manner, "Cheeky Irishman," which pleased the recipient no end. Most of the eight at our table were Geordies as was nearly all the *Polamhall* crew and they took it in turns to banter what had just taken place. "You're in there, Three O," and maybe he thought he was, but if he did, it was never going to happen.

At some stage, the Geordie lads broke into song with no objections from the owners. Their favourite was the 'Bladen Races' but we also had 'Glasgow Town, Lily Marlene' with assistance from the owners in German and numerous others, including Buddy Holly's 'All my love and All of my Kissing'.

At the height of the party, the Marine Superintendent, Mr Chapman, plus the chief engineer and virtually all of the engine room staff, which included the Donkey men and greasers, entered the big barn and occupied a large table close to ours. I imagine one man was left on board to make sure the Donkey engine kept running. Captain Armstrong along with Benny, would have been alone in his cabin.

Mr Chapman sent a round of drinks to the table and followed this up with his rendition of Elvis Presley's new song 'Are you lonesome tonight?' which received a great cheer. With the last song of the evening, we made our way back across the mini desert guided by the distant mast light of the *Polamhall*. Some of the Geordies were still singing the 'Bladen Races'.

Polamhall 19

Walvis Bay Southwest Africa, Early December 1961, Day 2:

After breakfast, I returned to my cabin and remembered I had put the 'United States' and 'ORIANA' in one of the big drawers beneath my bunk for safekeeping during our days riding the Cape rollers. I placed them on my cabin table and spent about five minutes admiring my handiwork. My daydreaming was interrupted by someone saying, "They look terrific, Sparks."

It was none other than Mr Chapman dressed in white overalls. He asked if he could come in and I said of course. He picked up the two models in turn and I could see he was wondering how he might gain possession of them, but I ignored the signals as these were my pride and joy. After a while, he said, "Must go, my boss, the chief, is waiting for me." The hammering and drill noises from the engine room had already started, but to this day, I've no idea what the repairs involved.

Chief Officer James decided to hold a lifeboat drill, excluding of course those in the engine room. The main part of the drill involved lowering one of the *Polamhall's* four lifeboats into the water. As was usual, the third officer on all ships was responsible for making sure the boats were up to spec.

This involved checking the provisions of hard biscuits, bars of barley sugar, etc., plus the fresh-water tanks. Other items were the oars, sail, flares, medical box, large matches capable of striking in gale force winds. The matches were about 8 inches long and the sulphur extended six inches down the stem. Once struck, they would keep burning in any weather.

My normal position during lifeboat drill would be in the radio room, but James agreed it was ok for me to participate along with everyone else. When I arrived, John and two deck crew were in one of the starboard boats, which other crew members were lowering over the side.

When it hit the water, John started up the outboard engine and let the painters go. The trio did a few turns around Walvis Bay harbour, before returning back alongside the painters.

Most lifeboat lowering and hoisting davits are motor controlled but ours weren't. Burly deckhands took it in turn to twist the big mechanical handles raising the heavy lifeboat at a barely detectable rate. I volunteered to take a turn and after about six twists I knew I had made a very stupid mistake. I could feel my arms aching and my breakfast about to make a re-visitation.

I persisted for a few more turns and then I had a light bulb moment! I told James it was most important we check out the lifeboat portable radio which was stored in the radio room. He agreed and instructed two of his staff to help me. When we returned with the SALVITA Radio, I decided rather than rig it in the lifeboat, which didn't look like it had been raised more than a few inches since my turn on the RACK, I would check it out on the boat deck.

With the assistance of my two new chums, we connected the short wire aerial to one of the stanchions and an earth connection to clean steel, after which I instructed them to turn the generator handles at a rate of about 30 revs per minute.

Let me pause and explain how the SALVITA works. It is or was a yellow coloured metal cylinder about three feet high and was eighteen inches in diameter. Its innards contained a transmitter and receiver tuned to the distress frequency of 500 KHz plus a long range 8 MHz distress frequency. The control section contained a tuning control and Morse key. Power was acquired by a hand generator hence my instructions to James's men.

The power output was only five watts which meant it could be lost in the din of everyone else's transmissions. To overcome this problem, all radio transmissions ceased by law between fifteen to eighteen minutes and forty-five to forty-eight minutes of every hour, and if you ever see an old ship's radio clock, note the minutes I referred to above are marked with a horizontal red triangle. So, to recap, imagine you're marooned in a lifeboat in the middle of a sea or ocean, and you wait for the silence period to start.

You tell two of those shipwrecked with you to start turning the side handles. The operator is wearing headphones and transmits SOS with name position and details of distress. He waits for a reply, because he's the only one who can hear or indeed understand the Morse language.

Everyone waits with bated breath for his reaction which hopefully will evoke screams of joy and laughter. Back to *Polamhall* Boat deck! I donned the waterproof headset and my two assistants turned the side handles as I transmitted to Walvis Bay Radio ZSV—*Polamhall* testing lifeboat radio, and I received an immediate QSL. We restored the aerial, etc. and returned the SALVITA to the radio room.

With the lifeboat eventually back in its blocks, lifeboat drill was over and I went to my cabin, lit a Senior Service and vowed never again to volunteer for lifeboat lifting.

Polamhall 20

Walvis Bay SW Africa, Early December 1961, Day 2 Afternoon.

It was a Sunny afternoon and some of us were sunbathing on top of the for'd hatch when the main engine turned over once, twice and then burst into full life with black smoke belching from the funnel stack.

With fingers crossed, we waited to see if it would keep going and it did. Sometime later, Derek the 4/E left the engine room and joined us. He was holding a mug of tea in one hand and a smoke in the other, and he looked in need of a shower. He knew we'd want to hear the latest news but drew out the moment by deliberately drinking his tea slowly, pretending not to notice our anxious faces.

I heard someone say, "Stop messing, Derek, and spill the beans."

"OK, so far so good, and the super and chief said we'll run it overnight and tomorrow morning we'll do the stress test. All being well, we'll sail at noon tomorrow for Dakar."

Dakar was new information, but the super decided, it would be a good idea to stop there for bunkers and fresh water, which would take no more than four to six hours and it was on our way to Middlesbrough.

That night we marched across the mini desert again for the big Dutch/German barn pub. The night was similar to the first, with the Geordie boys in even greater voice.

Sometimes even now, the 'Bladen Races' enters my head as a worm.

Breakfast over on day three, everyone prepared for the stress test. The engineers in the engine room, the chief officer with the Bosun and Able Seamen manning the anchor winch on the focsle head (this was precautionary only), the captain was on the bridge with an AB standing by to man the wheel if necessary, and John on the engine room telegraph. The voice pipe to the engine room was also adjacent to John for back up use if necessary.

Before the stress test began, the captain received confirmation from another Able Seaman standing near the stern, that extra ropes were attached to the after bollards, linked to two on the quay wall. The main engine stress test began by

129

the captain commanding 'Slow Ahead', and confirmed by John as he placed the Telegraph to 'Slow Ahead'. The engineers responded by turning big shiny steel wheels and levers in a similar fashion to the 'Wizard Of Oz'.

The *Polamhall* began to strain forward and the bollard ropes tightened. With the next command 'Half Ahead', the huge propeller turned even faster and the *Polamhall* vibrated in its attempt to break free. The next command 'Full Ahead', caused the propeller to turn at full speed which drew up silt and mud from the bottom of Walvis Bay harbour.

The *Polamhall* was almost jumping out of the water like a bucking bronco. After five minutes, everyone was satisfied the test was successful and John turned the telegraph to 'finished with engines'. Over the next couple of hours, the ship was readied for sea. Once lunch was over, the pilot came on board, the marine super departed for Johannesburg airport and a tug arrived to escort us out of the harbour.

I advised ZSC Capetown Radio and Walvis Bay ZSV our next port as Dakar for bunkers. I thought this would be my last contact with local station ZSV, but the next twenty four hours brought more drama, which proved otherwise.

Polamhall 21

Walvis Bay to Dakar December 1961:

The first day out and all was peaceful on our journey northwards in the South Atlantic. Our main engine was back to full health, Beaky had fresh seed and fruit that his daddy had bought in Walvis Bay, Captain Armstrong and Benny were listening to the BBC overseas service from London on his Eddystone Radio, and I sat looking through my large office windows onto the blue water where I could see the occasional albatross sweeping low over pods of blue whales.

Everyone on board was thinking of home, but it was still too early for anyone to have 'THE CHANNELS'. On day two, the calm came to a halt when Bryson came to my cabin and told me the captain wanted to see me in his cabin. When I arrived, he was talking to the chief and second steward who both looked worried.

One of the Able seamen, whose name I can't remember so I'll christen him Michael, didn't turn up for breakfast that morning and when the Bosun went to see where he was, found him in his bunk in a delirious state. Chief Steward Tom, as the *Polamhall's* paramedic, was called to assist and with muscle provided by willing hands, the sick sailor was moved to the isolation of our small three bed hospital.

I was handed a message which had been composed prior to my arrival. From memory, it listed symptoms of severe sweating, vomiting, severe headache, coming in and out of consciousness and difficulty speaking.

I called ZSV Walvis Bay Radio and after shifting frequency to 468 KHz where we could communicate without interruption, I sent the request for urgent medical advice. The operator at the other end told me to wait and it seemed an age before he came back. I imagine the station manager had to phone the local hospital.

When the reply came, it was from a doctor requesting an inventory of our medical chest. I acknowledged receipt and said I would revert ASAP. Tom, with the assistance of the second steward, made up the list as requested. From memory, it included oxygen, morphine, aspirin, Quinine and all sorts of other stuff with Latin names. I sent it on and waited for the reply.

The doctor thought our patient was probably suffering from Malaria, but we would need to keep him informed if the symptoms changed. He listed the procedure our paramedic with his two weeks training, should carry out and the medication he should administer. I took the doctor's reply to the captain's cabin and was invited to sit down beside our medical team.

Tom read the message and when he came to a part that said, 'mgs' he said, "What's that?" For about ten seconds everyone looked puzzled but simultaneously we all burst out laughing. I never saw Captain Armstrong so animated.

I'm sure the body in our hospital wouldn't have been too pleased to know he was in the hands of complete amateurs. Tom followed the doctor's instructions and the patient started to improve over the next few days, even to the point of being able to keep down some bread and chicken soup. My final message to ZSV was from Captain Armstrong to the station personnel and the hospital staff thanking them for their assistance.

Before we reached east of the Emperor Napoleon's last kingdom, the Island of St Helena, our patient, Michael, was well enough to sit out on deck and enjoy the sea air. He thanked everyone for looking after him. Some days in between watches, I would go and talk to him. He told me how his father was a Newcastle miner and encouraged him not to follow in his footsteps but to go to sea.

131

After a week, Michael was getting bored and wanted to get back to work but his immediate superior said no, as he was still too weak and might have a relapse. James suggested instead he might assist him with his paperwork and Michael jumped at the chance. Passing the chief officer's office every morning, I could see that Michael had taken to his new job like a fish to water.

He told me confidentially that he was now going to become a deck officer. I wished him well but didn't say his route from deck to bridge would be long and hard with years of study. Ian's journey was easier as he had a middle-class education and a Co. Apprenticeship.

We continued on a course for Liberia, passed through the doldrums and Equator, where we entered the Northern Hemisphere. On reaching Liberia, we hugged the West African coast past Freetown, Conakry and eventually Senegal, the former French Colony.

We entered **Dakar,** the large Muslim city with a very strong French connection. The oil and water tankers were waiting for us, and as we had run out of cigarettes, one of the local chandlers came on board with new supplies plus fresh fruit and vegetables. The cigarettes were *Gauloises* French manufactured and had the nickname 'Coffin Nails', and the reason soon became apparent.

They were very strong with loose packed tobacco which initially no one liked but soon became addicted. They exuded an atmosphere, which I imagine those who had frequented the 'Moulin Rouge' would have recognised. Our stay was short and with the call to prayer emanating from a local Mosque, we were on our way again.

Still hugging the West African coast, by Christmas week, we were passing through the deep-water channel, separating the Canary Islands of Tenerife and Gran Canaria. We switched on the Marconi Echosounder located in the chartroom, to make sure we always had enough water beneath us. The paper graph sketched the ocean bed which was occasionally interrupted by the echoes from schools of fish.

Steve, our on-board source of knowledge explained, the Canary Islands name had nothing to do with canaries, but the large dogs, which the original Spanish explorers found when they first discovered the Islands in the early 1400s. Latin for dog, 'Cane!'

We were north of the Canary Islands and west of Casablanca when Christmas Day arrived. We all wished each other a Happy Christmas and lunch that day was Turkey and ham, followed by traditional Christmas pudding, and on captain's instructions, there was beer and spirits for everyone above and below decks. The captain proposed the traditional toast to her Majesty the Queen and Wexford John interrupted with 'And de Valera?'

To which the Captain replied, "And de Valera."

The partying descended into something chaotic with everyone getting drunker by the minute. I refrained from drinking too much, conscious that I had watches to keep and always aware that one of my primary functions was to listen for ships in distress. As the party progressed, we were joined by deck and engine room crew.

The 'Bladen Races' was trashed out again, along with Elvis, Buddy Holly, Matt Monroe, Vera Lynn and many others. The cabin boy sang 'Henry the Eighth I am I am...Henry the Eighth I am', with actions which received a great cheer. At some stage, I went to the bridge and found Ian on the wheel and C/0 James in full charge which was just as well.

These were different times and such carry on these days would probably land people in jail. By the time we were abreast of the Straits of Gibraltar, everyone had the Channels. "What are the Channels?" It's the feeling that the ship will soon reach the English Channel and home.

After a long voyage, the anticipation of meeting loved ones again and nights at home excites mariners to the point where they can't sleep at night and they daydream by day. We passed up the Portuguese coast, Gentle Jesus, the Bay of Biscay and into the English Channel in early January 1962.

Our New Year's Eve celebrations were more muted than the 25th. with just one drink and the blowing of the ship's horn. We steamed up the Channel past the White Cliffs of Dover and into the North Sea, past the Thames estuary and on 6 January, we were boarded by the Middlesbrough pilot.

The final chapter number 22 to follow...please stay with me.

Polamhall 22

Middlesbrough, 7 January 1962:

Along with the rest of the crew, I went before the shipping master, who handed back my discharge book, once I signed the long document that he had put in front of me. I handed him the large stack of logbooks I had completed since first joining the vessel some seven months earlier.

Maybe someday in centuries to come (if they still exist), some student of marine history will read them and wonder where the bones of the author might lie. With bags packed, I said farewell to my cabin, Beaky and shipmates before descending the gangway for a waiting taxi and Middlesbrough railway station. I thought the *Polamhall* looked all the better for its Mina al Ahmadi paint job.

I knew the men I had just left would all see each other again, because they were employees of the Hartlepool Steam Navigation Co., but I would never see them again and they would never see me. I was just an appendage of radio stations moving from ship to ship. I boarded the train at Middlesbrough station and in less than an hour, I was in Newcastle and soon after that the Marconi Marine Office.

I handed in my paperwork and the chief cashier filled in my pay book, gave me a cash advance and advised the balance would be sent via a cheque in the post.

I was interviewed by one of the technical inspectors, and I advised him on the state of the radio station and spares required. With interview over, he wished me a pleasant leave.

Another taxi to the station and that night I was in Liverpool where I booked in to 'Anchor House' the Seaman's mission. As already advised, these were low cost establishments, I suppose, a two star level exclusively for mariners. The accommodation was very clean and adequate as was the food.

The staff were mainly middle-class girls, working part time, and I'm not sure if they were actually paid. The next day, I walked around Liverpool, had a haircut and took in a film at a London Road Cinema. That night, I boarded the Ferry 'Leinster' for Dublin, where I arrived the next morning.

I took a taxi from North Wall to Cross Guns Bridge, where the family were now living excluding of course Paddy, Eda, Seamus and George, who were all married. Under Nano's management, the large white building at Cross Guns Bridge had been built in the 1950s. There were two shops at street level both run by my mother, Agnes.

There was a large three bedroomed flat above. One half of the building sits on reinforced pillars as required by the CIE engineers. The main railway from Dublin to the west of Ireland runs alongside the building. The marble works of E. Rocca and Sons Ltd., occupied the land to the rear of the building.

After breakfast and a wash, I dressed in my best and walked down Whitworth Road where I waited on the bridge for my girl. We embraced and kissed, much to the amusement and delight of the passengers on a passing number three bus. We walked into town and passing the Gresham Hotel, I knew from the faces of the people passing by that we looked like a golden couple.

I enhanced that look, by lighting up a *Gauloise* which filled the air with the scent of Paris. If there is a God and there is a Heaven, maybe we'll be able to relive that lovely cold winter's day in Dublin in January 1962.

Typical Ship's Radio Station

Ms Scorton GWCT

South Shields Tyneside, Northeast England, 12 February 1962:

Having identified myself to the shipping master, I signed on the articles of the motor ship *Scorton*, owned by Chapman and Son Ltd. 'Newcastle Upon Tyne'. I left his office as its new radio officer. This was a fairly new ship, of about five and a half thousand tons.

MS SCORTON GWCT

Once on board, I introduced myself to some of those I'd be sailing with on the voyage to Tsamkong in Communist China and beyond. There was Captain Jones from Wales; a quiet man, and as it became clear during the voyage, a person of great knowledge and intelligence. You also knew instinctively that no one would ever question his authority.

Next came the chief officer, a Scotsman, whose name I forget, but I think it was Andrew. He was a man of medium height and normal weight, with a full head of grey hair, which made him look older than his years, which I estimate as

136

late forties. Andrew's wife was on board and accompanied him while we were in home waters.

His permanent companion was a yellow canary in a large cage fitted with bells, ladders and cuttle fish bone. He had regular discussions with Polly which I suppose was to their mutual benefit. I thought it odd that Andrew was older than most chiefs I had sailed with, but as he later informed me, he had refused a full command many times, preferring to remain as a chief officer.

One interesting thing he did relate was his first trip to sea as a deck apprentice trading in the Far East, lasted a full five years. Next in line was the second officer from Newcastle and I think his name was Nigel. He was about five feet five six inches in height and again not overweight.

I'm struggling to remember the third officer's name, but I think we all called him Benny. He was tall, of slim build and lived in a South Shields flat with his new wife. I know this because Benny took me home several nights for dinner and a bed in his spare room. As indicated in some of my previous stories, Geordie people are very kind and very sociable.

We four occupied four cabins two decks below the bridge with the captain's accommodation one deck above us.

Andrew's cabin, situated on the portside, was the largest with a double sized bunk, followed by Benny, me, and finally Nigel. After that on the starboard side, there was a small smoke room and a cabinet containing the ships library. All our cabins had portholes facing onto the main deck which allowed cooling breezes to flow through in hot tropical climes. We also had heavy curtains around our beds much like Mr Scrooge's in a 'Christmas Carol'. Very cosy!

The chief engineer and his staff lived in accommodation sited above and about the main engine. As the second most senior man on board, his accommodation, like the captains, was very spacious with a separate dayroom/office and an en suite bathroom. The chief engineer was a tall Dutch man with blonde coloured hair who only smoked cigars, and most days at meal times he drank wine from his personal cellar, if I can call it that. I can still see him roll his lips around his long-stemmed glass, with each sip of wine.

He and his staff occupied one of the two long tables in the saloon, with Captain Jones, Andrew, Nigel, Benny and me, at the second long table.

The chief steward had spacious accommodation, one deck below ours, along with the catering and deck crew members.

The radio room was located beside the chartroom. I was disappointed to find that my main transmitter was a Reliance, which meant that I would only be able to communicate to a distance of three to 500 miles. For anything beyond that, I would need the goodwill of GTZM colleagues operating with long range equipment such as Ocean or Globalspans. The emergency transmitter was a Solas which again was only medium frequency range.

I had Mercury, Electra receivers, which was fine. The Auto alarm was a Vigilant, which all ROA readers will know, can initiate many sleepless nights in heavy static conditions. We also had a Lodestone Direction finder and a SALVITA lifeboat Radio. The bridge was fitted with a Quo Vadis radar and Sea graph echosounder. There was no Dynatron radio for crew entertainment so those who could afford it, including the Captain, had their own Eddystone radios.

In the marine world of the 1960s, loading was still carried out by gangs of dockers using large quay wall cranes, which meant our cargo for China took over a week to load. Most nights, I went home with Benny to a nice freshly cooked dinner provided by his new bride. On reflection, I should have been bringing her a bit more than a small box of Black Magic chocolates. Young people don't really have a full appreciation of how to reciprocate.

There was one night which will live in memory till the day I die. Nigel and I went ashore together and after visiting one or two pubs, we wound up in a Workingman's Club. One of the barmen could see we were young and probably not used to drinking, and warned us not to have more than two or three bottles of Newcastle brown ale.

This is a strong drink brewed to suit the steelworkers of Northeast England. Nigel and I acknowledged the barman's advice and then stupidly ignored it. We left the Workingman's club at closing time assisting each other to stay upright. I remember that we met a man walking his Alsatian dog, with whom we both tried to engage in conversation, much to the amusement of his owner.

After that, I don't remember much till the steward called me with tea and toast the following morning. Observing my condition, he went away only to return shortly with a bottle of aspirin, for which I was grateful. I never did drink Newcastle brown ale again.

With loading complete, we exited the Tyne and entered the North-sea around 19 February 1962. I fired up the Reliance and advised Humber Radio GBR *Scorton* GWCT QTO Newcastle, next port Tsamkong China!

Our forty four day, 10560 nautical mile voyage, to the Far East, began with our holds jam packed with British manufactured goods, which would eventually wind up in cities, such as Peking and Shanghai. I was aware that relations between the UK/USA with China were strained, so whatever machine parts and spares we were carrying in wooden crates, would have received official approval in advance.

At a speed of 10 knots, we entered the straits of Gibraltar around 23 February 1962. I started to copy the Mediterranean weather reports from Malta Radio GYR.

As already implied, there was no great entertainment on the *Scorton*, so we had to make do with mealtime conversations primarily instigated by the captain and chief officer. On one occasion, Captain Jones listed a puzzle for all at his table to solve. We were given names of places and things, which when reasoned out gave us a sum of money in old coinage of pounds, shillings and pence.

For example, Royal Sovereign lightship would account for one pound and one shilling of the total end figure. We did very well, but could not resolve the last clue of north and south poles, which accounted for the last halfpenny.

Captain Jones eventually gave us the answer, which had taken even his quick brain over two days to figure out. HALF PENNY.......TWO FARTHINGS. ...
NORTH AND SOUTH POLES.

Andrew related how Admiral Cunningham inflicted heavy losses on the Italian fleet in March 1941 off the Greek coast. I moved that conversation on, as quick as I could.

During our Mediterranean voyage, we received some messages from the owners to the captain, but they were in code, which only he could decipher using the code book housed in his dayroom safe. Andrew, the chief officer, explained that some companies had cargoes stolen during the great depression, by other ships monitoring their plain English radio traffic and getting into port before them.

Those companies who had lost cargoes reverted to using codes.

Also, during this voyage, Captain Jones would hand me messages to send in Welsh. I had to relay some of these via **GTZM** ships with High frequency transmitters. Sometimes I copied replies to him which would also be in Welsh.

I would wait to see if he understood their contents which obviously, he did.

Sometimes, he would refer to the Llangollen Eisteddfod, which at the time meant nothing to me. I'll jump ahead a bit and say later in the voyage, I copied a message for him via Hong Kong naval base, which was again in Welsh and even though he was a very reserved man, he could not conceal his joy at its contents. I think he had been awarded some great honour as a Welsh bard?

He was very Celtic, which suited me because he would brook no criticism of anyone from a Celtic country.

Fourteen days after leaving the Tyne, we arrived at Port Said and waited in queue to enter the Suez Canal. We all had our money ready to buy from the local bumboats, i.e., cheap presents to take home plus tropical shorts and shirts. When we cleared the canal, we commenced our six day voyage down the Red Sea to Aden, where we arrived around 11 March 1962.

We again had to anchor and wait our turn to be called in. It was in between one of my watches, while standing on deck having a smoke, I noticed a light signal from ashore to the bridge of our ship—OPEN RADIO.

I was halfway up to the bridge, where Benny was coming down to get me. "Don, there's someone flashing a Morse message to us from ashore. Can you come and read it?"

"It's ok, Benny, I've already done so."

I contacted the shore station and received a message addressed to the captain for us to enter port.

Aden, 13 March 1962

Like many thousands of ships before us, we were in Aden to replenish our oil tanks for the long onward voyage across the Arabian Sea and Indian Ocean.

The loading took less than twelve hours, so there was no time for a shore visit.

We had to content ourselves with views of distant red coloured mountains and a history lesson from Captain Jones, part of which included the fact that rain in Aden is as rare as hen's teeth.

We journeyed in calm conditions across the Arabian Sea and two days later, when we were south of Socotra Island, we set a course southeast, which took us south of Ceylon (Now Sri Lanka) and into the Indian Ocean. After another course change, and a steam of six days across the Indian Ocean and down the Malacca straits, we arrived south of Singapore.

It was now near the end of March 1962 and very hot, as we were very close to the equator. With no air conditioning, the main relief from the heat was to leave open the forward-facing portholes. At this time, the chief's pet canary was

140

unwell. With assistance from the chief steward, they diagnosed the bird was egg bound, and they brought Polly back to full health with the aid of Vaseline and olive oil.

We entered the South China Sea and set a Northerly course towards the east coast of China.

Captain Jones gave me messages for Tsamkong detailing our ETA, etc. The MF band was saturated with static which made communication very difficult and many word repeats were required before a QSL could be agreed. I thought if only I had a HF transmitter life would be easier. That said, it did help that the operators in stations XJS and XSG transmitted very clear, very readable Morse.

The bursts of static also triggered false distress operation of the vigilant auto alarm. This meant the alarm bell in my cabin would frequently activate, wakening me from a deep sleep, and I'd have to run to the radio room even though it was always another false alarm. My shipmates weren't too happy and suggested I should switch off the Vigilant, but that would have been illegal.

We were advised in advance, not to take any photographs on our waterways passage up to Tsamkong and to do so would be considered a serious offence if we did. I suspect, our captain did not follow those instructions.

What nobody warned us about was, the 'Daily Telegraph' world maps which Nigel and I had pinned to our cabin walls. We entered Tsamkong in early April 1962.

Gangs of Chinese workers began the business of unloading the *Scorton's* belly load of goods as soon as we tied up alongside. They were all dressed in grey type smocks and hats. It was only when you looked carefully, that it became clear it was a mixture of mainly young men and women.

I noticed that every so often, either one or two of the workers would visit a small table, adorned with what looked like green tobacco and small clay pipes, in an area clear of the cranes. They would fill the pipes with a very small quantity of the green tobacco, then light it, take two or three puffs, put the pipe down and return to work.

Soon after arriving, I was in my cabin writing letters home and reading those I had received from home, when I heard Nigel, the second officer, in conversation with two Chinese officials. I couldn't make out what they were saying, but I gathered the men dressed in what looked like Army uniforms, were not pleased about something. I didn't have to wait long to find out, because I was the next person they came to interview.

Having requested and received permission to enter my cabin, they stood and studied the large 'Daily Telegraph' world map pinned to my Port bulkhead. After a brief silence, they started to point to two countries outlined on the map adjacent to China. "These are Chinese territories." I could see they were pointing to Mongolia and Tibet.

With that, they removed the large 'Daily Telegraph' wall map, with no objections from me. Nigel then told me his map had suffered a similar fate to mine. We wrongly assumed that was the end of the matter, but it wasn't. The next morning, we had to attend a hearing at one of the dining saloons long tables which was adorned with our 'Daily Telegraph' maps.

Captain Jones sat at one end and I could see he was really enjoying his role as one of the judges, while one of the army clad officials sat as another judge at the other end of the table. Nigel and I were invited to sit opposite each other at the middle section of the long table. The proceedings began with the Chinese official explaining that Mongolia and Tibet are part of the Chinese republic and are not independent countries as illegally displayed on our 'Daily Telegraph' charts.

Captain Jones was then invited to speak and in nuanced language understood by Nigel and me, we were invited to apologise for our ignorance and mistake in displaying illegal material. Once our apology was made and accepted, we left the two judges to finish the tea they had been drinking. As an aside, our maps were returned to us on sailing day with red crosses marking the offending sections.

During the day, we often met in the mess room with the engineers to discuss current affairs and exchange stories of previous voyages. In Tsamkong, we were joined by what I'll call two Chinese guards who spoke English in a passable fashion. Our initial interaction with the guards was restrained, but as time passed, we became friendlier.

They offered us their cigarettes and we reciprocated with ours.

Eventually, it was agreed everyone should smoke our higher quality Players and Senior Service brands. Our new Chinese friends were more than happy to accept this arrangement, particularly as we gifted them several packets each.

When we asked, what happens if they catch a lazy worker, "Do you send them to a Gulag?" They laughed and accepted the banter as a bit of fun, but we also knew not to overstep the mark.

There was no great shore entertainment, but within walking distance from the ship, there was a seaman's club well fitted out with quality low priced goods for sale. From memory, the chief steward bought a highly carved Chinese chest of drawers in high quality wood, which he considered to be an absolute bargain. Among the bits I and others bought was a tube of toothpaste about eight inches long which lasted me for the rest of the voyage.

The bar was stocked with drink, even cheaper than *Scorton* on board prices. The tables had propaganda magazines with stories of French Bishops and priests in Vietnam abusing young oriental girls which made us all laugh. Now I wonder?

On our walk to the ship each evening, the locals would give us no recognition, opting instead to look at the ground.

Once unloading was complete, we wished our guard friends goodbye, and commenced a short voyage to Hong Kong, where we berthed around mid-April 1962. The difference between Hong Kong and Tsamkong was difficult to believe. The port was crowded with ships of every nationality and planes were landing every ten or fifteen minutes.

The ferries from Kowloon to the islands were jammed with well-dressed people. The shops were full of merchandise, including transistor radios, and white goods of all sorts. The city at night was ablaze with neon signs and girls of easy virtue, but what happened in Hong Kong stays in Hong Kong.

The radio station had some faults including low power output from the Reliance transmitter, but these were soon sorted out by a technician from the local Marconi Marine office.

We left Hong Kong on 16 April 1962 and I advised the local station, ms *Scorton* QTO HONG KONG bound for Balikpapan Indonesia.

We sailed south for eight days down the South China Sea past the west coast of the Philippines and into Indonesian waters. Indonesia gained independence from the Dutch after the end of the Second World War, but in 1962, relations between the two countries was still a bit strained, unlike today. When we reached Balikpapan around the 22 April 1962, it was advised our Dutch chief engineer should remain on board.

This wasn't a problem, because we were only in Port for half a day to replenish our tanks with low priced Indonesian oil, which meant none of us could have more than a stroll along the quay wall.

We left Balikpapan and as we were now in British sea Area 7, I relayed a message to Sydney Radio via Darwin, next port Bunbury, Australia. With many course changes, we voyaged our way down past Bali and back into the Indian Ocean. I should have mentioned that Chief Officer Andrew was an expert at navigating by the stars, and took great pride in demonstrating this skill with accurate position fixing, during his 0000 to 0400 hours watch.

The Southern Cross shines brightly in the Southern Hemisphere which obviously helped.

We sailed down Australia's west coast past Perth, Fremantle and arrived in Bunbury around 5 May 1962.

From memory, this was a small very clean city and close to where the *Scorton* was berthed, fishing parties often departed in small boats. The sea off Bunbury must have been teeming with fish, because these same boats returned at sunset with the passengers struggling to carry their catches home to waiting families. The people were very welcoming and one Sunday a local couple took me and Andrew on a coastal tour.

It was their first car, a light green coloured Australian built *Holden,* and I could tell they were very proud to be now part of the motoring fraternity. Other memories include the soda fountains and every time I see the film 'Back To The Future', it somehow reminds me of a very pleasant stay in Bunbury, Australia.

Having discharged our Hong Kong cargo and back loaded with Bauxite (Aluminium ore), we left Bunbury and re-entered the Indian Ocean, to start a twenty six day voyage, towards the Horn of Africa and Aden in the Yemeni republic. When we reached British sea area 3, I switched stations from Sydney to Mauritius Radio.

The cargo of ore we were carrying turned us into a pendulum and we rolled incessantly for weeks before finally reaching Aden in early June 1962.

This was another half day visit to replenish our fuel tanks, after which we commenced a northerly journey to the Suez Canal via the Red Sea.

After a pleasant six days through calm seas, we reached the Suez Isthmus, where we were boarded by the first of our Egyptian canal pilots.

We exited the canal at Port Said and with Alexandria on our port side, we sailed on a westerly course towards Malta and Bizerte in Tunisia. I relayed a **TR** message to Portishead Radio as we were now in sea area 1. The music from those with Eddystone radios was often Arabic, but sometimes the captains was in English possibly, the Light Program, which in those days had a very powerful long reach on 200 KHz.

On one visit to his cabin, with one of his Marconigrams in Welsh, I could hear the latest craze music, 'Let's twist again', by Chubby Checker.

It was mid-June when we exited the Mediterranean Sea and entered the Atlantic Ocean. As all seafarers will tell you, at this point in a long voyage, everyone gets the channels. It's because the English Channel and home is getting closer day by day. Like children on Christmas Eve, it becomes difficult to fall asleep at night.

At least, the *Scorton* was back in waters where I had the comfort of communicating with my Reliance MF Transmitter. Once the ship passed Gentle Jesus off Lisbon and reached the southern end of the Bay of Biscay, I was able to talk with Land's End Radio GLD and Valentia radio EJK.

We passed Brest and entered the English Channel and when we reached the Thames estuary, the Gravesend Pilot came on board and took us up-river, and into the Royal Victoria docks.

Benny twisted the handle on the engine room telegraph to, finished with engines.

Our long voyage was over and on 21 of June 1962, we all signed off ship's articles as witnessed by the London shipping master.

I wished my Board of Trade friends a fond farewell and made my way by taxi to the Marconi Marine office, East Ham. With company paperwork complete, I made my way back by train and overnight ferry from Holyhead to Dublin, and two weeks leave with my girl, Rita.

You're probably thinking two weeks leave wasn't much after such a long voyage but in those days, there were hardly enough operators to man the thousands of ships in the British Merchant Navy, which was by far the biggest in the world. Marconi Staff clerks would almost plead for us to end our leave early.

As it happened, it suited me on this occasion, as I was granted study leave, to attend a three month Radar course at Kevin St College.

I'll continue this story with the....

Summer of Four Ships

I returned to the UK on 8 July 1962 and signed on the MV *Port Invercargill* GXCL at Immingham Docks on the Humber River.

PORT INVERCARGILL

I was the relief R/0 while the regular man was on leave. It soon became clear why the regular man was the permanent operator.

Port Line, one of the UK's most prestigious shipping lines, were the owners of this beautiful, twelve thousand ton vessel.

My cabin was palatial, with an extra-large single bed. The aroma of fresh coffee scented every part of the ship. There was one other occupant in my cabin.

A large green parrot! Immediately on my arrival aboard, I was visited by the chief engineer, who sought my approval to leave the second occupant in situ.

He explained he was looking after it for the owner, namely the man I was standing in for. I assured him I had absolutely no objection. He did say only he and a few others could handle the bird and if I wanted to retain my fingers, I should do no more than talk to it from a safe distance. No problem there either. Every day, the chief would release the bird from its cage and allow it to fly for half an hour or so within the confine of my room.

I won't list all the radio room equipment except to say it was very large and lacked for nothing. I was glad to be back in the company of a powerful, long range transmitter and two Atalanta receivers. The whole office including the door was sheathed in copper plate almost like an imitation of a Faraday cage.

The dining saloon was large, as the vessel on voyages to Australia, etc., was equipped to carry twelve passengers. The tables were adorned with crisp white linen cloths embroidered, with the Port Line Logo. The catering staff were Indian and Indian curry dishes were always on the menu. This ship had a purser who made sure the food was of the highest standard.

The *Invercargill* also had its own laundry room. Sometimes while on watch, I'd wonder how I might become a permanent staff member of such a lovely ship.

We left Immingham for Liverpool on a southerly route through the English Channel and Irish Sea. We entered the Mersey about two and half days later and tied up in Canada dock. A day or two later, we exited back into the Irish Sea on route to London.

I made sure to keep the station paperwork in good order and the equipment in a condition the regular operator would approve. My short career on the mv *Port Invercargill* ended at the Royal Victoria docks London on 22 July 1962.

The next time I heard about this ship was in 1967, during the six day war between Israel and Egypt. While passing through the Suez Canal, it got caught up in the conflict and was stuck with about twelve other ships in the Bitter lakes. The Suez Canal was closed for years after that and those ships caught up in the lakes began to deteriorate.

Unfortunately, my beautiful ship was one of them, and eventually Lloyd's insurance wrote all the vessels off as beyond commercial repair.

The 'summer of four ships' continued, when I signed on as relief officer, of the five and a half thousand ton, M.V. *Trelawny* GBNX—Owners—Hain Steamship Company. A very old British Company, who unfortunately lost many ships to the wolf packs during Second World War.

I signed on in Tilbury on 25 July 1962. The *Trelawny* was very similar in design to the *Scorton*, but I can't remember much about the radio room layout.

I do remember that several of the mates and engineers had their wives on board, none of whom seemed very friendly, but not rude. At night after dinner, we would all gather in the wardroom, to watch television programs such as 'Candid Camera, I Love Lucy' and 'Rawhide'. My attempts to make conversation with the young wives didn't progress beyond a brief reply of yes or no.

Perhaps they felt I wasn't a Hain Company man, or I was somehow an interloper on the regular R/O's territory. Of course it might also have been the Borgia, Henry the eighth factor.

Anyway, it didn't matter, because this was only a short home trade run to Hull, which commenced at the end of July 1962. I did no more than copy weather reports and send traffic information to Northforeland radio GNF and Humber Radio GBR, during the one-day voyage.

TRELAWNY

I signed off the *Trelawny* at the Hull Shipping Office on 1 August 1962 and reported into the Marconi Marine office, and that night I stayed in the Hull seaman's mission hotel.

The next day, 2 August 1962, I signed on the Ellerman Wilson Lines ship *Cavallo* GMQS.

I was now back on slightly more home turf as I'd already served on another of this company's ships namely *Livorno* GPWF.

MVCAVALLO

The *Cavallo* was one of the better ships in the Wilson line and I could see there was a pattern in the ships I was being sent to. The regular men now on leave were determined to make sure no one was going to take over their stations on a permanent basis and people like me were just jobbers!

This was a more comfortable ship than the Livorno and my fellow shipmates, including the captain, were very welcoming.

Most of the five days I spent on board was alongside in port.

On 4 August 1962, we left Hull and I called Humber Radio GBR to report *Cavallo* GMQS QTO HULL next port LONDON. The next morning, 5 August 1962, Northforeland Radio GNF called with a QTCl. We shifted to working frequencies and the message commenced D. Rocca *RIO*. It was a message to me from home wishing me a happy 21st birthday.

This was also the day the world lost Marilyn Monroe. I signed off the *Cavallo* at Poplar on 7 August 1962 and reported in, to the Marconi Marine office, East Ham.

It was in the East Ham waiting room that I first met John Harley who was doing similar relief work to me.

CITY OF WORCESTER

As both of us were in between ships, it was agreed we would have lunch together locally that day and we did. On returning to the office, we were both assigned to our next ships.

Mine was the *City Of Worcester* GHDC and I signed on at Poplar London on 8 August 1962.

This was a fairly new ship of over four thousand tons and part of the City Line fleet.

Another quality ship following the trend that started a month earlier.

I had a nice, forward facing cabin and a well fitted radio office.

Looking through my old discharge book, I can make out the captain's name as B. Waldie.

That night I had a visitor to the ship….none other than John Harley who had been assigned to a lesser vessel adjacent to the City of Worcester.

"How come a more senior man like me was not given this lovely ship, Donal? It just isn't fair."

I knew from his tone he was having a bit of banter.

We adjourned to the officers' mess, where the vessel's three deck apprentices were gathered and after a coffee break, it was agreed that we would all go into the big smoke, which we did by tube if memory serves me correctly.

A good night was had by all, but this was not the final encounter I was to have with John Harley.

The Worcester left London port around 10 August, and I switched on the Oceanspan transmitter and Atalanta main receiver. I advised Northforeland radio GHDC next port ROSTOCK EAST GERMANY VIA THE KIEL CANAL.

We sailed across the North Sea and arrived at the entrance to the Canal on 12 August. I sent and received messages for the Master via Norddeich Radio Callsign DAN.

After a very scenic 60-mile journey through German countryside, we reached Kiel and exited into the Baltic Ocean and later that day, we reached the port of Rostock in East Germany. In 1962, this was a communist state under the control of Moscow.

It hadn't progressed much since its takeover by Russia after the Second World War, whereas West Germany has resumed its position as one of the World's richest countries. Many East Germans lost their lives in a vain attempt to escape to the West.

On arrival, large quayside cranes began the business of unloading the goods we had brought from London. I took a lone stroll outside the docks where a man dressed in old fashioned clothes asked if he could buy the Inca block wristwatch I was wearing, or could I sell him some English cigarettes. Feeling sorry for him, I apologised but had to say 'no'.

That night, I accompanied some of the deck and engineering staff to a local club for foreign seamen. We had a good time and there were also local girls to talk to.

These were respectable girls, obviously, well educated, and took our banter in good part.

That night in the bar, I ran out of Marks, so I asked the barman if he'd change an English five pound note. He didn't say yes, and he didn't say no, but shortly afterwards I was requested to enter a side room by two men. We sat at a small table and they asked me to hand over the £5 note which I did.

They held it up to the light, felt it, turned it over and went away. Eventually, they returned and handed me East German Marks in exchange for my £5 note. The exchange was fair, but I was told I must not take any of the Marks out of the country.

This was not possible, as the bar prices were so cheap, and the remainder of my law breaking Marks, are still somewhere in one of my old suitcases.

We left Rostock and after a passage down the southern end of the Baltic and through the Kiel Canal we exited back into the North Sea sometime, on the 25 August. I called Stonehaven Radio GND and advised GHDC next port BIRKENHEAD LIVERPOOL.

We set a north-westerly course towards John O'Groats, after which, with many course changes we navigated the North Scottish coast and down through the Hebredian Islands, then onwards through the narrow waters, where Scotland and Ireland almost meet and are visible to each other on any day of the year.

We entered the Irish Sea and set a course that would take us north of the Isle of Man. On that warm sunny day in late August 1962, we passed west of Blackpool and the Tower was visible to the naked eye.

When we reached the Liverpool bar lightship, we were boarded by the Merseyside Pilot who took us up-river and into the Birkenhead docks.

I called Anglesey radio GLV and advised *City Of Worcester* GHDC QTP LNERPOOL AR.

I signed off the last of the four summer ships on 29 August 1962 and reported in, to Marconi Marine Pall Mall. The following morning, 31 August, I walked down the gangway of the Irish ferry mv *Leinster* and into a waiting Dublin taxi.

It was the first week of September when I entered the old 'Kevin St College of Technology'. With five other students, I then entered the Radar class room, where Dr Rice was awaiting our arrival. The room was full of test equipment such as AVO 7 multimeters, oscilloscopes and most importantly operational Marconi Mk 3 and Mk 4 Radars.

It was while I was completing my entry paperwork that a new person walked into the room. It was none other than John Harley.

"John, you didn't tell me you were doing the same Radar course as me."

"I'm not, Don. I'm one of the Radar instructors."

Cormount 1963

The Colliers—Cormount 1

Blyth Port, 4 April 1963:

Having paid the Newcastle taxi man, I turned to see the ship that was to be my home for the next four months. The Cormount, gross tonnage 2870, was built in the last year of Second World War and was now in the last year or two of its life. Towering above its holds were railway tracks and every so often a truck filled with coal would appear, and men covered in black dust would tip its contents into the holds of the waiting Cormount.

Coal dust was everywhere, and I wondered how I could avoid it and get down the gangway. As I was to learn later, Geordies are very kind and considerate people and the collier men operating the tipping machinery seeing my dilemma said, "Go on, son, we'll wait."

I nodded my appreciation and descended the gangway to be met by the second officer (I'll call him Michael). We introduced ourselves and he said, "Don't worry, Sparks, the coal is normally dampened before we take it on board but today is an exception." A few minutes later, I introduced myself to Wally, the chief steward.

He showed me to my cabin, which had been freshly prepared for my arrival. It was small but cosy with a high bunk at the end of which stood a large iron radiator.

Above the bunk there was an oil lamp. Wally, seeing the quizzical look on my face said, "Donald, you'll have to learn how to trim the lamp." Another quizzical look from me and Wally who had a great sense of humour smiled and said, "In port at 11:00 pm every night, the Egyptian firemen shut down the engine. They will give a ten minute warning by flashing the lights, so those left on board can light the lamps. Dinner will be served at 5:30 pm."

I thanked Wally and started the business of loading the contents of my suitcases in to very large and very heavy brown painted drawers.

My cabin was on the same deck as Wally, the chief steward, and also the chief and second officers. We all had portholes facing on to the main deck. The captain's cabin was on the next deck up, as was the dining/wardroom.

With my unpacking complete and dinner time approaching, I washed in my small hand basin and donned my uniform before ascending the steep stairs up to the captain's deck. Captain Jeffrey introduced me to the rest of the staff—chief officer whose name from memory was Bill; a man of medium build who sported a tidy looking moustache.

Second Officer Michael, again about medium height, and his age was about mid-twenties; the chief engineer whose name eludes me, probably about forty; a pipe smoking atheist intellectual and I suspect an avowed Socialist bordering on being a communist. His company was very entertaining.

With dinner over, it was time to sail. As we exited Blyth into the North Sea, I switched on my main transmitter, a Marconi Reliance, and informed Humber Radio GBR from Cormount GJGC QTO *Blyth* next port LONDON. Joining us on our voyage down the English East Coast were many other colliers. We were like a coal Armada sailing to feed the big smokes insatiable appetite for the black stuff.

Cormount Chapter 2

Blyth to London, April 1963:

We set course South for Flamborough Head which would take us past the Tyne, South Shields, Sunderland, Hartlepool, Whitby and Scarborough.

My office was long and narrow. It was so narrow in fact, that I had to step into my chair from the side, where seated like a Spitfire Pilot I could operate the equipment. The equipment, main transmitter was a Marconi Reliance, which was partnered with a Marconi CR 300 receiver. The emergency receiver was an Alert and the Auto Alarm was a type M.

I also shared the cabin with a Marconi SALVITA lifeboat transceiver. Best of all, though I was not aware of it at the time, was the emergency transmitter. Don't ask me to recall its name but I looked inside, and primarily I could see two very large valves which glowed like lamps when the equipment was switched on. How was the equipment switched on?

Well, under my desk was a very large motor which was the primary source of power. To activate this motor, you had to build up its speed via a heavy-duty rheostat. The noise built up slowly till the office sounded like a Spitfire engine and the deck vibrated like it was waiting for the chocks to be removed. I felt a great sense of power and decided to give it a test.

I called up CQ and requested a QSA/QRK? I got an immediate reply from one of the companion Armada ships who told me to go to a working frequency, 425 KHz from memory. My new friend, who was obviously familiar with this equipment, told me I was using a very old transmitter which was now illegal except in an emergency.

He also advised me that it was not stable on 500 KHz and might even interfere with those using 512 KHz. In other words, it could wipe everyone else off the air and best of all it sounded like a roaring MGM Lion! I nicknamed it the lion and I knew the Cormount had a dispensation for its use as we were close to being scrapped.

I knew I was allowed to test it as necessary and I decided I would also use it to receive early attention from East Coast stations, who would want to stop the Lion roaring as soon as possible. During the voyage South, I visited the bridge for tea and a chat with Michael, the second officer. From memory, the bridge was fitted with a DECCA Radar, possibly a D303 though it might have been a Marconi Quo Vadis.

Michael took me into the chartroom to show me the 'echosounder', which was part of the Marconi rental equipment. All I can remember was, its power source was dry and rechargeable wet batteries for LT and HT. To operate it, you turned a handle and looked at a spinning disk via a black visor. It was a bit like 'What the Butler saw'.

The CRT had an 'A' scan presentation and when a bottom echo was received, a vertical line would appear, to be measured again in a metric scale. There was also a DECCA Navigator, probably a MK4 and this was Michael's favourite piece of equipment, and probably the captain's and chief officer's too. Michael explained the workings of the unit. Three clocks—Red, Green and Purple read out signals from shore based stations and the navigator placed the coordinates on a DECCA chart, which gave a very precise ship's position.

This was a very expensive piece of equipment and I wondered why it was on board when we had three very competent navigators plus radar. The answer became clear as the weeks passed. Fog, which it seems to me, is a constant companion in season on the East Coast of England. As an aside, after my ten years on the Marconi shore staff, I joined the DECCA Radar Co. and rose through the ranks to become an area manager.

On one occasion, I was interviewed on TV to explain the history of the DECCA navigator. I told how it was designed by an Irish American engineer called O'Brien and an American engineer called Swartzkoph. They tried unsuccessfully to interest the American military in taking it on.

The story then goes that they were friendly with Bing Crosby and he was so impressed that he persuaded Sir Edward Lewis of DECCA Records, to fund its development. It was first activated militarily on D Day. O'Brien had a receiver at his UK home and knew exactly when the invasion commenced, which was a bit naughty! Anyway I digress, sorry. We reached Flamborough head and altered course for the Big Smoke.

Cormount Chapter 3

April 1963:

When we reached Flamborough Head, which was quite visible on our starboard side, we altered course for the Thames estuary. Soon after, we passed Felixstowe, Clacton on Sea, Southend on Sea and into the Thames. The Thames River Pilot came on board and took over our passage up to the Royal Docks (from memory?).

Although, Corys had many Collier ships, this pilot was invariably assigned to the Cormount. Allow me to call him Albert because he looked like an Albert. He entered the wheelhouse carrying a lot of newspapers, including the 'London Standard', which he handed to Captain Jeffrey.

This ritual had been his normal routine for years. He immediately lit up another cigarette, one of probably 60 to 80 a day. Wally brought him tea in his on board personal mug, which was the biggest I'd ever seen and he settled down to the task of instructing the helmsman—*starboard a bit…port a bit…steady as she goes*. I got into conversation with Albert and he loved to relate his personal history of the Thames which was most entertaining.

Albert was the very last freeman of the Thames. This meant he could set his own rate, whereas every other pilot was on a fixed salary as employees of the London Harbour board. I got the impression that Albert had made a very comfortable living over the years, though I suspect by his cough and chain smoking, this might have ended prematurely.

We arrived at the Royal Docks and after tie up, Wally announced dinner was ready. I would say this chief steward was the best I ever sailed with, because although there was no great choice, the meals were very fresh, very well cooked and presented.

After the meal was over, the table was cleared, and underneath was a large green baize cloth. The television was switched on and Captain Jeffrey went to his cabin only to return a few minutes later with a large pack of loose cigarette tobacco, plus skins, a Rizla machine and a pack of playing cards. He emptied the tobacco onto the baize cloth and spent the next half hour pumping out a very large number of homemade Virginia cigarettes from the Rizla machine.

These were to last him for the next twenty-four hours. When he finished, he opened the deck of cards and said, "Ok, let's play."

Along with the chief engineer and chief officer, I was one of the four players. The Poker session lasted several hours, and the stakes were small.

Cormount Chapter 4

London Royal docks, April 1963:

The card game continues. With every hand Captain Jeffrey lost, he would throw the cards down onto the baize, in a more cranky fashion, while invariably the chief engineer would lift the pot, while sucking on his pipe.

Bill and I were almost like observers, neither winning much nor losing much.

At one stage, Wally, the chief steward who had been watching Kathy Kirby on the TV show 'Stars and Garters', left the saloon and returned later with mugs of tea and bacon sandwiches. The game continued with the captain getting more agitated as his losing streak continued, till the last of his stash finally ended up in front of the chief engineer. With that, he lifted all the cards and walked out on deck and hurled the pack as hard as he could into the Thames.

He returned muttering, "That's it. No more, bloody card games!"

I could see Bill and the chief engineer smiling secretly while Wally mouthed in my direction, "Till tomorrow night." Apparently, this was not the first time the Thames wound up with a pack of playing cards, courtesy of Captain Jeffrey.

We shifted to watching the end of 'Stars and Garters' and sometime after 11, the lights flashed on and off. This was a signal from our Cairo shipmates that in ten or fifteen minutes the engine room would be shut down till 0600 the next morning. We bid each other good night and departed to our respective cabins.

On entering mine, I thought I had better light my oil lamp, which I did. It wasn't very bright and black smoke from the glass funnel soon filled the cabin, so I opened the porthole to avoid being asphyxiated. I now had the problem of how to get into my very high bunk, with its permanent bad weather sideboard. I could either draw out the large drawer beneath the bunk and use that as a ladder, or I could launch myself from the settee.

I chose the latter and once horizontal, it was quite cosy with shadows playing on the deck head and warmth from the water radiator located just inches from my feet. The next morning after breakfast, Wally asked if I slept ok, and I said fine except the oil lamp was a bit smelly. "No worries, Donald, I'll get that sorted." True to his word, the Bosun entered my cabin sometime later that morning, armed with fresh lamp oil and trimming scissors.

He set about his task like a lamp trimmer from some old sailing ship. First, he filled the reservoir with fresh oil and inserted a new wick. He then instructed me on the importance of using the trimming scissors till the wick was perfectly straight. He then lit the wick and refitted the globe. The difference was amazing.

There was no smell, no black smoke and the light was pure white. I thanked the Bosun, which was probably not necessary, as he could see how pleased I was with the knowledge he had just imparted. The cabin was even cosier that night and every night thereafter. This did change a little, however, and in fact quite a lot, with information imparted to me by Wally sometime later during one of our evening chats.

Cormount Chapter 5

London to Blyth, April 1963:

With our cargo of coal discharged, we sailed down the Thames estuary past Tilbury, Canvey Island and Southend on Sea, after which we set a course North towards Flamborough Head. I sent a TR message to GNF Northforeland Radio advising next port, Blyth. I copied the weather report from GBR Humber Radio and handed it in to the Bridge.

Reports of dense fog featured heavily on this report and it was not long before this was confirmed by the intermittent blowing of the Cormount foghorn. Many of the other colliers in our convoy were doing likewise and it was also important that every ship kept a careful radar watch. The colliers coming from North to South, would have kept to a different shipping lane than us, and even further off the coast were the multitudes of deep sea ships, heading to the four corners of the planet.

Sometime after passing Flamborough Head, the fog lifted and within binocular sight we could see some of our travelling companions. William Cory line sported very distinctive funnel marking of a white band on black and in the middle of the band was a white diamond shape. As usual, the second steward served up a very acceptable lunch that day.

In between watches, I often visited Wally in his cabin. He was a man probably in his mid-fifties. He spoke with a very Geordie accent through a toothless mouth. He said he could never get used to false teeth. Many people in this era had sacrificed their teeth to cheap toffee sweets and lack of toothbrushes.

Wally was a collier veteran whom I could listen to all day as he recounted his wartime experiences. In the early years, when the collier fleets bringing the vital fuel came to a bunch near the Thames estuary, the Luftwaffe would often strike and from memory, I think he recounted how one ship he was on was a casualty, but fortunately he was rescued probably by a fast naval patrol vessel. With the battle of the Atlantic raging, protection for the Newcastle fleets was limited.

Wally said, as time went on, some of the vessels got Oerlikon guns manned by two Naval ratings and some even got air protection in the form of single seater fighter aircraft being launched from the forward end of the ship, by a steam powered catapult. I'm sure Wally said the Cormount was fitted with an Oerlikon gun but maybe time is playing tricks with my memory.

One story he did tell is true. Some years earlier, the Cormount was on a voyage in the Baltic Ocean when the captain began to feel unwell and his stomach began to swell dramatically. He was examined by a doctor who didn't think it was cancer but as the vessel was due to return to the UK shortly, he should visit his own doctor to arrange a more definite diagnosis. The captain became very depressed and wouldn't be convinced it wasn't anything serious.

Wally tried his best to keep him calm but all in vain. One morning on the voyage home, he entered the captain's cabin with morning tea and found he wasn't there, so he entered his bathroom where he found the body hanging from the overhead pipes. I think the sadness of it all was still raw with Wally as he wiped a tear away.

Soon after we reached Blyth, there was a mass exodus from the vessel with everyone bar Michael (2/0), the second steward, and me dashing to catch buses and trains home. I remember Bill, the chief officer, lived in Sunderland.

Michael had to remain on board to oversee the loading and the second steward had to remain to serve our meals. I should also have mentioned the Egyptian fireman had to remain on board to keep the main engine running. They preferred to cook their own food, which was obvious from the few conversations I had with them.

After the evening meal with just me and Michael at the baize covered table, I could see that the steward wanted to say something, and he did. He asked if it would be ok if he also went home.

Neither of us objected, particularly as he gave us the keys to the galley food store. This was actually located beneath the galley proper and entered via a wooden grate on the deck. That night while watching telly, we enjoyed mugs of tea and bacon sandwiches dressed in brown sauce, which I had made for both of us.

As usual just before 11, our Cairo shipmates flashed the lights, so we proceeded to our cabins. With my newly acquired skill, I soon had the oil lamp glowing pure white. I again launched myself into the high bunk and settled in to reading one of Albert's newspapers.

Bearing in mind what Wally had told me about the toilet drama on a previous voyage, I was reluctant to extinguish my only light, and this wasn't helped by Michael in the adjacent cabin tapping on the bulkhead. I did eventually enter the darkness and pulled the covers over my head.

Cormount Chapter 6

The East Coast of England and Scotland During the Spring and Summer Of 1963.

We continued our five day round trips, between the NE and London. Sometimes instead of Blyth, we'd collect our cargos in Sunderland or Middleborough. If memory serves me right, the coal was sometimes crushed to a powder which invariably meant our destination was Battersea power station, where the crushed coal could be pumped into the furnaces and turned into electricity to power the Capital City.

There were times when we'd deliver to the Ford Motor Works at Dagenham. I can still see the huge Ford sign displaying its location. Other times we went to

Rochester. As it's one of England's very posh and ancient towns, it was lovely to walk around, particularly as the sun seemed to be always shining. Sometimes on the London trips, I would take the Bakerloo line to Kensal Green to visit my aunt Dotie who was married to Albert Crook.

Albert's claim to fame was his friendship with Billy Cotton when they served together during First World War and after that as London bus drivers. Albert ended his working life as a car delivery driver and loved telling how he once delivered a Rolls Royce. They had one daughter, Ellen, who became a teaching Nun at a London school called the Sisters of Mercy.

London was not unfamiliar to me, as I had been there on holiday in 1947 and 1954. At other times, I would visit other collier ships including the Flatties. The Flatties, these were ships with virtually no top structure which allowed them to sail under the bridges and access to the upper Thames.

Some of the radio officers I met were very interesting. For example, there was one chap poorly dressed wearing shoes that needed mending and everyone said he was a millionaire. He took every opportunity to visit the Stock Exchange and never left with less than he entered with.

Another vessel I visited a few times, the R/0 would not allow anyone to smoke and you'd be in trouble if you sat your mug of tea on any of the polished surfaces. His cabin and office were immaculate and even the antenna copper runs were colour coded. He had a bike which looked like it had just left the showroom. Even though I was on Home Trade pay, it was almost worth it to have comfortable communications with the shore stations.

I also had the MGM Lion and I knew I shouldn't, but just occasionally I'd switch it on and maybe call Stonehaven GND or Cullercoats GCC. The response was always immediate. The squeakiest hinge always gets oiled first. Who amongst us does not remember calling maybe Scheveningen PCH or San Francisco KFS more times than legal before receiving a reply?

Wasn't it lovely just to send PCH or KFS, then pause for a DE? Of course, the bloo…USA monitoring authorities always heard you over sending, which resulted in a Marconi request to ask why you broke the rules. I got a blue airmail once or maybe twice to explain myself. I felt like saying because if I didn't, I'd still be transmitting.

Of course, I didn't and usually replied 'Oh, I'm sorry I hadn't realised'. I apologise now to the more professional among you, who never broke the rules. I'll continue with chapter 7 later and the CAT CULL at BATTERSEA.

Cormount Chapter 7

Battersea Power Station; Now famous as The Museum of Modern Art, Summer 1963:

It was Sunday morning and I awoke to the sound of gunfire. We had been warned in advance, of what was to take place, but I had forgotten. I went out on deck, still in my dressing gown, and could see men dressed in navy overalls carrying guns, which they were using to cull the hundreds of feral cats, which had infested the large reserve mountains of coal.

I felt sorry for the poor creatures, but many of them were already in a poor state, thin with hunger and deformities. The chief engineer said it was probably the kindest thing to do.

It was probably also that day on our trip north that I handed Captain Jeffrey a Marconigram from head office instructing him to proceed to Methil in Scotland. It meant little to me, but it provoked a lot of groans and moans from almost everyone on board. "Methil? Oh no, not Methil." I felt safe in asking Wally why everyone was complaining about going to Methil?

"Well, Sparks, it means they won't be able to get home this trip." How awful I thought! I was probably the only one on board to be happy to be heading for the Firth of Forth.

That night alongside, with the cigarette making ritual over, the cards for the poker school were produced. Jeffrey was experiencing a reasonable run of luck, but this was about to come to an end as his kitty once again wound up in front of the chief engineer. That's it he said, no more and this time the cards wound up in Scottish waters. Bill smiled and Wally interrupted his TV viewing to whisper, "Until the next time."

Cormount Chapter 8

Port of Methil, Scotland, Summer 1963:

After breakfast on that first morning, as was usual, the cook came to the wardroom, with pen and paper, the purpose of which was to collect the cash for that day's horse bets. On board, the Cormount, there was a cohort of horse racing enthusiasts, who gathered in port to make out their betting slips, which were then taken ashore to the nearest bookie shop by whoever was available.

I was not one of the group, but I did pay a passing interest, and can confirm the return from the Queen's head, leaving the Cormount, was invariably much larger than those on the return journey. This had obviously been noted by the chief cook, who that morning made an announcement, "If everyone agrees I'll take on the betting book?" As all agreed the chief cook became the official turf accountant for the Steamship Cormount.

Things went well for the on-board bookie for several weeks, who ran his business from a small cash box. Little did he know that that cash box was about to be whisked away by an unexpected run of good luck by the Bosun. It was in Rochester I think when the first horse of the Bosun's treble bet ran home a clear winner as heard on the cook's Eddystone Radio.

When the second horse of the treble also pipped the post, the Cormount bookie contemplated a dash ashore to lay off horse number three, but time ran out. The gathering around the Eddystone grew with dribbles of sweat running down the cook's face. Some of us non cohort people felt his pain, which increased dramatically when horse number three, edged home by a short nose.

The winner cheered and the loser forlornly opened the small blue tin box, which was soon emptied of its contents, supplemented with a bit more from the cook's wallet. From then on, the tradition of the Queen's Heads leaving the Cormount for the local bookmaker shops resumed. And we also resumed our journeys up and down the English East Coast, until one day we received orders to proceed with a cargo of coal for Holland.

Captain Jeffreys couldn't contain his delight, because it meant the ship could take on a bond which Wally arranged. There were cigarettes at ten shillings for a carton of two hundred and bottles of whiskey and gin for seven shillings and sixpence plus other bits and pieces I can't remember. We journeyed up the Zuider Zee to a small port whose name now escapes me. In fact, I think it was so small we may have been the only ship there.

There was and presumably still is a bar very close to where the ship was berthed which meant a contingent led by Captain Jeffrey visited there every night to be served by a very friendly barmaid. We left this small port for Middlesbrough where we loaded another cargo of coal for a return visit. I wish I could remember where it was. We continued our normal routine of cargoes for the Royal Docks, where on one visit the second steward handed me an official looking letter.

I opened it hoping it wasn't a tax demand or whatever, but it was from the British Meteorological Office stating I was to receive an award for valuable work at sea. The second steward said I was going to get a medal. What would I get a medal for and I never did anything valuable at sea so it must be a mistake? "No Sparks, you're definitely going to get a medal."

The mystery was solved a few weeks later when the same second steward brought me another official looking parcel wrapped in brown paper. Well it wasn't a medal, but a very expensive world atlas, with an inscription on the first page—*Awarded To; Donald Dominick Rocca by The British Meteorological Office for his Valuable Work at Sea Aboard The SS Baron Ardrossan.* I remember when Captain Jeffrey saw it he wanted to buy it from me.

I know that Atlas is still lurking somewhere among all the cases in my attic. No doubt, most members of the ROA have similar books. On 2 September, 1963, I signed off the ss *Cormount* at South Shields and two days later, in the same port I joined the 3105 tonnes 'Hudson Strait'. This was a newer ship than the Cormount, with no loss of overnight power and hence no need for oil lamps.

I regretted I no longer had my MGM Lion but two Reliance transmitters and Mercury Electra receivers. What this ship did have was very unusual. At my first dinner on board, I noticed that the saloon had an actual fireplace which looked not unlike the one I had grown up with at home in Dublin. The steward kept it banked up with fresh coal and it looked and felt very cosy.

I was on board as the relief operator while the regular man was on holiday. I don't remember very much of the people on this vessel except as already said Geordie people are very friendly and very welcoming, and the men on the 'Hudson Strait' were no exception. I signed off at Blyth on 23 September 1963, and after I handed in my paperwork at the Marconi Marine Office, I made my way to the station and boarded a train to Liverpool and the overnight ferry to Dublin.

Sometimes looking back down the years to those collier days, I wonder…

'What became of the people we used to be?'

Irish Maple

Chapter One

Dublin Airport, Mid-January 1964.

IRISH MAPLE   W.S.P.L.

The KLM chartered Viscount roared down the runway before rotating and entered the sky above Dublin city, on route to Amsterdam. On board were forty men and I was one of them.

We were on our way as the relief crew of the mv *Irish Maple*.

This was one of about sixteen ships which made up the fleet of Irish Shipping Ltd. This was a semi state company which was formed during 1941, the year of my birth. Second World War was raging and most of the British Merchant fleet was engaged in feeding their people or at least those ships that weren't being sunk by the German U-boats.

De Valera and his government decided, that the only way we could survive was, to have our own fleet and Irish shipping was born. It was started with a ship purchased from the Greeks and with expertise provided by Riordans of Cardiff, more ships were added and soon the Irish Tricolour was sailing in Blue Waters.

Initially, we were allowed to sail in the British convoys, under the protection of the British Royal Navy.

Sometime later, this was changed to lone sailing by painting the Tricolour along the length of the hull, as a message to the German Navy that we were a neutral country. It didn't always work out, as some of our ships reported U-boat positions to the Admiralty in London, plus there were mercy missions where Irish ships rescued British sailors from the sea and lifeboats, after their ships had been torpedoed.

Usually the survivors were landed at 'Haulbowline' Naval Base Cork and repatriated back to the UK.

Anyway, I digress. Once the KLM Viscount landed at Amsterdam and taxied to the Schiphol passenger terminal, we passed through customs and a coach took us to the waiting *Irish Maple*.

Forty men with cases walked up the steep gangway to be met by a small number of the previous crew, who were keeping the ship alive.

Soon, these men would return to the four corners of Ireland, and a well-deserved rest. They had done their job well, because all cabins had been cleaned and the bunks made up with fresh linen. Once we had been fed, everyone took to their posts. The catering crew to the galley, the engineers to the engine room, the deck officers to the bridge and me to a very large radio room adjacent to the chart room.

My cabin was one deck below, with the captain the only other occupant.

Once I familiarised myself with my new station, I took to my bunk, and was asleep as soon as my head hit the pillow.

Chapter Two

Amsterdam, Mid-January 1964:

The first day.

A knock on the door and Second Steward Wally entered with morning tea. "Wakey wakey, Sparks. Rise and shine." Wally introduced himself and related how he had started his early career in the Irish army catering corp. I didn't know at the time, but I had good reason to be grateful to Wally later in the voyage, when he sorted out a problem I had after a night of youthful foolishness.

My cabin was not on suite but adjacent to it was a toilet and shower room, to which I had virtually exclusive use. As already said, the only other occupant of this deck was Captain Dwyer and he had a suite of rooms including a full bathroom.

Once showered and dressed, I descended to the dining saloon for breakfast and was shown to a long table already occupied by junior and middle ranking deck and engineer staff.

Willie Cummins—second officer, later senior captain with Irish Ferries. Jack Byrne—third officer, later promoted to captain. Peter Scott—senior cadet, Brendan Aherne—fourth officer. Others at this table included Engineers and two more deck cadets. Captain Dwyer's table included Chief Engineer Byrne and Chief Officer John Small.

Once I checked out the radio and radar equipment, I made notes of what Radio stations, etc., I'd be using during the voyage to the USA East coast, I decided to do a bit of sightseeing around Amsterdam. I couldn't help comparing its cleanliness to the litter strewn streets of Dublin.

A few days later, fully laden, we made our way down river and into the North Sea. I contacted Portishead Radio and advised we had left Amsterdam and we're now bound for Philadelphia, USA.

Even though Ireland was and is an independent country, our ships were allowed full access to the British Marine Radio Area scheme.

Within a few days, we were out of the English Channel and into the Atlantic Ocean proper. A blind sailor would have known this because of the heavy swell that rolled and pitched our ship from morning till night. Meal times could be a nuisance, trying to drink soup from a plate, determined to spill it anywhere but on to your spoon and sleep could be difficult when even with sideboards, we'd be thrown from our bunks onto a heaving deck. Many a night, I staggered back to my bed muttering expletives unrepeatable here.

Still for us seasoned seamen, it wasn't half as bad as for the new crew members who spent most of the first week talking to God on the big white telephone, "Oh God…Oh God!"

When we were South of the Irish coast, I contacted Valentia Radio EJK and sent messages from Captain Dwyer to Head Office Aston Quay.

As we were a weather **OBS** vessel, I also sent the report compiled by Willie Cummins Second Officer and this would have made its way to the Met office, to be part of Telefis Eireann's and B.B.Cs evening weather forecast.

Onward we ploughed through the grey Atlantic towards Philadelphia, where we arrived in the last week of January 1964.

Chapter Three

Philadelphia, Late-January 1964:

At a meeting in the wardroom, it was agreed that we would hire a television from one of the local TV shops. I collected the funds from the deck and engineer staff and using the on-board shore phone and Yellow pages, I started to make calls. The first shop that I phoned, refused to supply us with a TV, on the basis that, it wasn't worth it for such a short term rental, plus what would happen if we simply sailed away with it overnight?

This was a time when televisions were very expensive and very prized. I was better armed on my second call and offered to pay a premium plus assist with a temporary installation. This call wasn't going very well till the proprietor asked if my accent was Irish to which I said yes. "And are you on an Irish ship?"

Sensing I was on a winner, I informed him that we were all Irish and really loved the American programs. Within an hour, the sixteen inch black and white TV arrived and soon we were watching 'Bonanza, I Love Lucy, The Man From Uncle', plus daytime Westerns. This Irish loving TV man also fitted a TV in the crew mess room.

This was great and when we weren't watching TV, I tuned in the Dynatron Radio to Penn State KDKA, and instead of the dull rubbish transmitted by Radio Eireann, we had—Baby Love, The Supremes, House of the Rising Sun, The Animals, I Want to Hold Your Hand, The Beatles.

Speaking of the Beatles, they were on their meteoric rise to fame and particularly in America, teenage girls went crazy for their music. Our black and white television showed this when we arrived in New York, more or less at the same time their aircraft landed at Kennedy Airport, to hysterical joy from waiting fans.

Back to Philadelphia, we were advised to visit the Liberty bell and the place where the Declaration of Independence was signed.

No way were we interested in that sort of fuddy duddy stuff.

We were interested in burger bars, with red mock leather seats and loud juke box music, air conditioned cinemas showing 'My Fair Lady' and 'Dr Strangelove' and American popcorn. The 1960s was a time to be alive, though it was tainted with the recent loss of John F. Kennedy. Our Philadelphia visit was a bit spoiled on the last night, when Peter and I were returning to the ship by taxi. The driver seemed to get lost and pulling alongside a kerb, he said his shift was over and we'd have to hail another cab.

We stupidly paid him and waited for another cab that never came, so we started to walk. After probably two hours walking, we found our way back to the *Maple*. If there's a hell for bad taxi men, I hope he's still there.

The next day, we made our way down the Delaware River and back into the Atlantic Ocean. I advised Chatham Radio WCC USA and Halifax Radio CFH Nova Scotia Canada, next port New York.

Chapter Four

Philadelphia to New York, February 1964:

We sailed past Atlantic City on a heading Northeast, up past Long Beach and entered the lower bay where we picked up the first of our New York river pilots. He took us up the Hudson River where we anchored in the shadow of the 'Statue of Liberty', with instructions to wait until a berth became available. Normally swinging on an anchor can be boring but this was different.

Although, air travel was bringing the passenger Liner era to an end, by 1964 and we saw what was probably its closing stages, they came every day—the Queen Mary, The Queen Elizabeth, The France, Italian Liners, Dutch Liners, Hospital Ship 'Hope'; and as they passed the Statue, their large funnel horns blasted a greeting up the Hudson River towards the mighty skyscrapers as though to say, "Hello, Big Apple…we've arrived."

One day while seated in a deckchair enjoying the sights and sucking on a Lucky Strike, two of the Engine Room crew were doing likewise. These were mature men from Ringsend who joined as first timers in Amsterdam. "Tommy, isn't this wonderful. Did you ever imagine you'd see such a sight?"

"Not in my wildest dreams, Jack. Not in my wildest dreams."

Eventually, Port Radio instructed us to weigh anchor and make our way upriver where an empty berth was waiting for us.

There was still dollars in the TV float, so using the same trick I persuaded a local TV shop to supply us a short term rental sixteen inch. We were in the 'Big Apple', with TV, music by Elvis, and visits to the place where King Kong met his end. The Beatles had arrived to be met by thousands of hysterical teenage girls, and Bobby Kennedy was holding Election rallies in preparation for becoming another Kennedy President in 1968. This never happened because he was assassinated in that same year by one of the lunatic fringe.

The day after we tied up and with permission from Captain Dwyer, I made my way up to the Bronx and Rita's aunt, Rita's apartment.

This was a woman who immigrated to the States in the late 1940s and was now married to Eddie, a man of Polish extraction.

Their hospitality couldn't have been better, with highballs before and after dinner. In the evenings, Eddie would take me to the local tavern where he seemed to enjoy introducing me as Irish/Italian, which for some reason the company seemed to find very amusing! I still wonder why? Rita's two boys and daughter, Agnes, seemed to enjoy my visit.

During my metro train journey back to the ship, I noticed three young girls sitting opposite me and as they were leaving near Times Square station, they said, "Come and join us." Being recently married, this was an offer I had to politely refuse.

Our cargo discharged, we left New York and I reported to Amanganset Radio WSL Long Island next port Boston.

We sailed north past Nantucket Island and into Massachusetts Bay, where a Pilot boarded and took us alongside the University city of Boston. I couldn't help reflecting how in 1962, my Kevin Street Radar instructor Dr. Rice loved referencing the M.I.T. Boston, where major advances in Radar were made post Second World War.

Our stay in Boston was similar to Philadelphia and New York, and after a few days, we left with not much cargo but a heap of happy memories. I advised Halifax Radio CFH next port Belfast.

We set a course northeast and headed out into the usual heaving North Atlantic Ocean. With the prevailing westerly wind giving us extra speed, within seven to eight days we were off the Donegal coast and shortly after that, up the Lagan and a waiting Harland and Woolf drydock.

Rita arrived on board the next day.

Chapter Five

Harland & Woolf Shipyard, Belfast, End of February 1964:

The *Maple* sat in one of the large dry docks, probably the very one where the *Titanic* was built. Harland and Woolfs, probably the most sacred Orange ground in the world after the banks of Boyne and there we were, a large ship from the Republic of Ireland flying the green white and orange from the after flag pole. We were people from the happy part of the island and oblivious to the dislike of those men repairing and painting our ship.

Rita soon settled into the routine of ship life. There were other wives and girlfriends on board, but she far outshined them all and I pretended not to notice the attention she was receiving. There were visits to the Belfast shops during the day and parties at night in the wardroom.

With repairs complete and the *Maple* looking as good as the day she was born, we sailed down the Lagan and back into the Irish Sea.

I ran up the Oceanspan 7 Transmitter and Atalanta double heterodyne receiver—GPK Portpatrick Radio from EISL *Irish Maple* leaving Belfast, next port London. "QSL BV OM," came the reply.

When I finished watch that night, I found Rita in the chief steward's cabin along with a few others including the chief officer's wife.

The Chief Steward, Jack Doran, was a sophisticated man of the world, who shone in female company and that night he had a willing audience. He was also providing the drinks, which in Rita's case was a can of Coca Cola.

The next day after a breakfast of orange Juice, cereals, a full Irish toast and tea, we sat out on deck enjoying the sun and sea fresh air. While I was on watch, Rita had a nap or read one of her books.

After dinner that night, I left her in the wardroom where she and other wives enjoyed chat and Radio Luxembourg music from two large loudspeakers. That night, as I switched out the cabin light I noticed the ship was starting to roll gently but I kept this information to myself.

I needn't have bothered because when Wally entered the next morning with two cups of tea, the *Maple* was rolling pretty violently.

I showered and dressed, but Rita was still in the bunk. "I'm going down for breakfast. Will I bring something back for you?"

"Maybe some dry toast," came the reply. At breakfast, I noticed the rest of the wives were missing. As we rounded Land's End and entered the English Channel, the storm seemed to increase in strength and the rolling and pitching became more violent. After breakfast the next morning, the storm had eased a little and the White Cliffs of Dover appeared big on our port side.

I opened one of the windows a bit to allow nice sea air to enter the cabin and asked Rita if she'd like to sit up and view the White Cliffs.

"No, thank you."

"Are you sure?" This produced a silent stare from a pale face.

During the rest of that day, the storm abated and by evening time, my hungry wife was happily seated at the long saloon table, ready to be served soup followed by Beef and Yorkshire pudding.

The next morning, we tied up at King George V docks, London.

Chapter Six

King George V Docks, London, March 1964:

Loading of cargo commenced with goods we'd be taking to the opposite side of the planet, i.e. New Zealand and Australia.

The Irish Maple was going on a Shaw Saville Line charter. This was a premier British Shipping Co. with a cargo and passenger Liner fleet, so they would only engage quality ships like ours to carry their very expensive cargos.

The dockside cranes at times made loud blaring noises caused by heavy cables straining on bearing blocks. Rita asked what the noise was to which I replied, "We're loading Elephants for Melbourne Zoo."

"Really?"

As I couldn't keep the smile off my face, I received a punch on the shoulder.

Our days were spent touring around London with one visit to Harrods, where we couldn't afford to do more than have coffee and sandwiches. My pay had improved by this stage and it was supplemented by a monthly bonus from Irish Shipping Ltd. Pay rates were set by the British Board of Trade, which the Irish Authorities followed.

It was unheard of for shipping companies to pay over this rate, but ISL did and even though I was not a direct employee, but merely part of the radio/radar electronics rental package, they very generously included me.

At night, we would go to a cinema in Leicester Square or more often than not, we'd wind up at the new Seamen's Anchor House mission along with Peter, Jack, Brendan and others. Anchor House had just opened, and it was a luxury version of a Seafarers' Hotel with deep piled carpets and bars selling subsidised alcohol.

We were joined one night by one of my old classmates from Atlantic College. His name was Cyril Forde and a very entertaining character, whose company Rita really enjoyed. Cyril wanted to follow his brothers and become a deck officer rising to captain, but like many others with poor eyesight, he had to settle for second best and become an R/0. I should also say at this stage, Anchor House was run by Stella Maris, a Catholic institute.

When last orders were called, Cyril ordered a pint of Guinness which was placed on the table in front of him. He had only taken a first sip when, from across the room, a wall slid open to reveal a priest about to celebrate Benediction.

Most of the seafarers present took to their knees, though those of other faiths made a hasty retreat. Cyril participated, until after the host was raised and then said in a low voice while retaking his seat, "Ah F…this, I'm finishing my pint."

It was probably the only time in the world when during Benediction those close by, including our little group almost choked on suppressed laughter.

It was also on that very clear night, as we all walked down George V docks, that someone spotted *Sputnik* flying across the Horizon.

We gazed at the first and only artificial satellite circling planet Earth.

The days passed quickly and soon it was time to leave. Rita and I said our farewells at Euston Station, knowing it would be a long time before we'd meet again.

Chapter Seven

London to The Gulf of Mexico, March 1964:

We exited the Thames estuary and at Margate took a right hand turn for the English Channel. I advise Portishead Radio next port Curacao US Gulf for bunkers. I tuned in the Dynatron to BBC Radio and Cilla Black singing 'Anyone who had a heart' boomed into all the saloons and mess-rooms.

Sea conditions were calmer than our last trip in the channel. Captain Langran, who had joined us as the new master in Belfast, handed me messages for transmission to Aston Quay and elsewhere which I sent via Northforeland Radio.

Some time while on watch during our second day out, I received a request from Niton Radio GNI (on the Isle of Wight) to shift to working frequency 468 KHz, as he had a telegram for the master.

I complied and after copying the message, acknowledged receipt.

I read it twice before I put it in an envelope and proceeded to Captain Langran's dayroom where I found him working at his desk.

He read the message after which he lifted the internal telephone.

"Jack, can you come to my cabin immediately please." Jack, the chief steward, entered shortly afterwards and the captain handed him the telegram.

"Oh, dear God, that's sad, Sir. Will I bring him to your cabin?"

"Yes, Jack, and you had better stay, Donald."

A short while later, a worried looking Third Officer Jack Byrne entered the dayroom and was invited to take a seat. "Jack, I've received a telegram from head officer saying it was with great regret we must inform you that Captain Byrne (retired), died suddenly while at a church service last night."

There was silence in the room and Jack tried to compose himself with the news of his father's death. With a nod from Captain Langran, the chief steward handed him a glass of whiskey. I returned to my watch but a short time later, I was summoned back to the dayroom where the three men were still seated.

"Donald, is it possible you could get a link call through to Jack's family in Arklow?"

"Well yes, Sir, it is possible for the main transmitter to be switched to MCW to be used on Simplex Mode."

I could see Jack had been crying, but he did manage to tell me the number which I wrote down and suggested he follow me to the radio room.

I contacted Niton Radio and requested a link call to be put through to Arklow and what was our number in the queue. Knowing the situation, the operator said, "No queue for you, old man."

Soon after, Jack was talking with difficulty through tears to his mother and other family members.

To give him as much privacy as possible, I closed the door and stood at the far end of the office.

When he was finished, he thanked me and left to be alone in his cabin.

I called Niton Radio and requested the call charge, to which came the reply, "No charge, old man. Safe sailing."

There was sadness at mealtimes over the next few days, but as we headed south into summer conditions the mood changed back to normal. I copied weather reports from Washington Radio NSS and sent our reports to the Atlantic Weather ships and Horta Radio in the Azores Islands.

Within twelve days, we were passing between the straits of the Dominican Republic and Puerto Rico. Even with both cabin windows open it was very hot, which made it difficult to sleep.

Sometimes in the early hours after midnight, I would join Chief Officer Small on the bridge for a coffee. We would stand on one of the bridge wings talking. He smoked his pipe and I drank coffee from a large white mug.

Everything was silent except for the low murmur of the engine and soft lapping waves against the ship's hull. The sea was calm, lit by the light of the moon and the Gulf breeze blowing in our faces was heaven sent.

Soon we arrived at the Dutch Island of Curacao, where immaculately dressed in a white uniform, a Dutch Pilot navigated the *Maple* alongside the oil berth.

Chapter Eight

Curacao US Gulf, March 1964:

With our tanks replenished with fresh oil and galley store full of fresh food, we left Curacao to start our two-and-a-half-day journey across the north coasts of Venezuela and Colombia to Panama, where we dropped anchor among hundreds of other ships waiting to enter the Canal. It was almost a vision of what the Spanish Armada must have looked like.

The Panama Canal, one of the great engineering wonders of the 20th century, achieved with the mighty Yankee dollar and the loss of thousands of French and American lives to Jungle fevers and mosquitoes.

Before it opened in 1914, ships travelling from the Atlantic to Pacific had to round Cape Horn with its icebergs and mountainous seas. Many didn't make it, and many like Captain Bligh on the Bounty had to turn back and use the route via the Indian Ocean.

If a ship in the 1800s wanted to travel from New York to San Francisco, it took an extra four months round trip and a great deal of guts. It was, though, more commercial than trying to transport the same amount via the Rocky Mountains. Older men I sailed with, who rounded the horn, all said, "NEVER AGAIN!"

Eventually, I received a message for Captain Langran instructing us to lift anchor and proceed to the Canal entrance. Panama City was close by and it was said that many a young man seeking female comfort in that city, found he had become a film star on the return journey.

The Yankee dollar had bought something really impressive. We were whisked through giant locks, pulled through with the assistance of train like engines called mules, on the dock walls.

It wasn't long before we were free and after sailing through a Central American jungle, we entered the Pacific Ocean. The ocean was well named by the Portuguese Navigator Magellan, because it is peaceful and calm, and we were about to make our four week journey across it.

I called Vancouver Radio and gave him our position and next port Auckland, New Zealand.

Chapter Nine

Pacific Ocean, Early April 1964:

My job was to sit in a big office surrounded by high powered transmitters, expensive listening receivers and with pencil in hand, place an entry in the radio logbook every ten minutes. The trouble was, the normal 500 kHz babble of communications had dwindled to almost zero, with most of my entries saying, "All quiet, nil heard."

To relieve the boredom, I would often go on loudspeaker and join whichever deck officer was on watch. Sometimes, it would be Second Officer Frank Kelly and he would pass on his meteorological knowledge about cloud formations and how he and his colleagues were trained to look out for the first sign of a typhoon forming, which started with a small tornado in hot tropical waters. He never did find one. Other days, I joined in conversation with Chief Officer John Small.

It was one of his duties to keep the ship looking smart to which end and taking advantage of the good weather, many of the deck crew were painting the ship. If memory serves me correctly, some were even over the side on boards lashed with heavy ropes painting the hull. Wouldn't be allowed today, but John and the captain wanted to arrive in Australasia on the first Irish ship EVER there to look in pristine condition.

Although, the sea was millpond smooth and the sun shone from an almost cloudless sky, there were occasionally short bursts of heavy showers. To avoid these and allow the painting to continue uninterrupted, John would track the cloudbursts using the Marconi Mk 4 Radar and alter the ships course accordingly.

The younger painters were acquiring a sun tan by being stripped to the waist and boasting to each other that the Kiwi dolls would find them irresistible. One day while talking to John, I suggested I might paint my cabin to which he eagerly agreed. The next morning, the Bosun came to my cabin, in what I perceived as a grumpy mood and handed me an old paint brush along with two tins of paint.

When my morning watch finished, I activated the Vigilant Auto Alarm and commenced the decoration project by storing the carpet, curtains and bed linen, etc.

I softened up the old brush with turpentine which still didn't look great but when I opened the paint tins it was even worse. What I found was a sticky mess. I thought, "Well I may as well make the best of it."

I loaded the old brush with some of the sticky mess, but before I could apply it, Chief Officer Small entered the cabin and took it from my hand. His face grew red with rage and armed with the brush and paint, he left muttering, "I'll sort this out immediately."

It was only then I realised that in my innocence I had overstepped the mark into the Bosun's territory. Later, the Bosun's mate arrived, smiling I thought, with new paint and brushes. I recommenced.

I had visits from the cadets during the day giving their advice and I knew they were convinced an amateur like me would end up requiring them to come to my rescue. What they didn't know, because I never told them, was that I had been painting since the age of nine. Father Nano would have had me laying Terrazzo, if Mother Agnes hadn't intervened. I was the chief painter in Home Farm and had also painted the entire Rocca building at Cross Guns Bridge.

When I completed the painting in white and Greek blue, I started on the window brasses. First, I removed the old paint to reveal the brass underneath and then painstakingly brought the brass back to life finishing off with Brasso provided by Jack, the chief steward.

John said it looked fabulous and I could see he was thinking, maybe I could do the captain's accommodation, but thought better of it as it might cause a mutiny. I'm afraid the cadets weren't pleased with me as the chief officer thought the Brasses looked so good, he'd instruct them to do likewise in their cabins.

I was so pleased with my handiwork that I suggested I might paint the radio room, and almost before I finished the sentence John ran off to arrange new brushes and fresh paint. When I finished the radio office, including bringing back the Porthole brasses to the day they were born, I sat back and sucked on a Lucky, well pleased with myself.

As we sailed on down towards the Galapagos Islands, we lost our Dynatron Radio music completely, but Second Officer Kelly came up with a cunning solution.

Chapter Ten

Pacific Ocean, April 1964:

As already said, the further South we sailed, the less and less broadcasts we could receive, with the exception of some shortwave stations such as, 'The Voice of America', transmitting news bulletins, combined with American propaganda. The signals tended to fade in and out, with changing propagation conditions, which made listening for any length of time very annoying.

Again, as already said, Kelly had a solution! With the master's approval *Radio Maple* was planned.

One evening as we were passing south of the Galapagos Islands, Frank 2/0 and Jack 3/0 entered the radio room carrying Frank's state of the art Hi-fi equipment. We interfaced it into the Dynatron PA system and Radio Maple was born. We placed a music tape into the HI-FI; Frank spoke into the microphone 'Good evening, **Irish** Maple', and we could hear his voice booming through every speaker on board.

"For your entertainment, we now have Frank Sinatra singing, 'Young at Heart' from his film of the same name with 'Doris Day'." Other songs followed, interspersed with news from on board magazines and after a while, Frank allowed Jack and me to have a turn on the mic. We normally ran out of steam after about an hour, but the station was left in situ for the next evening's Radio Maple broadcast.

Reviews from all crew members were good, with some even passing written requests via Wally, the second steward. The second engineer loaned his special tape of Spanish guitar music which went down a treat.

As we steamed further South, passing 110 West we entered British Area 5, so I contacted Wellington Radio ZLW and advised our position and destination. ZLW would then have passed this information to Lloyds for general publication.

Chapter Eleven

Pacific Ocean, April 1964:

With the Galapagos Islands astern of us, we sailed on towards Easter Island and beyond.

Mealtimes were the highlight of the day with deck and engineer officers bantering each other about which job was the most important on board, plus their adventures on previous voyages.

Captain Langran, and hopefully he would approve of me saying so, was a very sociable ships master, a cultured man with great knowledge and teaching skills.

Many nights he would invite us to his dayroom, where we would all enjoy a few drinks and on occasion even sing a ballad or two.

In between watches during the day, I would join others in deckchairs on the boat deck and enjoy the sun and blue ocean. Flying fish were a common sight with the occasional shark coming to check us out. Just adjacent to my cabin was a door which opened out on to the top deck. At night after a cool shower, I would don my dressing gown and go sit on my own in a deckchair.

Apart from those on board, most of whom were asleep, there wasn't another human being for thousands of miles around. The skies were crystal clear and the Southern Cross vied with the Moon for attention. Shooting stars were common and the air was balmy, sometimes scented with the aroma of Copra.

Sundays were best because Jack would arrange for awnings to be erected on deck, below which a long table was placed and adorned with bottles of Gordon's Gin, Schweppes tonic and a silver bucket filled with ice cubes. The captain would sit at one end and his opposite number the chief engineer at the other end. The Gin and a cool Pacific breeze would soon put everyone in a very good mood. Even 3/0 Jack was becoming a little less bereaved.

When the dinner gong sounded, we would all repair to the dining saloon where again Jack and the chief cook would lay on, a special Sunday lunch of roast beef and Yorkshire pudding. Usually after this, it was siesta time for those not on watch, which unfortunately for me it always was.

On 19, April 1964, after a thirty eight day voyage from London, we entered Australasia and for the first time in history and since an Irish Ship flying a very large Tricolour of green, white and orange entered Auckland, New Zealand. News of our arrival preceded us and our welcome was astonishing.

Chapter Twelve

Auckland, New Zealand, April 1964:

I'll continue by repeating an account I wrote at the time which was subsequently published in the ISL house magazine. I believe sections of it were also covered by at least one Irish newspaper.

Anyway, here goes:

On the 12th of March 1964, the 'Irish Maple' left London bound for New Zealand via CURACAO and Panama and arrived in Auckland on 19th of April.

The reception from the Irish community in Auckland was overwhelming and I am pleased to report that we returned their hospitality by being Ambassadors in true sense of the word.

Suffice to say, that many, many hands were shook, and many parties, dinners and teas were attended by everyone aboard.

The Climax came on Sunday the 28th of April, when the lads of the 'Maple' played the Irish exiles in a game of Gaelic football. We arrived at Cornwell Park and the scene that lay before us was one that filled us all with pride. The Tricolour was very much in evidence and the sun shining from an umbrella blue sky reflected on the bonnets of some hundred odd cars. Loudspeakers placed around the grounds were announcing the arrival of the Irish team and many came to shake our hands and talk of home. While we talked, old Irish airs could be heard from the speakers.

The Irish exiles wore all white and the men of the 'Maple' wore white shorts and green jerseys. As the two teams paraded around the field, preceded by bagpipes and under the eye of a television camera, I'm sure many a person in the 500 odd spectators, was comparing it to an All-Ireland Football Final in Croke Park. When the teams reached the centre of the pitch, the band played the Irish National Anthem. All heads turned towards the tricolour and all stood proudly to attention.

Within seconds of the Anthem being played both sides took up their positions and Father O'Reilly from Cork threw in the ball. Within a very short time, the Aucklanders scored a goal, but the 'Maple' soon retaliated leaving the score one all. The Auckland team eventually won but our lads played a great game.

Particularly worthy of mention are Ken Edwards (Junior Engineer),

Jack Byrne (Third Officer), Peter Scott (Apprentice), William Boon (Able Seaman), Peter MacDonnell (Ships Carpenter) and Frank Kelly (Second Officer).

The result of the game was soon forgotten, for to all those present the only important thing of that day was the fact that 30 Irishmen had played a game of Irish football in a land many thousands of miles away from home.

Chapter Thirteen

Auckland, New Zealand, April 1964:

Continuation of Gaelic football match.

Father McHale gave a running commentary on the play. He faltered not once in his speech and he used the Christian names of all the players throughout. Had he remained at home, Michael O'Hehir would surely have had strong competition.

That night a dance was given in our honour.

This was held in the Irish Centre, which is a beautifully decorated and spacious hall. We were all made honorary members of the Society and given long white ribbons to designate same.

The emigrants besieged us with questions about Ireland and our ship.

The most asked question was, "When are you coming back and will more follow you?" We were more than pleased to answer all their questions. Many requested us to visit their relatives and friends back home, and we hope to be in a position, in the not too distant future, to carry out these requests.

The highlight of the night came, when Mr Vincent Mc Hale, the captain of the Auckland team, got up to make a speech. He said in part how thrilled he and every other Irish persons in Auckland were at having such an esteemed visitor as the *Irish Maple*. He ended by wishing us all a speedy return to Auckland.

Our Third Officer Jack Byrne thanked the Irish Society for the hospitality shown to us during our stay in Auckland, and concluded by saying that he and every member of the crew expressed a strong desire to return again soon.

After the speeches, songs were sung by both members of the Irish Society and members of the *Maple*. We were represented by Able Seaman Mr Tobin who sang opera good enough to grace the stage of La Scala. Able Seaman Mr Cousins played his harmonica.

More dancing followed mainly, CEILI which everyone thoroughly enjoyed, and finally the night ended with the playing of the Irish National Anthem.

Some of the special friends we made are:

Father Doyle, native of Enniscorthy. Father Hackett, a kiwi who became more Irish than the Irish themselves, during our stay.

Sam Bestall, Ex-Dubliner

Johnny and Mrs Kavanagh, Ex Arklow

Mick and Teresa Collins—Mick is a native of Killarney and a former Kerry Footballer, holding a senior championship medal.

Gerry and Anne Mc Caffrey—Gerry is a brother of Leo Mc Caffrey and is a singer of 'No Mean Ability' himself.

Mr Whooling, Ireland

Vincent Mc Hale, Ex-Mary's Footballer. Des Lee, Carlow

Jim Turner, Kildare

Mr and Mrs Coyne, Galway.

Before continuing, can I add something not said, almost sixty years ago.

Soon after the match started, the score started to become embarrassing in favour of the Auckland team, because as you'll see from above they had emigrant players, many of whom would have qualified to play in Croke Park possibly even on All Ireland day.

We did have Kenneth Edwards who played as a Dublin Minor and was in fact our premier player.

To avoid embarrassment, particularly as a clip of the match was subsequently played on New Zealand National Television, the referee halted the match and called the two captains for a conference on the side line. This resulted in a 50% exchange of players and jerseys.

Chapter Fourteen

Auckland, New Zealand, April 1964:

The last before departing for Christ Church.

There was one event, which took place and which I argued with myself, as to whether or not I should proceed in telling, lest it might hurt or offend those involved. My daughter, and proof reader initially said no but on reflection said yes but not to reveal any names.

The Great Love Affair

One day at lunch, a couple entered the dining saloon one of which we all knew as we'd been fellow travellers since Amsterdam and the other was a girl. I say girl but more than that she was stunning, and if memory serves me right a Nicole Kidman lookalike. Introductions were made and those at the table became more animated in their conversations with this uptown Kiwi girl, but she and her new love only had eyes for each other.

Sailing day arrived and we had a small gathering on the quay wall waving and shouting farewells, "Please come back soon," but this was never to be.

Uptown girl was among them waving goodbye to her lover, but this was not an end to their affair.

Chapter Fifteen

Christ Church, New Zealand, May 1964:

Again the Irish community in Christ church came out to greet us in a mirror image of our visit to Auckland. The love affair continued with a lot of understanding by Captain Langran in allowing generous leave to our young senior deck officer.

I pause here to say my proof reader has now changed her mind and told me to cease or scrap this part of my story. I would like to have continued but as a parting shot, I'll simply say…

Too many moonlight kisses cool in the morning sun; and this love affair was no exception with the final act played out later in the voyage at Macy's Store, Herald Square, New York.

I know because I was there.

Having unloaded the last of our cargo at Lyttleton, we re-entered the South Pacific Ocean and commenced our voyage on a North Westerly course towards Tasmania and Melbourne. I contacted Sydney Radio and advised the duty Officer, *Irish Maple* EISL QTO LYTTLETON bound for MELBOURNE.

This information soon found its way on to the pages of local newspapers. The result was when we entered Melbourne six days later, as the first ever ship into Australia flying the Irish tricolour, the throng on the quay wall was even greater than that in New Zealand.

Our six week stay was full of parties and receptions, including everyone on board being made honorary members of the prestigious Melbourne Celtic Club. From memory, this club was normally only open to those at the top of the social ladder. I still have my ribboned medal…somewhere.

More football matches were played during one of which, unfortunately, our star player, Kenneth Edwards, was injured and hospitalised. This resulted in him leaving part of himself in Melbourne, namely his spleen.

During the time of our visit, the famous Irish actor, Michael MacLiammoir, was on an Australasian tour performing, the 'Importance of being Oscar' to capacity audiences.

Captain Langran gave a lunch on board for MacLiammoir and his agent, Brian Tobin. Also present were Doctor Kearns Labour, M.P. for North

Melbourne and his wife. Some of the *Maple* functions were held on the bridge deck with my newly painted very large radio room being utilised as the bar area.

This was a good choice as the long desktops filled with state of the art marine communications equipment was of great interest to our visitors.

One abiding memory I have of Melbourne was our visits to the milkshake bars which of course sounds very innocent now.

After six weeks in Melbourne loading Australian iron for the booming Japanese economy, we left to the strains of an Irish piper and tears from the eyes of young girls who would never see their Irish sailors ever again.

I fired up my main Oceanspan 7 transmitter and Atalanta main receiver before contacting Sydney radio, *Irish Maple* EISL QTO MELBOURNE bound for OSAKA JAPAN.

We entered the Tasman Sea and set a course north towards the Great Barrier Reef.

Chapter Sixteen

West Coast of Australia, June 1964:

Before continuing, I must advise that what follows is based mainly on memories from almost sixty years ago, so please indulge me if it contains a few small inaccuracies.

We entered the Tasman Sea and headed north in the direction of Sydney. We stayed within binocular distance of the coast. It was now early winter in the Southern Hemisphere which was actually more acceptable than high summer.

All the days were sunny and in between watches we sat out in deckchairs overlooking a blue azure sea with the coast outlined in grey on our port side. Sometimes, with eyes closed, a cold Pepsi in one hand and a Lucky Strike in the other, what more could anyone want, except in my case the company of my beautiful girl, Rita.

At night, a few of us would sit in the same deckchairs and stare into the crystal clear sky while discussing how to solve world problems. Above us the Southern cross shone down like an elevated Pharos, as the arm of the Milky Way twirled its way through the night sky in a great half circle, and occasionally a meteorite would burn through the atmosphere, ending it's fourteen billion life in the blink of an eye.

Chapter Seventeen

Tasman Sea, Early-July 1964:

We continued up the west coast of Australia and as we passed Sydney, some said through their binoculars they could just make out the famous bridge towering over the construction site of the now famous Opera house. Sadly, all I could make out was a blur on the horizon.

A day later, we passed the city of Brisbane and some days later with the Great Barrier Reef on our port side and the coast no longer visible, we entered the Coral Sea. Still on a north westerly course with the islands of Vanuatu, and Solomon on our starboard side, we entered the channel between Papua New Guinea and New Britain before exiting into the Bismarck and Philippine seas.

As we crossed the equator, the temperature increased noticeably, though we were all well acclimatised to the heat by now. That said some nights the heat was so stifling you'd be lucky to get half a night's sleep.

We were then into British sea area 8 for radio communications so I contacted Singapore naval base and advised our position and destination—Osaka, Japan. We continued our voyage through the Philippine Sea past islands where famous American and Japanese sea and land battles had taken place only a few short years earlier. The island of Guam springs to mind.

We were still in typhoon season but were lucky apart from the odd short storm to have a safe passage. That said the bridge staff were always anxious to receive the weather reports I handed in from the British base in Hong Kong.

We entered the port of Osaka (from memory) sometime in late July 1964.

Chapter Eighteen

Osaka, Japan, Late-July 1964:

Looking back almost sixty years, memory fails me as to whether or not we also discharged into other Japanese ports, such as Nagoya. I know on later voyages aboard the Irish Spruce, we visited Hiroshima, Nagasaki and Tokyo, but that's a story for another day.

Our first day, an enterprising Japanese man set up a small pop up shop in the wardroom with approval from the captain and Chief Officer John Small. I didn't have a lot to spend but I did get some goods including small Japanese figures, paintings on silk and a ring for Rita with two cultured pearls in a twist arrangement. These items still exist somewhere within our family today.

Japan was booming with great shop prices selling state of the art cameras and transistor radios. I was with Jack, our third officer, when he bought his longed for, Canon camera. I bought Rita a Sanyo portable radio, which gave her great listening pleasure for many years. If in later years any family member finds it stored in the attic, please fit new batteries and remember us from many years ago.

At night, we would visit the local bars where there were always plenty of girls and the air was scented with perfume and the aroma from exotic cigarettes. I will say no more except that what happened in Osaka stays in Osaka.

It was early August 1964 when the last of our cargo from Australia was discharged and we left Japan empty ship bound for the Philippines.

I fired up the Oceanspan 7 main transmitter and informed Hong Kong Radio, Irish Maple EISL next port ILOILO.

5 August 1964. Somewhere in the Philippine Sea on the Western side of the Pacific Ocean. It was Kenneth Edwards 21st birthday and coincidentally it was my 23rd. Captain Michael decided to throw a birthday celebration for Kenneth starting that evening and what a night it was.

Some of the crew agreed to stay sober and run the ship while the rest of us got gloriously drunk and sang songs till the early hours of 6 August. With approval, I kept watch intermittently in conjunction with the Auto Alarm equipment.

The next day was quieter with everyone agreeing no more drink for a week or two.

Mid-August 1964, as we entered the South China Sea, the sea became rough and the sky was ablaze with large bursts of fork lightening.

Tropical rain reduced visibility to almost zero.

I was called to the bridge where Captain Langran advised me the MARCONI MK 4 Radar had packed in. At that moment, I thanked God for Radar lecturer Dr Rice and Kevin of St Technical College.

I examined the radar display and quickly diagnosed that we had Trace, grass, clutter control, range rings, range marker, heading line and a small centre Sun but no targets.

This radar had a built in Oscilloscope, possibly the only radar ever manufactured that did have one. I stopped the scanner rotation intermittently to check the A scan operation on the Oscilloscope.

NOTHING! I switched off all power and withdrew the top chassis of the transmitter unit, and as I did so I could see water dripping from the upper waveguide. I quickly re-engaged the top chassis and asked Jack to bring me a basin from the bridge toilet please.

With the basin in position, I again opened the waveguide and allowed its contents to enter the basin. By using a neon, I could see that the radar was producing transmission, but obviously not exiting the Scanner hog horn.

It was agreed I would climb the mast to check what might be happening at the scanner end of the radar.

Dressed in a black oilskin, I started my climb along with Fourth Officer Brendan Aherne, who was assigned to assist me. The ship was rolling heavily, torrential tropical rain was still falling, and the sky was intermittently decorated with bursts of bright forked lightening. To top it off, the bursts of thunder was deafening. Brendan and I had difficulty speaking to each other, so we reverted to hand signals. This all sounds very dramatic but we were children of the 1940s, and thought little of our discomfort or the danger of being toasted alive.

I examined the hog horn and found the heavy membrane covering it had been penetrated which allowed rain water to enter the waveguide which then ran down the length of the mast and in to the radar transmitter located in the chartroom.

I pause here to say how this happened. There is a breed of Japanese bird which had a fascination of pecking at MK4 hog horn membranes.

I later learned regular visitors to Japan knew to carry out a modification of replacing the membrane with hard plastic. I wish someone had told me!

I stayed on the platform covering the hog horn with my hand ,like the Dutch boy and the dyke, while Brendan went in search of some heavy plastic. On his return with plastic and tape, we patched the damage as best we could. That still left the problem of drying out the waveguide, and for those who don't know this was a parallel shaped solid 3 cm pipe, scientifically designed to guide the beam.

I suggested a hair dryer if there was such a thing on board, could be fed up the waveguide. The electrical officer said, "Hold on," and made a hasty retreat to his engine room store. He returned a short time later with a hot air blower which we connected to the bottom end of the waveguide. It was necessary for Brendan and me to make a few more hazardous trips up the mast to remove the plastic covering which allowed the hot moist air to exit into the South China Sea.

It took an hour or so for the guide to dry out after which the MK4 Display was back to normal, with ship and land targets painted in bright orange. We were all rewarded with glasses of Negrita rum.

The storm passed and sometime in the second half of August 1964, we entered Iloilo.

Chapter Nineteen

Iloilo, Philippine Islands, August 1964:

We tied up at Guimaras Island sugar pier, situated across the river from the mainland and the city of Iloilo. We came in empty ship but we'd be leaving loaded with sugar for New York.

Sugar was not a very profitable cargo but it covered running expenses plus a small profit which was better that sailing empty across the vast Pacific Ocean, and the very profitable cargo awaiting us in the USA.

We came from Japanese Pagoda towers and now we were enjoying the architecture of the old Spanish empire. Exotic flavours filled the air and trains running down main street alongside cars, scooters and bikes added to the exoticism. Soon after tying up, two armed men in uniform came up the gangway and ensconced themselves in the small officers' messroom. These turned out to be security guards which was new to me and why were they armed? The answer revealed itself that night.

The captain invited a number of us to his dayroom, for a few drinks, during which we could hear shots being fired. Everyone jumped up and went out onto the top deck. I remember there was Jack, Frank, Chief Engineer Michael Byrne and others.

Looking across the strait between us and the mainland was a long narrow vessel illuminated by a large searchlight under the control of our security guards. There was no visible sign of any one on board as the long vessel drifted under the power of a strong tide. Soon more shots were fired which elicited laughter and hand waving from young men lying flat in the bottom of the vessel.

These weren't just any young men, these were Pirates who regularly boarded ships to steal paint, ropes and anything else that was portable. The Pirate vessel soon drifted beyond searchlight range and we returned to a few more stiff drinks. Fuc…Pirates! That night and every night thereafter, I made sure to lock my cabin door.

Chapter Twenty

Iloilo, Philippine Islands, Continued:

The second night—all dressed up but nothing to do on Guimaras Island but how do we get to the mainland? The small river ferry we were hoping to use had stopped sailing as it was only used during daylight hours. The answer came from below…

"Vamos Vamos!"

Looking over the side, I could see the ships gangway had been lowered down to water level alongside which two boats similar to the Pirates were waiting. "Vamos Vamos," one of two small Filipinos shouted again. We needed no second invitation and soon most of the *Maples* crew was piling into the long narrow boats to be transported to the mainland.

As we approached the shore to the put, put, put of the outboard engine I wondered how we were going to get ashore as I could see no landing stage. The answer soon came as the two Filipinos jumped into the water and with more vamos, vamos…let's go, let's go, they loaded us one by one on to their shoulders and running through the water deposited us beside big waiting taxis. TAXIS! From memory, there were several black Chevrolets similar to those now gracing the streets of Havana.

They took off at high speed, on what was perhaps a fifteen minute journey, before stopping at a big wooden barn. Along with Jack, Frank, John and Brendan, we entered to be greeted by other crew members who had arrived before us. We sat down on long wooden benches above which were long rough wooden tables.

Barmaids came to take our orders and Rum was the preferred choice, which was very large and very cheap. In one corner of this not very upmarket nightclub was a three piece steel band, which started playing soon after we arrived. It sounded brilliant but perhaps the Rum helped.

One song was played several times:

I wish you bluebirds in the spring to give your heart a song to sing
And then a kiss but more, more than this I wish you love.
And in July a lemonade to cool you in some leafy glade
I wish you health and more than wealth I wish you love.

As the night went on, some of the *Maple* men who at home in small Irish towns would attend Sunday mass clutching their Missals lost all inhibitions and participated fully in what was offered to them.

The party ended as the dawn was breaking and waiting Chevys drove us back to where the now operational ferry took us back to Guimaras Island.

After a few more days enjoying the sights of Iloilo city and nights in the long wooden hut, we re-entered the Pacific Ocean, and set course due East towards Hawaii and the Panama Canal beyond.

Chapter Twenty-One

Philippine Islands to the Panama Canal, August-September 1964:

Every day was sunny, and every night was bright, as we made our way across the blue Pacific Ocean, birthplace of the MOON, towards the Hawaiian Islands. The sea was millpond smooth, allowing the *Maple* to glide smoothly through the water, at a speed in excess of 12 knots. I called the British Naval Station at Singapore and advised *Irish Maple* EISL next ports PANAMA and SAN JUAN PUERTO RICO.

I also advised San Francisco KFS with the addition that I would copy his Traffic lists. This information would be passed to the American Shipping Line, New York City.

As already said, the water was millpond smooth and in between watches, Jack Brendan and I would sit in deckchairs smoking Luckies, drinking Coke and sorting out the world's problems. The only interruption was the occasional flight of flying fish.

One day followed similar to the previous with Sunday drinks under the Irish Pergola remaining the highlight of the week.

The radio watches were very quiet except occasionally the air would burst into life when the operator of a ship within range would test his Transmitter. Sometimes we would exchange greetings and if he was Irish; the Morse exchange could go on for an hour or more or even longer if he was one of my ex Atlantic College classmates.

Our jobs were lost out to redundancy so these Morse code exchanges could not take place today.

It was nice at night to have a shower and sit staring at the stars sucking on a Lucky. Sometimes the air was scented with the smell of Copra from a nearby Island.

Sometime in September 1964 we passed south of the Hawaiian Islands and near September's end, we entered the Panama Canal.

Chapter Twenty-Two

Caribbean Sea, Autumn 1964:

We entered the Panama Canal, under the control of the American Pilot, who guided us through the Panama rain forest, and lakes and into the Gatun locks, after which we spilled into the South Caribbean Sea and set course northeast towards San Juan, Puerto Rico and the British Virgin Islands!

Puerto Rico an Island under American control bordering on becoming a State of the USA someday.

We arrived on a very warm Sunday sometime in early October. The purpose of our visit was to load up with fresh food and bunkers.

The city of San Juan is a tourist delight and I believe in those days the visitors were mainly rich Americans. They no longer had access to their previous tourist Heaven…Havana Cuba!

That night, Second Officer Frank and I toured the bars of the old town where some of the visitors listening to our accents interrupted our conversations to enquire who we were and where did we come from?

We told them about our ship and where we'd been and where we'd go next. New York City, Las Palmas Canary Islands, Tripoli and Marsa El Brega Libya, Barcelona, Spain. and Back Home to Liverpool.

"Wow, you guys are really something. What would you like to drink."

The next day, with the Maple freshened up with plenty of food and oil, we left San Juan and set a course north towards the 'Big Apple'.

Chapter Twenty-Three

Western Atlantic Ocean, October 1964:

Puerto Rico to New York City and Beyond.

As we steamed on a Northerly course towards the 'Big Apple', the days grew steadily cooler which made sleeping more comfortable.

As we were in British area 1C, I advised Portishead Radio GKS Bristol Channel and Chatham Radio WCC Long Island NY our position and destination.

We passed the Bahamas and the State of Florida on our portside edging ever closer to Hatteras Island off the coast of North Carolina.

The Gin and tonic Sunday morning gatherings on the boat deck had ceased but Captain Langran continued the tradition of evening discussions in his dayroom. I made sure the Dynatron Radio was always in tune blaring out 'Pretty

Woman, Twenty Four Hours From Tulsa, I Want To Hold Your Hand', plus many more.

This was music very much to our taste and when the day came when WINNS 1010 New York could be heard it got even better.

Finally after six days, we entered Long Island Sound and soon after we passed the Statue of Liberty before tying up alongside other ships flying flags from many other countries. The big passenger ships were still there, not knowing that their demise by, the Silver Birds in the sky, was imminent.

To get from the docks into the bright lights meant we had to pass through a dangerous neighbourhood. It was a bit like the Wildebeest crossing the Serengeti so we were advised never to walk alone.

We managed to hire a television plus a phone was fitted for crew use.

The 1964, World Trade fair was still running and Jack decided to pay it a visit. Many times, during the voyage, Jack talked how much he missed large cans of Guinness which I believe could only be bought in County Wexford. During his visit to the Irish Exhibition stand, he found what he was missing but paid a very high price for the pleasure of slaking his thirst.

I believe he paid $2 or $3 which was possibly ten times the Wexford price. We could have a good night out for $5, and in my case, enough left over for the train fare to visit Rita's family the next day.

Big iron suckers soon emptied our cargo of sugar from the Philippines and once the holds were cleaned the business of loading American goods for Spain and North Africa began.

We steamed back down the Long Island sound and into the North Atlantic, now loaded with a very expensive cargo under the control of American Line Shipping Inc…from memory.

I again sent TR messages to GKS and WCC.

The great circle journey was a typical Atlantic crossing with heavy radio traffic, the *Maple* ploughed through heavy seas some days and calm seas on others. I'm not sure how much it helped but the American owners sent daily reports for the captain's attention suggesting courses to steer for a faster smoother passage.

After about ten days, the Marconi MK 4 Radar pushing out forty kilowatts of power picked up the high mountains of Gran Canaria and soon after we were alongside the docks of Las Palmas.

This was a visit I wouldn't forget and even now almost sixty years on I awake some nights with its memory.

Chapter Twenty-Four

Las Palmas, Gran Canaria, October 1964:

The Canary Islands conquered by Spain in the 15th century and because Gran Canaria had such a large dog population, they named the islands—The Canaries, 'Canis'—Latin for dog.

During our stay, I learned that Las Palmas was famous for the production of walkie talkie dolls, so I decided to buy one. It was three feet tall with large Spanish blue eyes, and hopefully it still exists and is not now sleeping in an Irish refuse field.

In 1964, the holidaymakers had just discovered the Canary Islands. Visitor numbers were still small by today's standards and Las Palmas was the destination of choice. I imagine the large building cranes were only being erected in Tenerife and Lanzarote in anticipation of the millions, who now flock south every winter from the cold Northern climes of Europe.

We too were tourists and enjoyed mornings appreciating the old Spanish architecture and coffee at sidewalk cafes. Afternoons for non-watch keepers, were spent on the beach cultivating a tan and swimming in the sea.

At night, we'd tour the local bars, listen to Flamenco music and refuse to buy flowers from the basket sellers.

It then happened one night while Second Officer Frank Kelly and I were sitting in a bar when a basket seller came around.

This was a man, but he wasn't selling flowers, he was selling small black cute looking puppies.

"*Quanta Costa?*" I heard myself saying.

"Two hundred Pesetas, Senor."

With Frank doing his best to stop my foolishness, I handed over the money in Spanish notes and took possession of the dog.

On the walk back to the ship that night with Blackie whimpering silently under my pullover, I began to have regrets. Still I thought it'll be nice, until Frank reminded me the captain might not be too happy.

I hatched a plan. I'd house Blackie on a cosy blanket in the battery locker at the back of the wheelhouse and get him food and water from the galley.

This was fine for a while till I got into my bunk and I could hear him barking, despite my best efforts to placate him.

"Please be quiet or the captain will hear you; please, Blackie, please."

The next morning, Wally, the second steward, came into my cabin with tea and toast.

"Do you hear a dog barking sparks?"

"Wally, I did something silly last night."

Wally was sympathetic but still laughed.

"I wouldn't like to be in your shoes when the skipper finds out."

"You're a great bloody help. Thanks a bunch."

"You're welcome," and with that he left still smiling only to return a minute or two later.

"I'll take him, Sparks. It'll mean I'll have to hide him every Sunday during captain's inspection, but I'll manage that somehow."

Feeling guilty, but relieved, I retrieved Blackie from the battery locker, and handed him over to his new owner, who made a dash past the master's cabin before descending to the lower decks.

As it turned out, this was a love match made in Heaven. Blackie adored Wally and everyone on board assisted in making sure Captain Langran never found out...or did he?

After landing whatever American goods we had for Las Palmas sometime in late October, we re-entered the Eastern Atlantic and set a north easterly course towards the Moroccan coast. Within a few days of passing Marrakesh and Casablanca, we arrived off Tangiers and the entry into the Mediterranean Sea.

Chapter Twenty-Five

North African Coast, October 1964:

I contacted Valletta Naval base Malta GYR and advised our position and next port, Tripoli.

Sailing east through the Mediterranean Sea along the North African coast, we passed Algiers and within a couple of days we had Bizerte and the Tunisian coast on our starboard side. One of our on board historians pointed out the old ruined city of Carthage which was destroyed by the Romans in the Punic wars.

We set a course southeast and in less than two days, we tied up alongside the port of Tripoli in Libya.

Tripoli was not what I expected. It was beautiful with old Roman architecture and statues. There were tourists but not as many as I felt this place deserved.

One day, Frank and I went ashore to enjoy the sights, and found ourselves visiting the old **Medina** market place, which is more exotic than anything described in the Arabian nights. It was a place where a time traveller from a thousand years ago would feel at home.

I stopped at one stall and bought what I thought was a lovely head and face scarf for Rita. This was a big mistake, which I only found out about some years later and I'm going to pause my story here to relate why.

At home, Cheshire, England 1973, during our evening meal:

"Rita, I've never seen you wear that scarf I bought you in Tripoli."

"Donal, you've waited all these years to ask me that?"

"Well yes, Rita, you said it was lovely and I just wondered where it is now."

"Donal, do you think I was going to walk around Dublin looking like someone from Baghdad in the days of Sinbad the sailor."

"Oh, ok, Rita, and what about that lovely silk scarf I bought in Amsterdam in 1961."

"Donal that was more suitable to be worn by a street walker in the Pigalle district of Paris."

"Ok, Rita," I pretended, "and what about that lovely Kimono I bought you in Tokyo 1965."

"Oh God that was worst of all. A Kimono that looked like a shroud for a man and one foot longer than me."

Trying to suppress laughter, I asked, "And where are all those lovely presents now?"

"Well, Donal, when the people in the charity shops laughed and said 'no, love, we're not that desperate'! I Took them back home and even the children laughed."

"Ok, Rita, sorry," I said, knowing she had given me the greatest gift any man could ever have. **No more shopping ever again!**

It was simply a matter of money between the folds of a card which I didn't even have to buy as this task fell to my daughters. In the following years, whenever there was any complaints about presents I'd say. "Oh and aren't you forgetting about St Vincent de Paul?"

In way, we were both winners because Rita could buy whatever she liked and she was so beautiful and so glamorous, I loved being in her company. Sorry for digressing…

The *Maple* was emptied of more wooden crates of American goods from New York and sometime in November 1964, we left Tripoli for the Libyan eastern port of Marsa Al Brega.

The voyage across the Gulf of Sidra took less than two days and soon we reached the oil port where so many young British, German and Italian soldiers had ended their short lives.

During our stay while a number of us were enjoying a meal ashore, we got into conversation with some British soldiers. Towards the end of the meal, they suggested we return as their guests to the local British Army camp. This sounded a good idea as the night life in Marsa wasn't exactly what we were used to.

I'm not sure which of us went but I suppose Peter, Jack, Frank and me. From memory, the camp was close by and I think we walked to it.

Our hosts took us into a big hall which was full of British soldiers enjoying a night of beer and singing. Some were so enthusiastic they were even dancing on the tables. I imagine, their superiors turned a blind eye, as who in God's name, would want to be stationed on the edge of the Sahara desert.

For a while, nobody paid any attention to us until we started sharing our cigarettes. Our New York bond included Pall Mall, Chesterfield and Lucky Strikes. Theirs was Players and Senior Service.

"Are you guys Irish, and where did you get those cigarettes?"

Being Irish and in the middle of a British Military camp in North Africa, we were sparing with our reply which probably only added to the mystery of who we were.

They probably put two and two together and came up with something completely different.

Anyway it was probably the best night we enjoyed during our Libyan stay. Sometime late in November, we slipped the mooring ropes and as we left Marsa, I contacted Valletta Naval Base, *Irish Maple* EISL next port BARCELONA SPAIN.

Chapter Twenty-Six

Western Mediterranean Sea, December 1964:

As we made our way across the Western Mediterranean Sea, I copied a storm warning message from Valletta which I handed in to the bridge.

Captain Langran and Navigation Officer Frank studied it and decided we should alter course to the safety of the Bay of Palma Majorca.

We were high in the water as we now only had the remnants of the American cargo. Before reaching the safety of the bay, we took the full brunt of the storm and the *Maple* began heavy rolling and pitching. The catering staff had become used to calm seas and became a little blasé about securing the crockery much of which smashed onto the galley tiles.

With the storm over, we weighed anchor and hours later, we entered Barcelona on the northwest coast of Spain.

It was a brief visit as our remaining cargo was quickly discharged and the second engineer replenished his tanks with fresh oil for the journey home.

There was time for a visit to the Las Ramblas and a plate of paella.

After Barcelona, we headed south, down the Balearic Sea, onto the Costa del Sol, Benidorm, Alicante, Malaga, Gibraltar, through the Pillars of Hercules, and back into the Atlantic Ocean. At this point, everyone on board started to suffer with the channels.

The channels—this is the feeling that comes at the end of a long sea voyage and knowing you'll soon be back home among your family. The primary effect was an inability to sleep at night. It's the same feeling children go through on Christmas Eve awaiting the arrival of Santa.

We hugged our way up the Portuguese coast, past Lisbon, Santiago de Compostela and into the Bay of Biscay. We were now into winter and the Bay was rough but we didn't care as we were nearing home.

This was confirmed by the fact that communications to Valentia Radio EJK was loud and clear.

We were soon past Penzance at Land's End, into the Irish Sea and rounding Anglesey Island where we were boarded by the Liverpool pilot. He took us down the North Wales Coast and into the mighty Mersey and a berth in Birkenhead docks. It was 22 December 1964. An official from the Liverpool Mercantile office came on board and signed us off the ship's articles.

That same day, I reported into Marconi Pall Mall where I advised the Chief Inspector Bill Smith on the state of the station. With back pay in my wallet, I went for a haircut immediately followed by a trip to the B&I offices in Lime

Street where I booked overnight passage to Dublin and luckily one of the last remaining private cabins.

That night, having said goodbye to those of my shipmates not travelling home that night, I made my way to Trafalgar Dock, Liverpool and joined many more *Maple* crew members also making their way home for Christmas. The mv *Leinster* docked at the North Wall around 7 a.m. the next morning.

Once the ordeal of passing customs men, armed with sticks of coloured chalk rummaging through cheap brown cases of poor emigrants who could barely afford the price of travelling home, let alone smuggle anything of great importance was over, I hailed a taxi. Just as I was about to enter the back seat, "See you, Sparks. Good luck."

I turned to see who it was and there before me was Wally with Blackie by his side, almost fully grown now and adorned with a new Liverpool purchased dog collar.

"Goodbye, Wally, Happy Christmas. Adios Blackie."

Thanks for the memories!

MV Irish Spruce

EISR Cork, Early-January 1965:

IRISH SPRUCE   *Brownell Collection*

As I stepped from the late night train from Dublin to Cork, the rain started to fall and I debated with myself as to whether or not I should walk to the Verolme Dockyard, where I was to join my new ship or take a taxi?

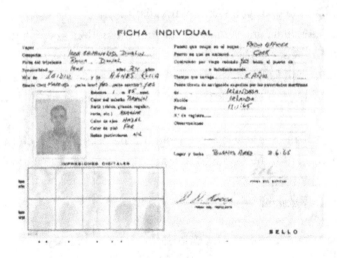

Before I could make a decision, a young man, about my own age enquired, if I was on my way to join the *Spruce*. I wondered how he picked me out from so many other passengers, but I suppose my navy blue overcoat was a giveaway. "Yes, I said," after which we introduced ourselves.

His name was Gerry Dorgan and he was joining as fourth engineer officer.

"Gerry, should we walk or take a taxi?"

"Walk," he said, "as it's not very far."

So, we started to walk, and as we did, the rain started to come down in walls of water, which quickly reached into our backs via our navy blue coats. To add to our discomfort, we had to stop every so often and rest our arms from cases filled with clothes for a year long voyage. "Gerry, I thought you said it wasn't far?"

"Ok, Donal, a little bit of a miscalculation, sorry." Eventually, we entered the shipyard and could see the *Spruce* was sitting high in one of the dry docks. As we entered the ship, we were met by the Chief Steward Tom Forde.

"You fellas look like drowned rats!" Tom as it turned out was an Irish shipping veteran and a very nice person who on this occasion provided us with towels to dry ourselves, after which he showed us to our cabins.

Mine was one deck below the bridge and close to the only other occupant Captain A.R. Evans.

This was a man of portly build in his early fifties from Wales.

After I changed into dry clothes and dislodged the contents of my cases into the wardrobe and drawers, there came a knock on the door and a man wearing third officers' braid entered.

"Hello, Don, I heard you were joining us."

"Hello, Peter, and congratulations on your promotion." Peter and I had sailed on the *Irish Maple* in 1963/4 and I was glad to see a familiar face.

"Donal, the chief officer is holding a welcome party and you're invited."

The chief officer was Mick O'Connell, and on this occasion, a very affable host.

It was about midnight when my head hit the pillow and I don't remember anything after that till the Cabin Steward Johnny Sexton entered the cabin with morning tea and toast.

The first day began.

Day one: Verolme shipyard, Cork Harbour, early-January 1965

On entering the dining saloon, I was directed to the captain's table where the captain was already seated along with his First Mate Mick O'Connell. We were soon joined by the rest of the deck staff—Frank Raftery 2/0, Peter Scott 3/0 and apprentices—Brophy, M. Larkin and David Collins.

Most of the talk was about what we had all done during the festive season.

The other big table in the saloon was occupied by the second most senior person on board, G. Cunningham, chief engineer, and his staff. I could hear Gerry relating the previous night's story of our long cold walk in torrential rain.

With breakfast over, I went to check out the radio room and bridge equipment.

It had the usual Oceanspan 7, Two Atalanta Receivers, Reliance Emergency Transmitter, Type M Auto Alarm, Lodestone Direction Finder, Alert Emergency Receiver, Dynatron entertainments radio and a SALVITA lifeboat radio.

The bridge equipment included a MARCONI MK4 Radar, Sea graph Echosounder and an ARGONAUT VHF.

While I was inspecting the equipment I would be responsible for, I could see there were two other men in the wheelhouse fitting a new DECCA Arkas J series Autopilot. One was a local Cork engineer and from memory, a UK engineer probably from their Liverpool branch.

When I returned to the radio room, I found a Marconi shore technician was in the process of fitting a Ferrograph tape player for crew entertainment. I think in fact he was a staff inspector called Bill Jones.

When he completed the installation, he handed me some tapes, one of which was Lena Horne singing her long list of songs—'Can't help loving that man of mine', The lady is a tramp, etc.

After a further three or four days in drydock, our voyage to South America and the Far East began.

It was a cold winter's day as we made our way down the river Lee and when we reached Cobh, the pilot wished us bon voyage before descending down the Jacob's ladder to the waiting Pilot launch.

I called Land's End Radio, GLD from EISR QTO Cobh next port VITORIA BRAZIL. I received a QSL and BV OM.

As we entered the North Atlantic, the *Spruce* began to pitch and roll in a winter storm that had been waiting for us. I secured my office chair with the deck chain, like many before me, and those who didn't often wound up being thrown onto the deck or worse still against the nearest bulkhead.

After my watch ended, I decided to visit the Marine Electrician Tom Coughlan. He was a first tripper, newly married and was homesick even before we left port. I found him still in his bunk and now he was violently seasick. I went to the galley and one of the stewards gave me some dry biscuits which I brought back to Tom, but he wasn't interested so I left him to sleep and told him he should start to feel better in two or three days. I regretted imparting this information as it provoked a further discussion with God.

As we sailed further south, the weather improved day by day and by the time we reached the Azores, we had gone from winter to spring, and by the time we reached Cape Verde Islands, we were back into summer. Tom was back on his feet as were all the other first trippers. The sea was now calm, and the skies were a deep shade of blue.

They say the loneliest man on a ship is the captain but after that I'm sure it must have been us operators.

Excluding passenger ships which had three or more radio staff, we had no one to talk shop with. I did have a junior radio officer on the mv *Baron Ardrossan* MSKP and if he ever reads this can I say, 'Didn't we have good times…particularly in Lourenco Marques, Mozambique'.

Now that Tom was better, I found him a good substitute and I think I managed to take his mind off his home sickness. I also promised I would get my wife to visit his which she later did.

When we passed the equator, the usual on board homage was paid to King Neptune and near the end of January 1965, we passed Recife, Salvador and finally on 28 January, we entered Vitoria bay where many ships were anchored waiting to be called into the port. There was no waiting for us and soon we were alongside where a cargo of iron ore was waiting to be loaded into our holds. We only had a couple of days to enjoy this small city with its Portuguese architecture before leaving fully loaded.

As we were now in British long range sea area 2A, I called the Naval Base near Capetown ZSC from EISR QTO VITORIA next port CAPETOWN.

I received the usual QSL and safe sailing OM.

As we were now in summer, the sea was calm, and it was possible to sit in our deckchairs on the boat deck drinking Coke and watching flying fish zoom over diamond studded waves, while lone albatrosses glided lazily in the sky.

We passed the small Tristan da Cunha islands in early February 1965 and entered Table Bay on 7 February, just astern of the passenger ship *Reina del Mar*.

Our Capetown visit was brief and with fresh bunkers and food we exited the bay and I called ZSC to advise next port Singapore.

We were now used to calm seas and balmy nights, and this continued into the Indian Ocean, till we arrived south of Madagascar and Mauritius. I had earlier passed a storm warning into the bridge, and the deck staff had taken the precaution of making sure the ship was properly secured. Then they hit us— Tropical storms Kathleen and Maureen.

They battered us senseless almost till we reached south of the Maldives' Islands. Everyone's good humour changed to, being a little bit cranky through lack of proper sleep. All reverted to good banter once Kathleen and Maureen abated, and Second Officer Frank plotted a course for Southern Sumatra which took us into the Java Sea and Singapore, where we berthed on 28 February 1965.

It was another two day visit with nights spent in the Merchant Navy club Connell House with its air conditioning in spacious bars and a long blue swimming pool.

Tom, the chief steward, regaled us with some of his sea adventures and when we returned to the *Spruce* at night, he would invite everyone to his cabin and entertain us further with his violin skills.

He was well known in his home county of Kilkenny as a violinist of some note.

On the day of sailing, Mick requested I join him on a visit to a local tailor shop and assist him in choosing a new suit. It was tropical weight, light shiny and bright, and I wished I'd had enough dollars to buy the same, but I didn't.

We left Singapore that night and I reported to the naval base GYS next port Chiba, Tokyo, Japan.

"Safe sailing, old boy," came the reply.

We entered the South China Sea and once we were abreast of Borneo, we continued our voyage towards Manila on a north easterly course.

The chief officer doubled the lookouts in case we became of interest to the Pirates known to frequent these waters.

We glided in blue seas past Vietnam on our port side on a course that would take us near to the island of Taiwan.

I consulted my copy of the Admiralty list of radio stations volume one and made a note of those stations to use during our tour of Japanese ports.

Time has eroded my memory as to which stations I did use but I do remember all the shore operators transmitted very readable crisp Morse code. It reminded me of the beautiful clear on-screen script, displayed at the start of Hollywood films.

In the first week of March 1965, we entered Tokyo Bay and as observed on the MARCONI MK 4 Radar a Racon was set out along the water before us like a magic carpet.

We entered the port of Chiba close to Tokyo and that night the young men of the *Spruce* with the unspoken agreement afforded to most seamen enjoyed the delights of perfumed bars and female company.

Similar nights followed in Yokohama, Yawata, Hiroshima, Nagasaki, Osaka, Kobe.

On 17 March 1965, just as we were entering Yokohama, I copied a message via Hong Kong addressed to Captain Evans. It was an instruction to all the ships in the fleet to celebrate St Patrick's Day in the same way as 25 December.

Tom, the chief steward, made sure there was plenty of Turkey and ham for all hands followed by a couple of cans of Guinness export.

That night, Ireland came to Yokohama and for all the right reasons I'm sure a few of its residents may still remember it.

Towards the end of March 1965, with the land of the Rising Sun astern of us, we set a course back south towards the Philippines and the South China Sea.

In early April, we arrived in Malaysia via the Malacca straits where we loaded timbers at the island of Penang for Mozambique and South Africa.

It was now the monsoon season, and every day around mid-afternoon, we could see the rain in the distance before it actually arrived.

When it did arrive, it was torrential after which it disappeared virtually in a matter of seconds.

With our cargo of exotic timbers, we left Penang and north of the Malacca straits we entered the Indian Ocean and set a course southwest towards Madagascar.

As we were now in British sea area 3, I contacted Mauritius Radio and advised *Irish Spruce* EISR next port LOURENCO MARQUES MOZAMBIQUE.

I received the usual QSL BV.

As already said, we were in the monsoon season and I knew it was important to copy the twice daily marine weather reports from Mauritius.

During our long passage across the Indian Ocean, the deck staff with the captain's approval set up a small swimming pool between two of the after hatches.

It was only about three feet deep and twelve foot long, but once filled with seawater, it looked great and made a welcome respite during those long hot muggy days and nights.

We voyaged southwest past the Maldives, Seychelle Islands and the Mozambique Channel before entering Lourenco Marques at April's end 1965.

LM (now Maputo) was the capital city of the Portuguese colony Mozambique. It was a free and easy living city with the best music radio station in the Southern Hemisphere. It attracted many tourists from South Africa, who wished to escape the more staid way of living in their own country.

After two days in LM, we sailed for Durban where we arrived on 8 May 1965.

A local school teacher, Basil Sheedy, and his friend, Peter Murphy, arranged a reception for us at the Mayfair Hotel where Peter was the manager. Unfortunately, I over indulged with too many bottles of Castles. We knew the vessel was scheduled to sail at 2300 and as the night progressed, I kept a nervous eye on Chief Officer O'Connell to see when he was going to make an exit.

Eventually, he did and we all made our way back to the docks accompanied by many of our party friends.

The *Spruce* sailed about ten minutes after our arrival. When we were opposite Brighton beach, I advised ZSD DURBAN Radio, *Irish Spruce* EISR next port CAPETOWN. I never realised until then that an inebriated person who has difficulty in speaking will struggle just as equally on the key.

I had just fallen asleep when the second mate shook me awake as the captain had messages to send. I struggled to the radio room in my dressing gown and switched on the Oceanspan 7, and composing myself as best I could I again called ZSD QTC 2.

Looking back with the benefit of almost sixty years, I suspect my opposite number in the radio station realised my predicament and was very tolerant till eventually, I managed to sign off. The next day, I swore never again to repeat my youthful stupidity and I never did.

Our visit to Capetown, the Tabletop City, was brief and on 8 May, we were back in the South Atlantic again. I advised the naval base at SIMONSTOWN S.A. *Irish Spruce* EISR, the next ports are in BRAZIL AND ARGENTINA.

It was now winter time, in the Southern Hemisphere, so the seas were rough, which once again meant everyone on board got a little bit cranky, due to disturbed sleep and long sea watches. My hours were, two hours on and two off, over a 14 hour day. Of course, we also had callouts even during our time off to attend to Radar breakdowns, etc. Most radio officers had an additional Ministry of Transport Radar Certificate qualification for which they received a small addition to their pay.

During our twelve day voyage, Captain Evans entertained us with stories of his adventures, during the many years he spent on the South American coast.

We re-entered Vitoria in late May 1965, and an adventure with Scott I'll remember till the day I die.

Vitoria, Brazil, May 1965

The Scott adventure began when Peter 3/0 announced after lunch that it was time to get fit, and would I accompany him on a trek over the hills of Vitoria. I readily but stupidly agreed. As it was Ascension Thursday, I thought it might be a perfect day to ascend the heights of Vitoria.

Suitably attired but with no water or food, and a few Brazilian reals in our pockets, we started our journey at 1300 hours. I bravely followed in Peter's footsteps. Even though we were both over six feet tall, I struggled to keep up with my companion's fast pace. After a harrowing climb, we reached the summit of Vitoria's highest peak at 1400 hours.

Why do I say harrowing? Well, the mountain was guarded by wild goats and when we weren't running from them, we had to endure passages through dense jungle like foliage. Scott was still quite cheerful, and very witty, but nagging doubts as to the wisdom of the expedition began to creep over me.

However, the tranquillising effect of the beautiful view was sufficient to boost my flagging enthusiasm. Ten minutes later, we carried on regardless, with me following in Peter's three feet strides.

Three hours later, after covering 10 to 15 miles of hot dusty terrain, the navigator politely informed me he was under the impression we were lost.

Not only were we lost but very, very thirsty. Eventually, we found a local tavern which we entered with some strange stares from old men playing cards on one of the cheap wooden tables. We slated our thirst with a few San Miguel beers the first of which made me feel like John Mills downing his Carlsberg in the film 'Ice Cold In Alex'.

After our second, or possibly third, bottle of San Miguel, we planned our next strategy, which was a fatal mistake. We left the tavern with an exchange of nods to the old men and proceeded on our journey. A short time later, we entered a large compound with grey buildings and bars for windows. Men in prison uniform some at eye level were laughing and shouting something in Portuguese to us. "Peter, let's get out of here."

Before he could answer, a prison guard arrived also laughing, "Sair, Sair."

We didn't understand what he was saying but as he was pointing towards a big gate, we suspected he wanted us to leave. We quickly complied and made a hasty retreat through the big gate with 'Bye, Johnny', and more laughter coming from behind the barred windows.

It might have been better to remain as our next encounter was with a local swamp. Signs depicting skulls and crossbones confirmed we were actually entering a swamp. We took a reciprocal heading and at 2000 hours, tired, thirsty, hungry and exhausted, I vaguely remember staggering up the *Spruce* gangway with words of encouragement from Peter. Second Steward Johnnie Sexton thoughtfully kept two dinners warm for us, which we gratefully consumed before crashing with an early night.

After our Ascension adventures, I always made sure to hide from Scott during daylight hours in port.

As Peter is now in Heaven, maybe someday we can meet up again and enjoy another day walking through the stars.

Vitoria, Brazil, 1965

It was winter time in the Southern Hemisphere, but at twenty degrees south, it's difficult to know when the seasons change. The weather was glorious on the morning we exited the port of Vitoria, and once we dropped off the pilot, the *Spruce* set a course which would take us down the coast of South America.

As we were in British sea area 2A, I called the Naval base, ZSC at Capetown and signalled *Irish Spruce* EISR QTO VITORIA next port RIO DE JANEIRO. QSL BV OM, came the reply.

We arrived in Rio de Janeiro to be greeted by Christ the Redeemer holding outstretched arms at the top of a large mountain. As we only had a small amount of cargo to discharge our visit was brief with only one night ashore to enjoy the night life of this wonderful city. The bar we went to was full of mainly British seamen.

Some of them were DBSs (DISTRESSED BRITISH SEAMEN). These were seamen who had overslept and failed to return to their ships before sailing time.

The code of the girls from Brazil was to look after their needs until the embassy or ships agent could arrange their passage back to the UK normally on another ship.

Unfortunately, they would receive a bad discharge report limiting the quality of future ships they could sail on, plus they would suffer a fine which would be deducted from their back pay.

In the meantime, they could enjoy female company, complimentary drinks from fellow seamen including the crew of the *Spruce* and days on the Copa Cabana beach. Unfortunately, we had no time to visit the beach as the next morning we set sail for Santos where we arrived a day later.

Santos Brazil, Late May 1965

It's most famous inhabitant and possibly the greatest footballer ever to have lived was Pele. He had reached the pinnacle of his career where he remained for many years dazzling spectators and breaking goalkeeper's hearts, excluding England's legendary Gordon Banks, who made possibly the greatest save in history at the 1970 Mexico City World Cup. Thereafter, Banks and Pele remained lifelong friends.

We only spent a few days in Santos, but one episode does come to mind.

Tom Forde, chief steward, gave a party in his dayroom. Present was Mick O'Connell the chief officer, Frank Raftery 2/0, Peter Scott 3/0, Gerry Dorgan 4/E, plus a few others whose names time has erased from my memory.

Tom entertained us with his violin playing sometimes accompanied with a song from Gerry. It was during one of these renditions that a man and woman appeared at the open door. Tom stopped playing and the man at the door said, "Sorry to interrupt, gentlemen, but we've come from Sao Paulo. My wife is Irish and when we read your ship was in port, we felt we'd have to come and visit if that's ok?"

"Certainly, it's ok."

We made room for them on the long green settee and Tom filled two glasses with Guinness export which he handed to them.

The man from memory was from the USA, where I'm guessing he met his Irish wife. He had a law practice in Sao Paulo and from the expensive clothes and jewellery they were wearing, I imagine a very successful practice. His wife spoke with a mid-Atlantic accent, which reverted to inner city Dublin, after three or four of the very strong Guinness beers. He was a bit reserved, but she made up for this by telling us about their mansion in the city and her team of servants.

At some stage, the chief cook entered the company to discuss the next day's menu with the chief steward. Almost immediately his expression took on a quizzical look. "Mary? Is it yourself Mary?"

Looking a bit flummoxed, she hesitated before answering, "Yes, Johnny, it is me."

"Isn't it a small world that we should meet after all these years, thousands of miles from home?"

We could see Mary wished it was an even bigger world when Johnny started to relate their growing up years together in East Wall Dublin and embarrassing stories I better not reveal here.

Tom saved the situation somewhat by suggesting he and Johnny should discuss the menu list in the dining saloon. On his return, he poured Mary a large gin and tonic which allowed her to revert to kind.

The party ended with the sound of the dinner gong when everyone including our visitors took to seats in the dining saloon.

When dinner was over, we accompanied our new friends to their limousine, parked near the end of the gangway. My last memory of them is, the big red tail lights exiting the quay wall.

I'll pause here to relate a brief encounter my girl, Rita, and I had with the chief cook during Christmas week 1965.

O'Connell Street was packed with people enjoying the festive season. As we were passing the Metropole cinema and restaurant, I could hear someone shouting, "Sparks, your tart is lovely." I acknowledged Johnny with a wave. As we walked on, Rita was silent for a while and then said, "Who was that person calling me a Tart?"

I explained the connection after which we both laughed. "Rita, any chance of you becoming my Tart?" This resulted in me suffering a bruised shoulder!

We left Santos on the 30 May 1965, and set a course southwest which would take us past Mar del Plata and onward towards our next port.

I fired up the Oceanspan 7 and advised Simonstown Radio South Africa, *Irish Spruce* EISR QTO SANTOS next port BUENOS AIRES. QSL safe sailing OM, came the reply.

On our three day voyage South, during my morning watch, a knock came on the office door, to which I answered, "Come in." It was one of the Able Seamen. "Sorry to disturb you, Sparks, but can you put the music back on, please?"

I remember replying, "But the radio is on."

This was incorrect as when I checked the Dynatron Radio was in fact dead. I told my visitor I'd check it out once my watch ended. I could see he was a bit disappointed with this news as entertainment on cargo ships in those days was limited to a small library, usually run by the third officer and whatever broadcast radio stations, we operators could tune in and feed into the ship speakers.

When my watch was over, I started to check, why the Dynatron was not coming on. I could see all the valves were cold, so I lit up a Lucky Strike and contemplated my next move. I knew from previous vessels there had to be an AC power source coming from somewhere. Most ships, in those days had 110 or 220-volts DC power supplies, but the Dynatron required AC power, which came from a rotary converter, but I'd never seen its location.

I asked Tom, the marine electrician, if he knew where it was which he didn't. By this stage, a number of my shipmates became interested, particularly Captain Evans, who liked listening to the BBC overseas service when it wasn't fading in and out too much. I think it was Mick, the first mate, who eventually said, "Try looking at the top of the engine room," and when we did there it was, a smallish Rotary Converter with 220 volts DC in and 220 volts AC out.

It wasn't rotating. We could see the brushes were worn and the commutator looked in a sad state. Tom agreed to overhaul it in his workshop, so we started to free it from its bench mount, during which it became apparent how Mick knew its location. We found a parasite cable running from the motor straight to his cabin and his personal radio. Tom spent the next few hours dismantling the converter and rebuilding it as almost new.

Later that day, the Dynatron and Mick's radio were back on air blasting out Spanish music like 'The Bossa Nova' and 'Spanish eyes'.

We entered the River Plate on the morning of 2 June 1965.

Soon after passing Monte Video Uruguay and the wreck of the German Battleship Admiral Graf Spee, we arrived in Buenos Aires.

Buenos Aires, 2 June 1965

Before being allowed ashore, we had to be checked out by what from memory were immigration officers or possibly the local police. Everyone was photographed and fingerprinted. This data was then transferred on to a passport which also included a full description of the holder. Captain Evans validated the information with his signature.

Although, Peron and Evita were long gone their legacy lingered on. We were warned what areas we should not enter and if we visited a bar where the owner was remiss in not paying police protection money, it might result in one or more of us being removed from our bar stools, and next morning wind up sweeping Buenos Aires most famous thoroughfare—Avenida 9 De Julio.

That night with our new Argentinian seamen's shore passes and a few Pesos tucked into our wallets we went ashore to enjoy the delights of the Paris Of The Southern Hemisphere.

The comparison is well deserved, but in those places where Tango music was being played and patrons were laughing and joking it all became very silent when men in police uniform entered. We instinctively knew to keep our heads down knowing one word out of place could result in us holding the wrong end of a brush.

With a fresh cargo for South Africa and the Far East, we left Buenos Aires in June 1965. I advised ZSC Capetown that our next port would be Capetown. The operator mustn't have been too busy because realising we were Irish and a premier Rugby nation he wanted to engage in a conversation about the sport. Because of Apartheid, South Africa, also a premier Rugby nation, were excluded from participating in any of the international games.

My opposite number was obviously a mega fan. I mentioned when growing up I used to see Dr Carl Mullen every day as he was a neighbour in Home farm and that seemed to please him. Carl was part of the famous Irish team who won several Triple crowns in the 1940s. I was glad our Morse code exchange ended after that, as I wouldn't have been able to feed much more information, to this rugby starved enthusiast.

The South Atlantic Ocean

Time passed slowly as we spent long boring days staring at grey rolling seas. We did have Lena Horne coming out loud and clear on all the mess room speakers but even her dulcet tones were starting to wear a bit thin. There were of course the albatrosses zooming down to wave height, and occasionally a visit from a curious humpback whale.

It was late June 1965 when we again entered Capetown.

Capetown, June 1965:

The ship's agent came on board with post from home, which is one of the highlights of a seaman's life. I was in the middle of reading mine from Rita when I was called to the captain's cabin. When I entered, I was introduced to the ship's agent. A telegram from Captain Evans I had sent to ZSC a few days prior to our arrival listing all our food and fuel requirements included a request to arrange a Radio Survey via the Irish embassy in Johannesburg.

The Agent said the Irish embassy had ignored his request, but the British agreed to assist. Either a Harp or Crown made no difference to me, so long as we were allowed to operate legally.

The next morning, a man with a British rather than a local accent arrived to carry out the inspection. He was about fifty years of age of medium height, who wore glasses and carried a briefcase containing papers and radio test equipment. I had requested Tom to arrange a tray of tea and biscuits to be available on his arrival.

As he sipped his tea, he asked when the staff member from the local Marconi Marine office would be arriving. I said I didn't think anyone would be coming. This produced a silent reply and I thought this is not a good start. Perhaps it was an insult to his dignity that someone more senior than me was not in attendance.

As the survey progressed past testing the Autokey and SALVITA lifeboat transceiver, the man with the spectacles seemed to soften a bit. By the time he entered the battery locker to check dates and specific gravity readings, he was quite chatty. We returned to the radio room where he inspected the mandatory spares including the phosphor bronze emergency aerial.

He started to complete the paperwork, including our new licence, and said everything looks fine. Then just before he finished off, he said, "I think perhaps you should carry an extra 807 valve or perhaps two." The 807 valves were the output stage of the Oceanspan 7 main transmitter. I volunteered to go and get some from the local Marconi Depot, but he said no they must arrange delivery prior to the vessel sailing.

The agent who was still on board, contacted Marconi and an engineer brought the new 807s on board later that day. Tom provided him with silver tray service, and I related how the surveyor insisted on the spares being delivered by the office rather than me collecting them. This produced a wry smile, so looking back sixty years I suspect there were issues between the two parties.

On our last night, I decided to walk alone through the city and with my few remaining Rand maybe take in a movie at one of the local cinemas.

I wore my red pullover cricket player style wrapped around my shoulders.

I hadn't been walking very long when I saw him. He was black and very tall probably a member of the Zulu tribe. He was naked from the waist up and shivering with the cold as he huddled close to a building in a vain attempt to acquire some shelter. People of black and white passed him without a glance.

When our eyes met, I could see he was hurt by the expression of pity in my eyes. I reached to undo the red pullover but changed my mind and like everyone else, I just walked on. Even after all these years, I can see his hurt look and many times I've wished I could turn back time and hand over that cheap red pullover.

The next morning, the rope men released the *Spruce* from the quay wall and the pilot guided us out of port and back into the South Atlantic Ocean.

South Atlantic Ocean, 1965:

We left Capetown and as we were still in British sea area 2, I advised ZSC next port Singapore.

We sailed on an easterly course, along the South African coast, for one and a half days and when we were south of Port Elizabeth, Frank, our second officer, set a course Northeast, which took us into the Indian Ocean, and calmer waters.

This time tropical storms Kathleen and Maureen were a distant memory, and each day followed, more or less as the one before. When we reached 30 degrees south, I started copying the weather reports from Mauritius, and also advised our position and destination.

In between watches, I would visit the wheelhouse and the officer of the watch and I would talk mainly nonsense about world affairs. It was pleasant at night with a full moon shining on a calm sea to sip tea from a large mug and listen to waves gently lapping on the *Spruce's* hull. The temperature rose higher every day and as it was now the monsoon season, torrential tropical rains would sometimes reduce visibility to a few miles, and even our 50 kilowatt Radar struggled to differentiate between sea clutter and ship targets.

I suppose we needn't have worried because it was rare to spot another traveller in this vast ocean. There were one or two nights on Peter's watch when he would call me to assist on the Aldiss lamp. We would exchange messages with a passing ship giving our name and where from to where bound.

It was August when we re-crossed the equator, and soon after that we were back in the Malacca Strait before again reaching Singapore.

Singapore, August 1965

The weather was hot which is not surprising as we were very close to the equator and the mosquitoes were happy to accept our donations of fresh blood. They particularly liked wrists, ankles and the soft skin surrounding the eyes. The bites were bad enough, but it was impossible not to scratch when they started to heal. We drank lots of Schweppes tonic water for its quinine benefits in avoiding malaria.

We again availed of the facilities offered by Connell house but for a change some evenings we would take a rickshaw to streets lined with wok restaurants, where the air was scented with the smell of curry and prices were very reasonable.

Some others took rickshaws to forbidden cinemas followed on occasion to Houses of the Rising Sun.

With cargo discharged and the *Spruce* replenished with fresh food, oil and water, we left Singapore and entered the South China Sea. I called GYS Singapore and advised next port Nagasaki. Our 12 day voyage took us past Vietnam, Luzon, Taiwan and Okinawa.

It was summer again, not that we were aware of the seasons because apart from the monsoon rains, every day was hot and Sunny.

It was late August when we tied up alongside in Nagasaki. All the devastation of the atomic disaster twenty years earlier seemed to be gone.

After breakfast on the first morning, lots of the crew were congregating in the wardroom, where again a local vendor, with the chief steward's approval, had set up a very enticing display of his wares. There were plastic figures of Geisha Girls, Samurai warriors, Japanese travellers, paintings of Mount Fuji on silk cloth, cultured pearl rings and many other cheap goods.

I was never a shopper, so to me this was a great way of acquiring gifts for my family back home. They were gratefully received and some even survive to this day, albeit mainly in forgotten drawers.

After Nagasaki, we steamed for about half a\ day to Hiroshima—the city where the first atomic bomb in history was dropped at 8.15 a.m. on 6 August 1945. This was the city where the mighty Japanese navy set out to successfully destroy the US Pacific fleet at Pearl Harbour on Sunday, 7 December 1941. The city paid the price of the terrible American revenge.

When we arrived, Japanese efficiency had restored the city, almost to its former glory. We had a couple of nights ashore. The air in the bars we visited always had a perfumed aroma. This was added to by the scented cigarettes the girls were smoking. I tried one of these cigarettes but quit after the first two drags, and lit up a Senior Service instead.

On returning from a visit to the toilet the barmaid, for hygiene reasons, always presented us with a hot wet hand towel on a silver tray. Maybe chief medical officers could suggest this practice in the fight against COVID?

We left Hiroshima for Kobe, where we tied up on the same day.

Kobe, September 1965

While cargo for our next voyage was being loaded, we enjoyed the sights and sounds of this beautiful Japanese city.

I particularly remember the restaurants where steaks were served on very hot ribbed pig iron metal plates. The steaks were gourmet standard and for many years I wondered how this was possible? The mystery was solved recently while watching a food program on TV when the presenter explained how Kobe cows were reared totally stress free, and fed a special type of grain and milk.

It was October 1965 when the *Spruce* loaded with wooden crates full of Japanese goods exited back into the North Pacific Ocean. We were now in British sea area 8 so I called the Naval Base in Hong Kong on 8MHz and advised *Irish Spruce* QTO KOBE next port VANCOUVER CANADA. Our two week voyage, across the North Pacific Ocean commenced.

North Pacific Ocean, 1965:

The Spanish explorer, Magellan, named it well, because it is Pacific, and I have no memory that we encountered anything of interest during our long crossing. It was pleasant to sit on deck at night under a starry, starry sky and wonder if other beings were doing likewise on some other far off worlds.

There were no weather reports to copy and most of my ten minute log entries said *nil heard*. Very occasionally while sitting in a daydream in front of one of the two Atalanta receivers, the speaker would burst into life causing me to almost jump out of my skin. The signal would have come from a nearby ship testing one of their transmitters, probably an Oceanspan or if it was a passenger vessel a Globalspan.

About six days after leaving Kobe, we crossed the International dateline and entered British sea area 6. I called Vancouver and gave him our QTH and advised I would monitor his traffic lists. Having crossed the dateline, my fourteen hour day, reverted to a very early morning start.

We arrived in Vancouver B.C. sometime in October 1965. To us this was a city like home where everyone spoke English, and excluding the difference in our accents no one would have taken us to be anything but Canadian.

What did surprise us was, members of the Irish community coming to visit us. These immigrants probably emigrated to Canada in the 1950s and were delighted that a little bit of Ireland had arrived on their doorstep. They arranged parties for us and I could see they now had middle class homes and an income to match. They blended in well with this very British Canadian Provence.

It took over a week to discharge our Japanese wooden crates during which time 'love stories' began particularly between the *Spruce* catering staff and the Vancouverite girls. I knew from previous experience that these affairs were going to end in quay wall tears but who was I to burst the bubble of young men going about in a dreamlike state. Remembering a story told by Welsh Captain Jones whom I sailed with on the mv *Scorton* GWCT, I hoped those in love wouldn't be foolish enough to jump ship.

Captain Jones had an incident in Canada when two of his crew didn't turn up at sailing time. His solution was to inform the Mounties that he was treating them for an STD, and this resulted in the culprits being marched on board some hours later.

With our holds empty, we travelled the short distance across the bay to Vancouver Island and Cowichan bay where we started to load Seaboard Timber for Liverpool.

Cowichan bay was and is primarily a tourist resort. We tied up alongside a long wooden jetty. Our new location presented a problem for those in love but a local ferry back to the city provided the answer. The visitors no longer came, and the parties ended, but we were in a tourist resort.

We were able to hire small boats with outboard engines and go fishing for salmon. It was also interesting to talk with the local Indians whose ancestors probably peopled this area thousands of years ago.

The banded timbers for Liverpool loaded slowly into the holds of the *Spruce* and after that timbers began to be stacked on to our deck space. It rose to a height just below the bridge with access walkways for the crew.

Eventually, we were ready to go with all crew members present.

It was November 1965 when we left Cowichan Bay, and I advised Vancouver Radio next port Panama Canal.

USA West Coast, November 1965

Our ten day voyage down the American West coast, began with a full crew, that is to say, none of the love affairs resulted in anyone doing something stupid. I fully expected at least one or two *Spruce* members to request a Marconigram be sent to the girl of their dreams, but no one came.

I subsequently heard on the grapevine that plans had been made by some, for a Vancouver reunion in the spring of 1966, with jobs already secured. It would have been very easy, in the mid-60s, for anyone Irish to emigrate to Canada and hopefully, there are now people alive today in British Columbia, because an Irish ship of no great importance, visited there in 1965.

So, to continue:

Within a very short time, we were off the State of Washington heading south. Although, it was winter, the sea state was calm and the weather balmy with a very comfortable temperature. We hugged the coast past the State of Oregon and after three days we were abreast of San Francisco Bay. I had been copying the weather from radio station KFS.

On our fifth day south, we passed Los Angeles and San Diego. The weather was getting noticeably hotter.

We were now off the Mexican coast and once past the Gulf of California we edged in much nearer to the land and so near in fact that at night, we could see shore lights on the horizon. Eventually, a highlight arrived when Acapulco appeared on our port side. It was easy to understand its attraction mainly for American tourists as the sea was crystal clear and occasionally marlin sword fish would appear close to the *Spruce*.

We steamed for another five days down the Central American coast, past Guatamala, El Salvador, Nicaragua, Costa Rica. Finally, arriving at Panama City. With a pilot on board, we journeyed through Loughs, Lakes, Jungle, through the Gatun Locks and into the Caribbean Sea.

We were now back in long range radio sea area 1C and with the Oceanspan set to 16, or maybe it was 22MHz, I called Portishead Radio (in the Bristol Channel) GKI from EISR next port SAN JUAN PUERTO RICO.

We voyaged across the southern Caribbean Sea on a north easterly course for about four days, before tying up in San Juan where we stayed overnight to fill up on fresh food and oil. We in fact took on more than was intended. There was time for one night ashore, where we joined American tourists on a pre-Christmas break.

It was now early December 1965 and on leaving the Island of Puerto Rico, I advised Portishead Radio next port LIVERPOOL.

A special request was made to Chief Engineer Cunningham and Second Engineer Burke to put the boot down and get us home for Christmas. A smile was the reply, but it was known or suspected that the engineering staff always kept a secret oil reserve for homeward bounders. They must have complied because the noon positions as plotted by the deck officers showed an extra 20 nautical miles or so per day.

It was about two days after leaving San Juan that it was revealed what extra we had taken on at that port.

It was an Able Seaman on the after deck enjoying a cigarette and the last of the setting Sun who discovered him first.

"Take me to the captain, Sir," a tall Blackman said to him in a strong Caribbean accent. The Able Seaman, whose name I can't remember, said later he almost swallowed his cigarette with fright. The uninvited guest was interviewed by Captain Evans and other senior officers in the wardroom. His name was Paddy Reilly. I kid you not, and he hid either in the hold or among the timber deck cargo for more than two days.

He was fed and given a bunk in the *Spruce's* small hospital which was better than the ABs cabin who first found him. I sent a message from Captain Evans to head office at Aston Quay, Dublin, including the information that our new arrival was a British subject with a British passport. I think he was from the British Virgin Islands.

Head office replied they would inform the Department of Foreign Affairs who in turn would advise the British authorities.

Paddy settled into life at sea very well assisting the Bosun's team in making the ship spic and span for our arrival home.

There was good banter between him and everyone else on board, but he was very lightly dressed, and as we journeyed further north the temperature fell more and more day by day. Paddy was grateful for the extra warm clothing provided by Chief Steward Tom, accompanied with a half case of Guinness export.

I have no memory that we encountered any storm of note, but the North Atlantic is rarely anything but rough. By the time we passed the Azores, everyone had the channels, but we were grateful to the engineers for speeding us home as quickly as possible.

Soon we were steaming up the Irish Sea and down the coast of North Wales. Captain Evans prepared a Marconigram for the Liverpool Agent which I sent to GLV Anglesey Radio.

It was 21 December 1965 when we tied up in Garston Dock, Liverpool. Two men dressed in uniform came on board and accompanied our new crew mate Paddy to a waiting car on the Quay wall. I'm sure as a British passport holder he was fine, and did no more harm than hitch a free lift to the mother country where maybe he still lives.

That same day, a Marconi assistant inspector came on board to check out the station. He introduced himself as Mac, and little did I know, but that he was to be a colleague of mine for the next ten years.

The next day, I packed my cases and bid farewell to all those with whom I had shared a circumnavigation of planet Earth.

The shipping master came on board and once I handed him my large stack of radio logbooks and signed off ship's articles, I was free to descend the gangway to a waiting taxi, which took me to Pall Mall and the Liverpool Marconi office.

I handed in my accounts to the Chief Clark and reported the state of the station to the Desk Inspector Bill Smith. After that, I enjoyed the rest of the day walking around the centre of Liverpool, and that evening a ferry to Dublin where I arrived to enjoy a very happy Christmas 1965.

The *Irish Spruce* was to be my last deep sea voyage, as I returned to Marconi Liverpool in January 1966, where I was employed as a Marine technical assistant, until the mid-70s.

Today is 15 December 2021.

I'm in my 80th year, and still working on ships, albeit now almost as a hobby.

When people ask, "When are you going to retire?"

I tell them, "I don't know, but maybe when the last of Camroc Ltds twelve remaining customers cease to call, or more likely when I enter the Silent Key honours list of QSO." THE RADIO OFFICERS ASSOCIATION.

CPSIA information can be obtained
at www.ICGtesting.com
Printed in the USA
LVHW040537120423
744131LV00004B/52